Roman and Civil Law and the Development of
Anglo-American Jurisprudence in the Nineteenth Century

Roman and Civil Law
and the Development of
Anglo-American Jurisprudence
in the Nineteenth Century

M. H. HOEFLICH

THE UNIVERSITY OF GEORGIA PRESS
Athens & London

© 1997 by the University of Georgia Press
Athens, Georgia 30602
All rights reserved
Designed by Walton Harris
Set in 11/14 Janson by G&S Typesetters, Inc.
Printed digitally

Printed in the United States of America

Library of Congress Cataloging-in-Publication Data

Hoeflich, Michael H.
Roman and civil law and the development of Anglo-American
jurisprudence in the nineteenth century / M. H. Hoeflich.
        p.   cm.
Includes bibliographical references and index.
ISBN 0-8203-1839-6 (alk. paper)
    1. Law—Great Britain—Roman influences.
    2. Law—Great Britain—History—19th century.
    3. Law—United States—Roman influences.
    4. Law—United States—History—19th century.
        I. Title.
KD540 .I164 1997
349.42'09'034—dc20
[344.2009034]   96-5522

British Library Cataloging-in-Publication Data available

To Karen, my one true love, now and forever

CONTENTS

PREFACE

This book has been a labor of love for over a decade. It has been a work done in stolen moments, moments not occupied by the demands of administrative duties. It has also benefited enormously from the assistance of many individuals. I have been blessed to have superb assistants at three universities. I owe a great deal to Jan Sanderson at Illinois, Janice Herzog at Syracuse, and Sandy Patti, Lynn Heskett, and Fran Hewitt at Kansas. I have also been enormously aided by student helpers. I owe a debt to the work of Gony Frieder, a member of the Class of 1996 at George Washington University Law School who spent hundreds of hours putting together footnotes and references, and to Charles Cassassa, Shawn Stogsdill, Scott Jarboe, and Rick Gier for editing and citation duty at Kansas. I also wish to thank Mary Burchill for preparing the index.

Many of my friends and colleagues have contributed greatly to this book. I must thank, above all, Alan Watson of the University of Georgia and John Cairns of the University of Edinburgh for their kindnesses and constant assistance, including reading and commenting on the whole of the book. I am also greatly indebted to Stephen Presser, Jim Brundage, Matthias Reimann, Bill Weicek, Joe McKnight, Ken Pennington, John Langbein, Charlie Donahue, Dick Helmholz, and Hans Baade for comments on various pieces. To Professor Peter Stein of Cambridge University I owe a double debt. First, he has been a source of encouragement to me since I first attended his lectures more than twenty years ago. Second, the influence of his own researches, which he has generously sent me over the years, are felt throughout this volume. Peter Stein has been the pioneer in the subject; I merely follow in his footsteps. Similarly, I must acknowledge several of my teachers: Richard Luman, who first put me on the path toward being a historian, Walter Ullmann, who taught me how to write history—and how not to, John Crook, who guided my first faltering steps in the study of Roman law, and Geoffrey Elton, whose kindnesses to a foreign graduate student can never be adequately repaid.

In the past ten years I have benefited greatly from the kindness of countless colleagues and students who tolerated my insistence on writing this book, often at the expense of doing my decanal duties. I am greatly indebted to them.

I must also acknowledge those who provided me with financial support for research on this book. My gratitude is due to the National Endowment for the Humanities, the University Scholar Program at the University of Illinois, the Delmas Foundation, and the American Philosophical Society.

Finally, there are two debts that I can never fully repay. I have already thanked Alan Watson for his assistance with this book. But Alan has been my true friend for over fifteen years and has always shared his knowledge and his books and his research with me. No one could have a better colleague and friend. Finally, my wife, Karen, has always been there for me, good times and bad. She is my one true love.

Portions of this book first appeared elsewhere in earlier versions. Chapter one is published with the permission of the *American Journal of Legal History*, portions of chapters three and four are reprinted here with the permission of the *University of Illinois Law Review*, and chapter two, which first appeared in *The Reception of Continental Ideas in the Common Law World, 1820–1920*, edited by Matthias Reimann, is published with the permission of Duncker and Humblot.

I recall a poem of Catullus wherein he speaks of the process of sending his words out into the world. It is a frightening process, no matter how often it is done. I send the words contained in this book out to you, reader, and ask that you be merciful. What errors there are are mine alone.

Roman and Civil Law and the Development of
Anglo-American Jurisprudence in the Nineteenth Century

Origins

Common lawyers have since the sixteenth century prided themselves on the uniqueness of their legal system and the legal profession both in England and in the United States. Nevertheless, in spite of a professed insularity, the best common lawyers and legal scholars have long been beguiled by Roman law and its modern counterparts, collectively known as civil law. Perhaps the greatest historian of the common law, F. W. Maitland, pointed out in his lectures on the Renaissance in English law that it was possible until the sixteenth century to argue that Roman and civil law were actually part of the law of England and, indeed, seemed for a time a possible replacement for the English common law, though that never took place.[1] There has never been a full reception of Roman or civil law in England or in the United States (though that, too, was a possibility for a brief period in the aftermath of the Revolutionary War and the bitterness many Americans felt toward England and all things English).[2] But although there has never been a full reception of Roman and civil law in the Anglo-American world, the influence of these alien systems has certainly made itself felt.

It has become a commonplace of our legal historical scholarship in the past few decades to relegate the influence of the Roman and civil law to a very minor, indeed trivial, role in the development of law and juristic thought in the Anglo-American world. Of course, no one can deny the history of the civilian jurisdictions of the United States during the nineteenth century or of the civilians and their court systems in England until the dissolution of Doctors' Commons in 1858. Beyond this, however, few have been willing to tread. The best known of the histories of American law, Lawrence Friedman's magisterial study, virtually ignores the influence of Roman and civil law on common law thinking in the United States.[3] The English legal histories of this period, even those as comprehensive as Milson's or Holdsworth's, betray a similar and misguided prejudice.[4]

There have been voices in the wilderness. Roscoe Pound, whose work is considered in the final chapter of this book, recognized early in his career that Roman and civil law did play a key role in the development of American law, as did more recently Peter Stein, himself a holder of the civil law chair at Cambridge.[5] Most recently, specialized studies on the subject have appeared, but these studies have not been systematic.[6] They have served the important function of drawing attention to the historical problem but have not attempted to explore it in detail. It is the purpose of this volume to do precisely that.

The thesis of this book is quite simple. Although Roman and civil law were not received into the Anglo-American common law during the modern era, they did, in fact, exercise a significant influence on the thinking of some of the most important jurists and legal theorists of the nineteenth century in both England and the United States and, thereby, did indeed play a significant role in the development of Anglo-American law and jurisprudence.

The approach taken in this book is biobibliographical. I have not attempted to examine in detail the effects of Roman and civil law on the development of substantive areas of Anglo-American common law. Such is certainly possible in some areas. One could, for instance, detail the development of American water law during this period and mark those points at which Roman and civil law ideas are most definitely present.[7] Similarly, one could look at the development of commercial law or conflicts-of-law doctrine in both the United States and Great Britain and illustrate those principles now accepted in the common law that derive from Roman or civilian models.[8] Obviously, it is necessary to touch upon such matters when discussing the works of jurists who wrote in these fields, but to do such a study properly one would have to examine the entirety of the case law and legislation in these areas and see at what points Roman and civil law concepts entered into the common law tradition. Similarly, I have not attempted to do more than touch upon the influence of Roman civil law in actual court opinions. Professor Richard Helmholz, in a recent, brilliant article, has laid the groundwork for such a study.[9]

In this book my aim has been rather different. I believe that the development of law can be studied best in terms of people, and especially those who devote their lives to thinking and writing as well as practicing the law. It is fashionable among legal historians today to denigrate the history of doctrine as old-fashioned and a preoccupation with the personalities of the law and the legal profession as antiquarian. These historians favor the use of statistics and the close study of vast masses of case law to determine what the law actually was in practice.[10] Certainly, the social history of law has an important place in legal history, but one must not forget that law, as Professor John Baker has remarked, also has an intellectual side.[11] The history of legal doctrine may seem to some to be old-fashioned, but it is valuable nonetheless.

There are two ways in which one may study the history of doctrine. One is to study doctrinal development in the evolution of cases and legislation. This, as I have noted, could be done for the history of the influence of Roman and civil law in the Anglo-American world.[12] To do so would present several serious methodological problems, however. It is often extremely difficult to trace the origin of a particular line of case law down to a definite incident of borrowing because most judges of this period did not acknowledge whence they acquired the particular principle with which they were working. In some cases, of course, it is possible, such as with certain areas of commercial law or with conflicts of law. Usually, however, it is impossible to distinguish between a case of parallel development and a case of direct influence.

A second way to examine the history of the influence of Roman and civil law on the development of Anglo-American law, however, is to study the great lawyers and jurists, to learn what they studied and wrote, and what, through their teaching and writing and by example in their practice, they helped to convince other lawyers was important. I have taken this second approach in this book, writing a history of the "high culture" of the law in Great Britain and the United States and studying the works of those individuals who most shaped that high culture.[13]

To understand the influence exercised by Roman and civil law ideas on the development of law and legal thinking in the nineteenth century in England and in the United States it is necessary to begin with a brief overview of the state of Roman and civil law studies in these two nations during the eighteenth century. England had, from at least the twelfth century, when Azo began to lecture at Oxford, a flourishing civilian tradition. The civilians had their own Inn at London, Doctors' Commons, and a monopoly on law teaching at the two universities.[14] They exercised exclusive rights in the ecclesiastical courts as well as in the courts of admiralty and the vice-chancellorial courts at the universities.[15] As a result of this civilian tradition there flourished a small industry in producing books about Roman and civil law to help train would-be civilians. Moreover, in Scotland, Roman law continued to be taught as a basic legal subject and the Scots professors and lawyers often exercised some influence below Hadrian's Wall.

In addition to this exclusively civilian tradition, during the sixteenth century there was a serious attempt to receive Roman law into the common law, if not explicitly to supplant the common law by the Roman.[16] This, too, brought forward a number of volumes, such as Robert Wiseman's small tome on the "excellency" of the Roman and civil law.[17] Although this drive to receive Roman and civil law was ultimately unsuccessful, it did lead, as Daniel Coquillette has demonstrated, to a lasting influence of the civilians upon their common law brethren, felt particularly in certain areas and in the work of certain judges such as Lord Holt.[18]

By the eighteenth century, however, the law in England was in a state of disrepair. Legal teaching at the universities had virtually ceased, the Inns of Court were moribund, and the standards for admission to the Bar were scandalously low.[19] Learned lawyers were few and far between, and, therefore, it is not at all surprising that there was little activity to be discerned in Roman and civil law. Several treatises by civilians were published, but it was not until the end of the century, when such men as Sir William Jones and Lord Mansfield came into their own, that any serious work appeared. Nonetheless, by the end of the eighteenth century and the beginning of the nineteenth, the winds of change and of reform were beginning to be felt in England. Mansfield was on the bench, legal treatises were beginning to be published, chairs in English law had been established at the universities, the University of London had been founded and three legal chairs established, the Inns were beginning to teach again, and standards for the Bar were being raised.[20] Reform in law and legal education was in the air, and with this new trend, interest in Roman and civil law began to make itself known again. When John Austin first gave his lectures on jurisprudence at London—and repaired to Germany to ensure that they would be sufficiently learned—it was clear not only that the common law was going to be revitalized but that Roman and civil law would play a role in the intellectual currents that accompanied that revitalization.

In the United States developments were somewhat different. Until the middle of the eighteenth century the American legal profession closely resembled that of Great Britain, as befitted a colonial Bar, except that education was less sophisticated and the level of practice in all but the largest eastern cities was well below that in London. But the generation of lawyers that came of age at the middle of the century was also to be the generation who made up the core of the Founding Fathers. These men were not only trained in the common law but were steeped in the legal and political philosophy of the Continent and much taken with the Roman model of a republic and with the legal system and lawyers that made that republic great.[21] The debt of the Founding Fathers to theorists such as Montesquieu and their admiration for Roman orators such as Cicero is well-known.[22] In addition, the learned lawyer in America at the middle of the eighteenth century was trained in the classical tradition and knew best the Bible and Latin prose literature.[23] It is not at all surprising, therefore, to what degree this interest extended to the classics of Latin legal literature.

This interest in and knowledge of Roman and civil law in the generation of the Founding Fathers was not particularly scholarly. The best of them, perhaps, had more than a passing acquaintance with Roman and civil law. The example that comes most easily to mind is Thomas Jefferson. After he graduated from the College of William and Mary, Jefferson studied law with George Wythe.[24] Wythe, as Hamilton Bryson has shown, was no stranger to Roman and civilian legal learning.[25] Perhaps it was under Wythe's tutelage that Jefferson learned something about these alien systems. In later life he had cause to use this knowledge. In 1772 Jefferson was retained to obtain a divorce for Dr. James Blair of Williamsburg. Unfortunately, Virginia law was adverse to such an act. Jefferson's notes reveal that he had recourse in the matter to civil law sources as the basis for his arguments in Dr. Blair's favor. He cited Samuel von Pufendorf and Barbeyrac as well as the Frederician Code of Prussia. He also cited the Roman law several times, but these citations were most probably drawn from Pufendorf as well.[26] Later, in his celebrated legal battle with the noted Louisiana lawyer Edward Livingston, Jefferson again called upon his knowledge of Roman law to argue his case.[27]

An example of another of the great lawyers and statesmen of the late eighteenth century who studied Roman law is John Adams, who has been called the "Justinian of Braintree, Massachusetts." When Adams decided to seek admission to the prestigious Suffolk County Bar, he approached Samuel Gridley, a prominent Boston lawyer, for support. To impress Gridley, he had prepared himself to be grilled on Latin literature and Roman law. Thus at his interview with Gridley he was able to say that he had been reading Cicero and Justinian's *Institutes* with Vinnius's notes. Beyond this rather pragmatic approach, Adams did, in fact, study a number of Roman and civilian texts, and his notebooks, in Coquillette's words, "demonstrated a good knowledge of Roman contract and bailment principles." In several cases—especially admiralty cases—Adams put this knowledge to use.[28]

Clearly, in the late eighteenth century the best American lawyers were familiar with Roman and civil law. It was gentlemanly and connected to the eighteenth-century love of the classical world. It was useful when arguing cases in courts that used civil law, such as the admiralty courts, or when the common law was adverse to a litigant's position, such as in the case of Dr. Blair. It was also, as revolutionary fervor grew in the colonies, politically acceptable because it was the law of the great early republic upon which so much of the new republic was modeled, and it was not the law of the enemy, England.

The results of this late eighteenth-century attraction of American lawyers to Roman and civil law were several. First, this interest meant that the subject would be studied. Jefferson, in a letter to a young friend on the best method to study the law, urged that Roman and civil law be a part of any beginner's education.[29] The College of Philadelphia included the study of civil law in its curriculum by the end of the sixth decade of the century.[30] Second, this interest led to the importation of Roman and civil law books into America, which would have been costly at the time.[31] Several of the great early collections of Roman and civil law books in America were begun in this period.

Thus by the beginning of the nineteenth century there was already a fair bit of interest both in the United States and in England for Roman and civil law among lawyers and jurists. It is interesting as well that many of the motivations for this interest, for example, the political and social significance of these subjects, were important on both sides of the Atlantic. But interest in Roman and civil law did not end with the death of this generation of lawyers and jurists in the early nineteenth century. On the contrary, it grew and expanded, and by the end of the nineteenth century, Roman and civil law had become an accepted part of the background and education of lawyers in both countries.

Indeed, the nineteenth century brought with it both continued interest and new reasons for Anglo-American common lawyers to become interested in Roman and civil law. In the United States the new century saw the incorporation into the nation of vast territories such as Florida and Louisiana that had formerly been under civil law. It saw, too, the defeat of U.S. forces at the hands of the British, which engendered a revulsion among many for all things British and, for a short period, opened the possibility that the new republic would wholly reject the English common law tradition and adopt the civil law. In both England and the United States, the new century brought with it the winds of educational reform for lawyers and a concomitant search for a more "scientific" approach to law, a search that often led to Roman and civilian writings.[32] In the United States, too, the unique southern literary and legal culture and the eventual rejection of things northern led to closer ties with Scotland and the Continent and a new appreciation for Roman and civil law among its best lawyers and jurists. In England, as in the United States, furthermore, the legal reform movements often embraced Roman law and Roman and civilian legal ideas as their models.

As the century aged, even more uses for Roman and civil law were discovered. These subjects came to be seen as the basis for university legal education and for the development in England of general jurisprudence. In both England and the United States, Roman law especially came to be seen as the quintessential core of comparative law studies, a subject much in favor as the new colonial empires expanded and grew.

In other words, throughout the nineteenth century there was a vital Roman and civil law tradition in the Anglo-American world. It was never dominant, and at times its vitality was confined to only a few brave souls. Never were the country courthouses in either England or the United States filled with learned Romanists or civilians. Nevertheless, Roman and civil law studies never disappeared from the Anglo-American scene. Books and articles continued to be published, young lawyers continued to toil at the sources, and experienced jurists continued to take inspiration from these alien texts.

Certainly, it would be an indulgence of the grossest historical fallacy to suggest that Roman and civil law were ever received in the Anglo-American world in the nineteenth century. But it would be nearly as inaccurate to suggest that they played no role in the development of Anglo-American legal thought. In the pages that follow, the extent to which they played such a role is detailed.

1

Roman and Civil Law in the Anglo-American World Before 1850

JOHN AUSTIN AND JOSEPH STORY

This chapter examines the work of two well-known nineteenth-century jurists and their use of Roman law. The first, John Austin, held the Chair of Jurisprudence at the University of London, was a teacher of John Stuart Mill, a follower of Jeremy Bentham, and one of the most influential legal theorists of the past two centuries. The second, Joseph Story, was both the first incumbent of the Dane Professorship at the Harvard Law School and an associate justice of the Supreme Court of the United States.

During the past two centuries interest in the history of both the English and the American legal systems has revived. This renaissance of legal historical studies, however, has scarcely encompassed Roman and civil law.[1] Comparative law studies, long the refuge of Romanists and civilians, are on the decline. The most influential histories of English and American law during the past few centuries generally discount the place of Roman and civilian ideas in the history of the Anglo-American common law. This "conventional wisdom" is misconceived. Roman and civil law are a significant part of our intellectual heritage.

Both Austin and Story were major figures in legal education and in the development of legal scholarship. This chapter examines the place Roman and civil law held in their thinking and writing and how foreign law entered the Anglo-American legal tradition at an early and formative period. In so doing it challenges the prevailing scholarly view that foreign law played little part in the development of Anglo-American common law. If two major figures in that development knew and used Roman and civil law, however, their influence cannot be ignored. Indeed, neither Story nor Austin worked in an intellectual vacuum. At the same time, the other extreme view that Roman and civil law were of overwhelming and dominating importance to the work of men like Story and Austin is inaccurate. The true significance of Roman and civil law in the writings of nineteenth-century jurists is far more complex.

John Austin and Roman Law as an "Ordering Principle"

John Austin was born in 1790, the son of a well-to-do merchant family.[2] He was called to the Bar in 1818. For approximately seven years he had a moderately profitable practice in equity. During this period he became close friends with both Jeremy Bentham and James Mill and was caught up in their interests in political and legal philosophy as well as law reform. Indeed, from 1821 until 1822, Austin acted as tutor in law to his friend's son, John Stuart Mill. During this period, too, Austin began his literary career, publishing articles on law in the *Westminster Review* and the *Parliamentary History and Review*. In 1827, through the intervention of various members of Bentham's circle, Austin was appointed as the first incumbent to the Chair of Jurisprudence at the University of London. He did not begin lecturing until 1828, however, and in the interim traveled to Heidelberg and Bonn, where he came under the influence both of the German Pandectist movement, dedicated to exposition of Roman law and its application to modern law, and the historical school of jurisprudence founded by Gustav Hugo and Friedrich Carl von Savigny.[3]

When he returned to London, Austin commenced the lectures upon which his later fame as the founding father of the school of analytic jurisprudence rests. Although his first course was deemed a success, by 1832 attendance had dropped off and, in failure, he resigned his chair.

In 1833 he served on the Benthamite-inspired Criminal Law Commission but quickly resigned and in 1834 attempted once more to lecture on jurisprudence at the Inner Temple, but again met with failure. For the next twenty-five years Austin accomplished little of note. Much of the time he lived in Germany, supported by his wife's translations. From 1834 until his death, he made no lasting contributions to law or legal scholarship. He died in 1859, depressed and convinced of his failure. Unfortunately, it was not until after his death that his position as the preeminent English legal philosopher of the nineteenth century was firmly established.[4]

To understand Austin's use of Roman and civil law and their place in the development of his jurisprudential ideas, it is necessary to assess the extent of Austin's knowledge and expertise in these subjects as well as to understand the tasks he set himself in his *Lectures*. It is also necessary to place the *Lectures* in their historical and philosophical context.

Austin trained to be a lawyer by reading law at the Inner Temple but had no university education. He studied Roman law during 1821–22 with John Stuart Mill as his pupil, but these seem to have been relatively elementary studies centered around Johann Heineccius's *Elementa Iuris Civilis*, an eighteenth-century Roman law "nutshell" based on Justinian's *Institutes*.[5] His major contact with Roman law came during a stay in Bonn before taking up his duties as professor of jurisprudence at London. As Andreas Schwarz points out, during Austin's residence at Bonn, that city was not a center of legal scholarship.[6] At that time in Germany, two schools of legal thought were in conflict: the traditional natural law school and the new historical school of jurisprudence, founded by Hugo and the then young Savigny.[7] The historical school marked a significant break from the natural law tradition. Followers of Savigny and Hugo argued that to understand a legal system it was necessary to see that system in its historical development and to recognize that legal doctrine was not plucked from some Platonic ideal legal heaven but was rather the end product of a society's development. Thus followers of the historical school looked to changes in society and to particular national characteristics such as language, religion, and geography to understand the development of legal doctrine. The historical school's influence had yet to be felt in the law faculty at Bonn in 1826–27, but in the history and philology faculties Gottfried Niebuhr and A. W. Schlegel were partisans of Savigny.[8]

For the most part, however, the lawyers at Bonn were supporters of the *Naturrechtslehre* (natural law). This, in itself, is significant, for Roman law and Roman legal terminology provided the basis for natural law discourse, if not its substance. Austin also studied with a young *Privatdozent* (the German equivalent of a university instructor) at Bonn, whom Schwarz believes was probably Ludwig Arndts, later to become a noted civilian legal scholar.[9] Schwarz surmises that Austin's studies at Bonn were not profound, that they were centered around elementary texts, perhaps including the recently rediscovered text of the *Institutes* of Gaius, a classical Roman jurist.[10] Indeed, Schwarz was able to examine the Roman and civil law books once owned by Austin and acquired by the Inner Temple after his death and, unfortunately, lost during the Second World War. These volumes, about one hundred in number, consisted mainly of elementary treatises and systematic encyclopedias of Roman and civil law, as well as more specialized treatises such as Immanuel Kant's *Metaphysik der Sitten*. Schwarz reveals that the most heavily annotated volumes were the elementary and encyclopedic works and suggests that several, including Nikolaus Falck's *Juristische Encyclopaedie*, exerted great influence on Austin's thinking.[11] Certainly the references contained in the 1869 edition of the *Lectures* bear out Schwarz's remarks.[12]

It is interesting that Austin chose to learn his Roman law in Germany rather than at home. There may be several reasons for that decision. First, English legal education, both in the civil law and in the common law, was at a low point in the 1820s. Instruction at the universities and at the Inns was haphazard and rarely sufficient to produce a learned practitioner, let alone a learned jurist and professor. Indeed, the creation of Austin's chair at London was one of the earliest formal efforts to stem this downward educational trend. Second, the German lawyers and law schools were just entering their most creative period.[13] Savigny had published his famous first work only a decade before. News of the German renaissance in legal studies reached Great Britain quickly and obviously motivated Austin.

One should not make the mistake of thinking that Austin's interest in Roman and civilian legal ideas was unique in his period. Indeed, a chair in Roman law had been created at London and both Oxford and Cambridge had the Regius chairs, whatever the quality of the current incumbents. Indeed, because of Britain's own civilian tradition and the existence of lectures on Roman law in Scotland, as well as at Oxford and Cambridge, Austin had available to him a native English civilian literature. He had access, of course, to the work of the great sixteenth- and seventeenth-century civilians such as Robert Wiseman, William Fulbecke, Thomas Wood, and Sir Arthur Duck, as well as later treatises such as Alexander C. Schomberg's *Historical and Chronological View of Roman Law* and Samuel Hallifax's *Analysis of the Roman Civil Law*, based on his Cambridge lectures.[14] Of course, these domestic efforts were squarely in the English civilian tradition, written to instruct would-be practitioners in the ecclesiastical and admiralty courts. No doubt Austin knew these books but sought out German scholars to gain a more thorough and scholarly understanding of the philosophical basis of Roman and civil law.

In sum, Austin was not, by any means, a learned civilian either on the English model or like his Continental colleagues. Nevertheless, he had a secure knowledge of the basic concepts of Roman law, understood the broad categories and technical vocabulary, and probably had mastered the elementary principles contained in Gaius's *Institutes*, Justinian's *Institutes*, and the elementary German Pandectist works of the early nineteenth century. Indeed, the fact that he owned one hundred books on Roman and civil law in his personal library is both unusual and significant. There is no evidence, however, either from his letters and library or from his references in the *Lectures*, that his knowledge went beyond this modest level. Indeed, in the *Lectures*, references to Gaius and to the modern civilians such as Nikolaus Falck, Ferdinand Mackeldey, and Johann Heineccius abound, but citations to the *Digest* or *Code* of Justinian, the major Roman legal codifications necessary for all but the most elementary understanding of Roman law, are rare. Thus all the evidence suggests that Austin's knowledge of substantive Roman law was not sophisticated. He mastered only its systematic philosophical aspects and its vocabulary.[15] Yet his knowledge of Roman law was at least equal to that of other English common law legists.[16] It was also, because he had contact with the systematic efforts of Germany's modern Roman lawyers, quite different from the knowledge of his English civilian counterparts.

On the simplest level, in his *Lectures* Austin was attempting to fill a job description. Austin's was one of three professorships created in the new law faculty. His was the chair of jurisprudence. The others were chairs of English law and of Roman law. His task, therefore, was not to lecture on the substance either of English or Roman law. Rather, it was to expound on the subject of jurisprudence. Fortunately, Austin himself suggests what he believed jurisprudence to involve in his reconstructed essay "The Uses of the Study of Jurisprudence." Austin tells us, in the opening of this essay: "The appropriate subject of Jurisprudence, in any of its different departments, is positive law: Meaning by positive law (or law emphatically so called) law established or 'positum,' in an independent political community, by the express or tacit authority of its sovereign or supreme government."[17] Although he considered other topics to be part of jurisprudence or necessarily to be discussed in connection with jurisprudence, it is clear that Austin's main concern was to discuss positive law, rules of conduct established by a sovereign addressed to a particular class of persons carrying a sanction for disobedience or deviation.

Within this broad definition of jurisprudence the work itself can be further divided into two parts, the lectures that make up his *Province of Jurisprudence Determined* and the remaining (and more numerous) lectures. The *Province* is, in many respects, as much a work of political philosophy as of law and shows strong Benthamite influence.[18] The other lectures, called by W. L. Morison the "main course," deal with legal categories and distinctions, the rights and duties of persons, questions of substantive law and procedure, and special topics such as codification.[19] Again, it must be emphasized that the *Lectures* are not a work of substantive law in the same sense as a modern treatise is. A reader learns virtually nothing of the common law as it was practiced in Austin's day. Case citations are exceptionally rare and fact patterns virtually nonexistent. One could not study Austin's *Lectures* as a preparation for practice, as one could, for instance, study William Blackstone's *Commentaries*.[20] One might learn, for instance, what it is to speak of a servitude but nothing of how to create one. Rather, the main course is an elaborate essay in definition and logical systematization. Austin himself, in his "Outline of the Course of Lectures," stated:

> Expounding the principles and distinctions which are the appropriate matter of general jurisprudence, I shall present them abstracted or detached from every particular system. But when such a principle or distinction, as so abstracted or detached, may seem to need exemplification, I shall also endeavor to present it with one or both of the forms wherein it respectively appears in the two particular systems which I have studied with some accuracy: namely, the Roman Law and the Law of England.[21]

Austin's other task, as revealed in the main course of *Lectures*, was nothing more or less than an attempt to construct an elaborate and logically consistent edifice of rules and principles upon which to analyze and understand law generically and the common law specifically. The very essence of the *Lectures*, especially the main course, is abstraction, the process of exposing rules and principles of law separate from the fact patterns or transactions to which they might apply.[22] It was for this task that his rudimentary knowledge of Roman law was so perfectly suitable.

The historical context of Austin's attempts at systematization in the main course of the *Lectures* is fairly clear. In the early nineteenth century, the common law in England still labored under the medieval system of the forms of action.[23] This system was, in fact, highly unsystematic in the sense a "system" was understood in Austin's time. It developed within the legal and political environment of conflicting jurisdictions which dominated English law during the later Middle Ages and the early modern period. Its structure was entirely pragmatic and chaotic if viewed in the abstract. Different forms of action existed for different fact patterns. To have a cause of action justiciable in a royal court, it was necessary to make the facts of one's case, as presented in the pleadings, fit a particular form of action. By Austin's day the system was in its last years, later to be overthrown by the series of statutes culminating in the Judicature Act of 1873. By the beginning of the nineteenth century, it was clear to many interested in law that the forms of action were internally incoherent, premised not on logic or consistency, but rather on the quirks of historical accident and procedural fortuity.[24] What was needed was an overarching and consistent system to bring order out of the chaos.

Several English civilians had earlier attempted to impose order on the common law through the use of the structure of Justinian's *Institutes*. Thus John Cowell in his *Institutiones Iuris Anglicani* of 1605 and Thomas Wood in his *New Institute of the Imperial or Civil Law* of 1705 both attempted to systematize English law to make it more palatable to both university-trained and simple common lawyers seeking order in the chaos of case and statute. Sir Henry Finch in his *Nomotechnia* likewise attempted to impose order on chaos.[25] Sir Matthew Hale, in his *Analysis of the Law: Being a Scheme or Abstract of the Several Titles and Portions of the Law of England, Digested in Its Method*, published in 1705, again tried to bring order to the common law, this time, as Alan Watson argues, with little recourse to Roman models.[26] And, of course, William Blackstone in his writings and, above all, in *An Analysis of the Laws of England* first published in 1756, as well as in his magnum opus, his *Commentaries on the Laws of England*, first published from 1765 to 1769, provided a set of categories, based in part on Roman law, for English law.[27]

With the exception of the openly Romanist treatises of Cowell and Wood, the attempted systematizers developed rather different structures, albeit based to some extent on basic Roman legal ideas. Finch's system is unique, Hale's system is his own, and Blackstone's is sui generis, as both John Langbein and Duncan Kennedy have observed.[28] Austin's system, too, differs in detail both from its predecessors and in its use of Roman and civilian models. Nevertheless, it is crucial to recognize that, in spirit, all shared a common ideal: the reduction of the seeming chaos of the common law to an orderly system with rules and principles consistently applied. It is equally important to recognize the role Roman and civil law played in these attempts.

Like the historical context, the philosophical background of Austin's systematizing efforts in the *Lectures* is relatively clear-cut. There are several obvious influences. First, of course, come Bentham and the Utilitarians. Bentham, as part and parcel of his work on codification, recognized the importance of deriving a system of categories and logically connected rules from the confusion of case law and statute that constituted the common law.[29] Austin was clearly a part of this tradition. Indeed, in his *Lectures* he carefully analyzed the need for codification and attacked the anticodification opinions of Savigny.[30] In fact, the Benthamite tendency toward codification led not only to attempts to construct actual codes but also, in 1867, in the wake of several failures at codification, to a movement to construct a "digest" of the law, "which would be a condensed summary of the law as it exists, arranged in systematic order, under appropriate titles and subdivisions, and divided into distinct Articles or Propositions."[31] This effort is, of course, perfectly understandable. Bentham and his followers recognized that it would be wholly impossible to achieve a successful codification of law without first developing a system of categories and subcategories within which to construct the code. The utility of the system of categories developed would ultimately determine the success of the code. A useful and logical system might not ensure a successful codification, but an illogical or inconsistent system would guarantee the failure of a proposed code. Roman and civil law, especially on the German model, presented a ready-made structure for such systematization.

Another factor that influenced Austin toward an attempt at systematization in his *Lectures* was the general intellectual fascination of the day with science and the scientific method. Although in the United States we are accustomed to place the movement toward development of a "scientific jurisprudence" in the latter half of the nineteenth century in the works of men such as Christopher Langdell at Harvard, the "scientific" ideal in law developed earlier in England and on the Continent.[32] The notion of a "science of law" as it developed in the later nineteenth century drew much from experimental science and from evolution theory. Langdell looked to the law library as a laboratory for this new science.[33] The scientific idea of law as it developed earlier in England looked more to scientific efforts at taxonomy and classification going on at the time. Austin's work anticipates the efforts of later positivists. For Austin it was scientific to derive a "taxonomy" of law, a systematic structure in which principles and rules could replace genera and species. Furthermore, Austin himself, in the third of the *Lectures*, refers to mathematics and geometry, in particular, as models for a "science" of law.[34] Science was precise and deductive. From general rules specific results could be logically derived. Above all, mathematics and science were deemed to be principled enterprises. Patrick Atiyah has described Austin's period as an "Age of Principles," and law, "like the other moral sciences . . . began to seem like a set of principles, deduced from the basic ideas of natural law, a vast set of self-consistent rules, each deriving some authority from a principle."[35] Even though Austin rejected much of the natural law tradition, Atiyah's remarks would appear to be applicable to Austin's works, if one substitutes for natural law the notion of positive law promulgated by a sovereign.[36]

In this "Age of Principles," a final possible influence on Austin's decision to create a taxonomy of the common law in his *Lectures* could have been the political dimension. Duncan Kennedy has argued that an underlying purpose of this work was to create a logical set of categories for the common law to preserve the political status quo as it existed in eighteenth-century England.[37] In Kennedy's view, the very elaboration of a complex structure of law carried with it a hidden agenda with significant sociopolitical consequences. Arguably, the same could apply to the system developed by Austin in the *Lectures*. Undoubtedly, the substantive content of the *Lectures* tends to perpetuate and legitimate a legal system skewed to favor, for instance, the propertied classes.[38] It is difficult, however, to argue that this was Austin's conscious intention in the main course of the *Lectures* because these reveal, if anything, a strong lack of interest in substantive law but rather focus on vocabulary and categories. It is undeniable, however, that in the lectures in *The Province*, Austin's jurisprudence is firmly conservative and has unavoidable political and social ramifications.[39]

Against this background, one can describe the way in which Austin's *Lectures* are an exercise in systematization and legal taxonomy. They are not systematic quite in the style of Hale's or Blackstone's *Analyses*. The *Lectures* go beyond mere arrangement of the law into headings. Hale in his *Analysis* and Blackstone in his text of 1756 both limited their tasks to a mere arrangement of the law under general headings. Blackstone, in his *Commentaries*, of course, went further and produced a treatise of substantive law organized within the categories established in his *Analysis*, a treatise designed to acquaint the would-be lawyer with English law as it was practiced. Hale's *Analysis*, though unique in its conception and execution, used some of the Roman institutional categories as inspiration, as W. G. Hammond has persuasively argued.[40] Blackstone also used Roman sources, to a degree, both in his categories and in substantive areas, such as the law of *ferae naturae*,[41] but his *Analysis* and his *Commentaries* are predominantly domestic and differ in significant respects from Hale's earlier work.

In the main course of his *Lectures*, Austin used Roman and civil law in several ways. First, Roman and civil law provided both an inspiration for and a source of Austin's scheme of abstraction and systematization. Second, Roman and civil law provided the logical and precise set of legal terminology necessary for exposition and explanation of the system developed by Austin. Third, in those areas where Austin's efforts transcended systematization and exposition and concerned substance, Roman and civil law also provided both vocabulary and rules.

Taking the latter category of borrowing first, anyone reading the *Lectures*, in even a cursory manner, must be struck by the number of instances in which Austin borrowed directly from Roman and civil law on substantive issues.[42] For instance, the concept of a juridical entity enjoying the rights of the status of "person" in the common law was rare and never fully developed before the nineteenth century. On the Continent, however, the civilians had created the legal fiction of a juridical person, called by Hugo and Savigny *die juristische Person*.[43] Fictions, as lawyers know, are immensely useful, for they allow lawyers to fit new concepts into existing legal categories rather than having to construct a whole new structure within which to place them. This particular legal fiction permitted rules and principles directly recognized as applying to natural persons to be applied to juridical persons as well, thereby obviating the need to create a whole new set of rules applicable to them. In cases in which a rule applicable to a natural person would be inappropriate for application to a juridical person, an exception could be created. One could thus have general principles subject to exceptions rather than a series of less inclusive categories. In short, the fiction of juridical persons served to simplify immensely any systematic exposition of the legal system. Thus it is not at all surprising that Austin adopted this civilian concept in his *Lectures*.[44]

Another example of such substantive borrowing from Roman and civil law for the purpose of simplifying the task of systematization is Austin's adoption of institutional writings on the sources of law. The accepted sources of common law have always been problematic, especially because of the lack of any written constitution and the dependence on custom and usage. Although attempts at devising a rigorous set of rules regarding sources of law had been made before Austin's time, none was very successful in England.[45] On the Continent, also, many legal scholars had puzzled over this issue, and it had become traditional to use Roman ideas about the sources of law, at least as a starting point, because of their apparent simplicity and consistency.[46] Austin, following Continental models, chose to frame his discussion of legal sources, not on English tradition but on Roman and civilian ideas, and to divide the sources of law on Romanist models, that is, statutes, cases, jurists' opinions, and the like.[47]

In determining the basic categories to draw a "map of the legal system," Austin again drew heavily on Roman and civil law.[48] Austin's treatment of the systematic nature of law goes far beyond the efforts of either Blackstone or Hale. Austin's analysis of law was, first, rights-based. He rejected the basic dichotomy postulated by Blackstone both in his *Analysis* and his *Commentaries*. Blackstone believed that law could be divided into two categories, the first concerning rights, the second concerning wrongs.[49] Austin believed that this was a fundamental error. He believed that a discussion of wrongs, as well as remedies and sanctions, must necessarily be subsumed under the category of rights, for it was from the basic concept of a right that the notion of wrong was logically derived.[50] Austin's rejection of Blackstone's first dichotomy and focus on rights, it may be suggested, followed the spirit of the civilian writers especially, whose emphasis clearly was on the concept of "right" (*jus* or *Recht*); and yet he carried these ideas farther than had his Continental predecessors.[51]

The second of Blackstone's major dichotomies, the distinction between the law relating to persons and the law relating to things, Austin accepted, albeit with differences. This basic division of the legal system into two categories was the fundamental dichotomy in Austin's systematic treatment of law and legal categories. Here Austin both followed as well as deviated from his Roman and civilian models. The Roman and civilian institutional writers from Gaius and Justinian to Heineccius and Falck premised their analysis of legal systems on a trichotomy, the division of law into laws relating to persons, laws relating to things, and laws relating to actions (*jus personarum, jus rerum, jus obligationum*).[52]

The division of law into these three basic categories was a fundamental tenet of Roman and civilian legal philosophy.[53] Austin accepted the first two categories but believed that the category of law relating to actions had to be subsumed under the first two as arising necessarily and directly therefrom.[54] Thus if one were to construct the beginnings of the civilian institutional scheme of a legal system, it would look something like this:

LAW (BASED ON RIGHTS)

Relating to Persons   Relating to Things   Relating to Actions

Austin's scheme, in contrast, looks like this:

RIGHTS

Relating to Persons   Relating to Things
Actions Pertaining Thereto   Actions Pertaining Thereto

To the present-day common lawyer, Austin's scheme seems, perhaps, the more familiar. Here, again, Austin started with a focus on Roman and civilian models but domesticated them for an English audience.

Indeed, a close reading of the *Lectures* makes it clear that Austin used his sources creatively, accepting those distinctions, rules, or principles he found useful and rejecting those he found illogical or inconsistent. Again, although the Roman and civilian lawyers accepted another basic legal dichotomy, that between public law and private law, Austin rejected this definition.[55] His analysis supporting the rejection is premised on the notion that public law, excluding criminal law, is actually law concerning the sovereign.[56] Since the sovereign is a person, what the civilians deemed to be public law was simply a special subcategory of the law of persons and should be treated as such.[57]

Roman and civil law served Austin in his *Lectures* on two levels in regard to his efforts at systematization. First, they served as living proof, at least to his mind, that it was possible to reduce a complex legal system to fundamental principles and rules, as in geometry or other fields of mathematics. Roman law, to Austin, was paradigmatic. It was proof that law could become a "moral science." Thus Austin could escape from the pessimism that had led Thomas Wood, a hundred years earlier, to write that "it has been thought impracticable to bring the laws of England into a Method."[58]

On the second level, Roman and civil law went beyond a paradigmatic role for Austin. It became a quarry for jurisprudential and systematic thinking. Learning on the systematic nature of Roman law, especially among the Continental institutional writers, was highly developed. Analysis of the utility of various legal categories, for instance, of dichotomy and trichotomy in law, regardless of the particular law in question, had become an important part of civilian scholarship. In developing the distinctions and categories of the main course of his *Lectures*, Austin had an active and full civilian tradition upon which to draw. That he did so is clear and that he did so selectively and creatively is equally clear.

Andreas Schwarz, among others, has suggested that Austin was little more than a disciple of Bentham and a supporter of systematization of law, borrowing mechanically from the Roman jurists and German civilians, for instance, from the writings of Falck.[59] Falck was a law professor at Kiel and the author of a popular academic text, his *Juristische Encyclopaedie*, the second edition of which was published in 1825 and which Austin studied.[60] Some of the sections of this treatise must have been of interest to Austin. The first chapter, "Von den Theilen der Rechtswissenschaft" ("On the Divisions of the Science of Law"), would have been particularly interesting to him. In this chapter Falck established, for instance, the dichotomy between public and private law and the distinction between the law relating to persons and that relating to things. But here, again, it is wrong to assume that Austin slavishly followed his civilian models. For instance, Austin stated forcefully that a proper jurisprudential discussion must first consider the law relating to things and then move on to the law of persons, subsuming that law relating to actions under both heads, as noted above.[61] Falck, closely following Roman law, adopted the tripartite structure of persons, things, and actions, in that order, an organizational scheme rejected by

Austin.[62] Falck, as well, accepted the distinction between public and private law which Austin rejected in his *Lectures*.[63] Thus, although Austin depended heavily on Roman and civilian institutional writings, including Falck's, in charting out his "map" of the English legal system in the *Lectures*, it was dependence in the form of intelligent borrowing and adaptation, not servile imitation. Even though Austin's knowledge of substantive Roman law was not profound, he was able to use the systematic writings of those more learned than he as a starting point for his own jurisprudential system. He was not an English institutionalist grinding out simply an English translation of a German treatise. On the contrary, he used the German works to develop his own English theories.

Finally, it is necessary to consider briefly the second part of Austin's efforts in the *Lectures*: the development of a precise vocabulary in which to discuss law and laws. From one perspective, the *Lectures*, other than those in *The Province*, could be characterized as an attempt to create a working vocabulary of precise terminology for the legal philosopher. Here, too, Austin used Roman and civil law extensively. Austin did not attempt to twist and distort Roman legal terms so that they would carry common law meanings. His stated goal, to create a system of legal rules and principles abstracted from the sordid intricacy of the English common law, prohibited such an approach. On the contrary, Austin devoted much of the *Lectures* to explaining what he believed the terms to have meant to Roman jurists. These definitions, in the abstract, became for Austin the building blocks of any legal system. When he felt dissatisfied with a particular term and believed that the jurists' definitions were logically deficient, he argued against their usages in regard to Roman as well as common law.[64] In effect, much of the discussion in the *Lectures* is a dialogue about law in the abstract, about its system, between Austin and his predecessors, dead some fifteen hundred years.

Why did Austin employ Roman legal vocabulary rather than his own English? The answer again can only be speculative. One might suggest that once Austin made the choice to adopt a system inspired by Roman categories, he could not use English legal vocabulary with any hope of success. English legal language in the early nineteenth century was still dominated by the conceptual world of the forms of action, of writs, and of tenures.[65] Because he rejected as chaotic and logically deficient the classification of law by the forms of action, any attempt to use English terminology steeped in them would have subverted his efforts at systematization. Austin needed terms that could be both precise and free of connotations incompatible with his scheme of systematization. Austin needed to develop a systematic terminology that could serve as a set of abstract rules and principles applicable, in theory at least, to the analysis of any legal system, including the common law. Roman legal terms, both because they had been developed within the context from which Austin's system derived inspiration and because they could be precisely defined without the English connotations that were anathema to Austin, were perfect. Of course, the utility of these Roman terms to Austin stemmed, in part, from his ignorance of the nuances of Roman law. Austin's audience, however, was undoubtedly no more familiar with Roman law than he was.

An example of how Austin preferred the greater precision he perceived in Roman legal terminology is to be found in his discussion of the terms "creditor" and "obligor":

> "Creditor" is the correlative of "Debitor" and applies to any person who has jus in personam. The French "Debiteur" and "Creancier" have precisely the same meanings. The English "Obligor" and "Obligee" ought to bear the same significations. But, in the technical language of our Law, the term "obligation" or "bond" has been miserably mutilated. Instead of denoting obligatio (as correlating with jus in personam,) it is applied exclusively to certain unilateral contracts evidenced by writing under seal. Or, rather, it is applied to the writing under seal by which the unilateral contract is evidenced. That is to say, it is not the name of an obligation, but of an instrument evidencing a contract from which an obligation arises. And, in consequence of this absurd application of the term Obligation or bond, the well-constructed expressions Obligor and Obligee are also completely spoiled. If it were used properly, the term "Obligee" would apply to any person invested with jus in personam. And the term "Obligor" (as the correlative of "Obligee") would apply to the party lying under

the corresponding duty. But, in consequence of the narrow application of "bond" or "obligation," the term "obligee," with its correlative "obligor," exclusively applies to persons who are parties to certain contracts: namely, such unilateral contracts as are evidenced by writing under seal, and are couched in a peculiar form: That peculiar form being not less absurd than the absurd application of "bond" or "obligation" to which I have pointed your attention.[66]

It would be an overexaggeration to suggest that Roman and civil law completely dominated John Austin's thought and writings. On the contrary, Austin was a trained barrister, and as much as he attempted to put a Roman stamp on his work, fundamentally it remains the work of a common lawyer.[67] Andreas Schwarz has argued that Austin's work has about it a "foreign air" and has, as a result, met with resistance in Anglo-American legal circles. To the extent that Austin's work shows clear traces of Roman and civilian law and vocabulary this is undoubtedly true. Nevertheless, Austin did not attempt simply to write an English-language civilian treatise. The main course of the *Lectures* is an attempt to domesticate foreign law, using Roman and civil law notions to improve the common law. Thus, ultimately, Austin's work must be seen as that of a man oriented toward the common law but drawing upon the civil law. In concept and in exposition, the main course of Austin's *Lectures on Jurisprudence* betrays their mixed heritage and the major influence of Roman and civilian learning. It is interesting to speculate as to the overall significance of this foundation law of the Anglo-American school of analytic jurisprudence in Roman and civil law. Perhaps most important is that Austin became convinced that he could achieve his task of systematization based on the Roman schema. No one before Austin came close to constructing an abstract, systematic exposition of law as a series of rules and principles. The works of Wood, Corwell, Finch, Hale, and even Blackstone failed to give the law even the appearance of a science. Neither Bentham nor his other followers were able to construct such a system. Austin, in the main course of his *Lectures*, came closer to success in this endeavor than any of his predecessors or contemporaries. If modern legal philosophers now judge Austin's work harshly, that judgment ought not to denigrate the intellectual achievement in its own historical setting. Equally, we ought not to neglect the influence exerted by Roman and civil law in making that achievement possible.

In conclusion, there is, perhaps, some irony to be found in Austin's use of Roman and civil law in producing his *Lectures*. Austin's knowledge of foreign law was superficial. He never mastered the intricacies of Roman substantive law. His learning could not have competed with that of the Continental civilians such as Falck, Mackeldy, or Rosshirt. Yet the superficiality of his knowledge may, in the end, have been precisely what made his *Lectures* possible. Had Austin truly mastered Roman and civilian legal scholarship from the perspective of the new "historical" school he might well have lost his belief in the systematic, logical, and consistent nature of Roman law. In a very real sense, Austin was a direct inheritor of the tradition that believed Roman law to be *ratio scripta*, the incarnation of legal reason and system.[68] In fact, classical Roman law is highly inconsistent, ambiguous, and filled with illogic.[69] Its system is superficial and its consistency disappears on close examination. That Austin knew Roman law only in its institutional guise as expounded in elementary textbooks and in its German modernist incarnation kept this truth from him and made it possible for him to attempt systematization as he did. Perhaps much of our present-day criticism of Austin's work as too simplistic and reductionist could be leveled as well at his use of Roman and civilian sources. Regardless of what criticism we make, however, the text of the *Lectures* bears strong witness to the use of the sources.

Joseph Story and Roman Law in America

Joseph Story is far better known to American lawyers than is John Austin. Born in Marblehead, Massachusetts, in 1779, he graduated from Harvard College in 1798.[70] From 1799 to 1801 he studied for the Bar in the offices of Samuel Sewall, and he began the practice of law in Essex in that latter year. In 1805 he was elected to the state legislature, where he served until 1808, when he was elected to Congress. In 1811, at the age of thirty-two, he became an associate justice of the United States Supreme Court, a post he retained until his death in 1845. In

1829 he was elected to be the first incumbent of the Dane Professorship of Law at Harvard. Beginning in 1832, he published a series of
Commentaries on legal subjects: on bailments in 1832, on constitutional
law in 1833, on the conflict of laws in 1834, on equity pleading in 1835,
on equity in 1836, on the law of agency in 1839, on partnership in
1841, on bills of exchange in 1843, and on promissory notes in 1845. If
Austin's life was dominated by failure, Story's was filled with success.

Despite their differences, Austin's and Story's careers have remarkable parallels. Both were early and important legal educators. Both
held chairs at prestigious universities. Both were authors of significant
legal treatises. Today Austin and Story are recognized as two of the
most substantial legal intellects of the first half of the nineteenth century, and the works of both are accepted as fundamental contributions
to the Anglo-American legal heritage. As described above, Austin's
Lectures are suffused by Roman and civil law. In this second part of
the chapter, the influence of Roman and civil law on Story's works will
be outlined, analyzed, and placed in its historical and philosophical
setting.

Story's Knowledge of Roman and Civil Law

Unlike John Austin, Joseph Story had no special training in Roman
and civil law. It is unlikely that during his undergraduate years at Harvard College he devoted much, if any, time to foreign sources and legal
systems. During his apprenticeship to Samuel Sewall he may have encountered civilian sources in his work on commercial law or admiralty,
though it is again unlikely that he had any formal training in these areas.[71] Nonetheless, with the zeal common to those who teach themselves, Story seems to have collected civilian writings with a passion
from an early date. We find him writing to Nathaniel Williams in
August 1812, for instance, requesting that Williams purchase a copy
of Cornelius Bynkershoek's works for him.[72] In an 1818 article in
the *North American Review* regarding David Hoffman's *Course of Legal
Studies*, Story shows a surprising breadth and depth of learning in the
civilian writers on commercial law and admiralty.[73] In an address titled
"Progress of Jurisprudence" presented to members of the Suffolk Bar
in September 1821, Story again showed the extent to which he was

aware of the importance of the civilian influence on common lawyers such as Lord Mansfield and Sir William Jones.[74] Indeed, subsequently, in a letter to Edward Everett concerning acquisitions for the newly founded Library of Congress, Story was insistent on the importance of Roman and civilian materials for American lawyers and law libraries.[75]

Of course, a tradition of interest in Roman and civil law was present among American jurists before and contemporary with Story. The generation of the Founding Fathers, men such as Jefferson and Adams, took a great interest in these subjects. Indeed, it is likely that Story's early experiences with Roman and civil law closely resembled those of his fellow Massachusetts citizen John Adams.[76] Thus, in showing an interest in these topics, Story followed in the footsteps of men such as Adams, Jefferson, and Wythe, but, as shall be apparent, he carried this interest further than they did.

It is also important to realize that Story was, like Austin, not unique in his period for his interest in Roman and civil law. Peter DuPonceau in Philadelphia and James Kent in New York both knew and used Roman and civilian ideas in their writings.[77] Indeed, Kent often used a French citation to "bully" his colleagues on the New York court to agree with an opinion.[78] Chancellor Kent, author of the famous *Commentaries on American Law*, first professor of law at Columbia, and longtime member of the New York judiciary, was well-known for his interest in Roman and civil law.[79] According to John Duer, Kent's first interest in the Continental jurists derived from his interest in French literature, an interest fostered by his friend Alexander Hamilton.[80] But his distinction for his interest in both Roman and civil law exceeded his literary fame:

> During his clerkship, he adopted the law of nature as a favorite study, and it was a study that he never abandoned. At a later period . . . his attention was directed to the Jurists of France, and with the writings of the principle—Domat, Emerigon, Valin, and Pothier—he had become thoroughly conversant: nor is this all. His understanding had assented with a full conviction to the opinion of Sir Matthew Hale, that without a knowledge, and that not slight and superficial, of the Roman law, our own law is never to be comprehended as a science . . . and following the advice of

Selden, and the examples of Hale and Holt and Mansfield, he had devoted and continued to devote, a considerable portion of his time to this important study. The Institutes, Pandeils, and Code of Justinian, as the writings of the great modern Civilians, by whom these immortal monuments of human wisdom, then vast repositories of legal science have been explained, methodized, as illustrated, became the subjects of his frequent personal and diligent meditation.[81]

Even in the substantive areas in which Story's use of Roman and civil law was most important, for instance, commercial law and conflicts of law, his contemporaries were doing the same thing. But Story's influence, because of his remarkable career and the equally remarkable volume of his publications, was clearly greatest and he did more, as shall be demonstrated, than other Americans of his period to further interest in Roman and civil law in the United States.

We are fortunate to have some knowledge of the books on Roman and civil law available to Story during the period when he was writing his *Commentaries*. In 1835, Harvard published a general catalog of its law library to which was appended a supplement listing two gifts of foreign materials.[82] The first, and larger, was the Livermore Collection, bequeathed in 1833 by a prominent Louisiana attorney, alumnus of Harvard, and legal author, Samuel Livermore.[83] The second, a smaller gift, came from none other than Story.

Both the Livermore bequest and the Story gift, recorded in the 1835 *Supplement to the Catalogue of the Law Library*, consist almost exclusively of foreign law books, principally from the sixteenth to eighteenth centuries. They are noteworthy for being antiquarian and do not reflect the scholarship of the latter half of the eighteenth and beginning of the nineteenth centuries. Although volumes by Giuseppe Casaregis and Hugo Grotius are present, for instance, the only text by Robert Joseph Pothier is his edition of the *Pandectae Justinianae*.[84] The wealth of antiquarian Roman and civilian materials, however, was virtually unparalleled in America at the time. Furthermore, more recent civilian works were clearly available to Story, albeit not from Harvard collections. The library of the Boston Athenaeum, for example, was rich in the more modern civilian texts.[85] In addition, Story must have possessed a substantial collection for his own use, as his citations in the various *Commentaries* testify. For example, in the *Commentaries on the Law of Bailments*, Story cites Jean Domat, Robert Joseph Pothier, Arnoldus Vinnius, Viscount Stair, J. G. Heinnecius, Samuel Hallifax, the French *Code Civil*, the Louisiana *Code of 1825*, and Lord Erskine, as well as Justinian's *Digest* and *Institutes*.[86] In the *Commentaries on the Law of Agency*, Story cites Domat, Bernabe Brisson, both the French *Code Civil* and the *Louisiana Code of 1825*, R. J. Pothier, J. G. Heineccius, Stair, Samuel Livermore, and Jacques Cujas, as well as the *Corpus Iuris Civilis*.[87] In the *Commentaries on the Law of Partnership* Story went a bit further afield. He cites Pothier, Samuel Pufendorf, Domat, Vinnius, the *Code Civil*, J. B. M. Duvergier, J. M. Pardessus, Erskine, Stair, A. Duranton, the *Louisiana Code of 1825*, and, of course, the *Corpus Iuris Civilis*.[88] To give one more example, the *Commentaries on the Conflict of Laws* are rife with quotations from civilian scholarship. Indeed, this work contains an index of forty-five authors cited, including Pothier, Heineccius, Ulrik Huber, Cujas, Pufendorf and Johannes Voet.[89]

Perhaps as important as the books in his and other libraries was that others in his circle were greatly interested in Roman and civil law. In Cambridge Story was well acquainted with two notable Romanists, John Pickering and Charles Follen.[90] He also came to know well another young German émigré who would himself become a noted civilian in the South, Francis Lieber, discussed in Chapter 2.

John Pickering was a native Bostonian, born in 1777 and educated at Harvard.[91] He was a successful practicing lawyer with a taste for the classics and an extensive knowledge of Roman law. His best-known work on the subject is his essay "The Civil Law," published in the third volume of the *American Jurist*.[92] This essay is an assertion of the necessity for American lawyers to study Roman and civil law and a paean to the revival of its study in Europe. It shows a remarkable knowledge of the subjects and of the modern literature thereupon.

Charles Follen was a German émigré, born at Romrod in 1796 and forced to flee Germany—where he had been lecturing on Roman law at Jena—who eventually made his way to the United States in 1824.[93] On his arrival he became a protégé of DuPonceau in Philadelphia, himself a jurist of note and one of the most learned civilians of his day.[94] Through DuPonceau's influence, Follen was appointed as professor of German at Harvard. His appointment there, however, specifically envisaged his teaching Roman law at the law school, which he did for the brief time he remained in Cambridge.[95] Lieber, another German émigré, carried on an extensive correspondence with Story and introduced him by mail to a leading German jurist of the day, Carl Joseph Anton Mittermaier.[96] This correspondence led to Story's becoming an editor of and contributor to Mittermaier's *Kritische Zeitschrift für Rechtswissenschaft und Gesetzgebung des Auslandes* and enabled Story to keep up with contemporary German scholarship.[97]

Thus, even as Story was beginning work on his great *Commentaries*, in which he would use Roman and civil law so well, he was surrounded by others both conversant with and supportive of such efforts. Undoubtedly, these personal contacts helped further his professional labors.

It becomes obvious, then, that Story had more than a passing acquaintance with Roman and civilian scholarship. Sympathetic colleagues and needed books were available to him and, judging by the frequency of citations to leading civilians, he had discussed these matters and read the books and digested the knowledge they contained. Surprisingly, there is a complete absence of German-language civilian scholarship in Story's works, no doubt because he never learned to read German.[98] In this Story was much different from John Austin, upon whom contemporary German civilian scholarship was directly influential.[99] The *Commentaries* also make it relatively clear that Story's knowledge of Roman law was derived from primarily secondary rather than primary sources, as was Austin's; his main reading and his main analysis centered on the civilian tradition rather than profound reading of the primary Roman texts. In this, he was, perhaps, a lesser Romanist than Pickering or Follen. Again this is fully understandable, for the civilian texts were those most easily accessible to an American lawyer, even to one who could not read German.[100] Although the various *Commentaries* do contain frequent references to Roman rather than to modern civilian sources, there is little indication either in the text or in the notes that Story found these primary sources on his own rather than being led to them by civilian writers of secondary textbooks.[101]

Thus, if asked to characterize Story's knowledge of Roman law, one would have to say that it was superficial and was derived from reading in the modern civilians but was relatively great for a practicing lawyer. His knowledge of the civilians, especially in the substantive areas that interested him, however, was extensive. Certainly, it was great enough that he felt comfortable in expounding substantive Roman and civil law doctrines in his *Commentaries*.

The Impact of Civilian Literature on the Treatise Format Adopted by Story

It has long been recognized that Story's *Commentaries* mark one of the first significant departures in the standard form of legal literature away from either the digest tradition or the multivolume, comprehensive commentary tradition.[102] The first, the digest tradition, was one of the oldest forms of Anglo-American legal literature, having much in common with the late medieval and early modern abridgments such as that of Anthony Fitzherbert.[103] The multivolume comprehensive commentary tradition was more recent, springing from Blackstone's *Commentaries on the Law of England* and Chancellor Kent's *Commentaries on American Law* and having some connection, perhaps, with the literature exemplified by Sir Edward Coke's *Institutes*. The form that Story adopted did not fit exactly within either of these traditions, for although Story called his books commentaries, they were, in fact, in the phrase of T. F. T. Plucknett, textbooks, or, as A. W. B. Simpson would have it, treatises.[104] The textbook, as defined by Plucknett and Simpson, is a monograph, beginning with a definition of the subject and proceeding "by logical and systematic stages to cover the whole field." The various *Commentaries* published by Story between 1832 and 1845 certainly fit this definition. Neither Plucknett nor Simpson, however, explicitly addressed why Story chose this new format.

Several reasons may be adduced for Story's choice of form. First is the purpose for which the *Commentaries* were written. Superficially, they were written to fill Story's need for teaching materials. Unlike Austin, Story was to instruct students in substantive areas of the law to prepare them for practice. Already by the time of Story's appointment as Dane Professor the movement for university legal education was strong in the United States, as opposed to England, where university lectures on the law were still intended mainly for laymen.[105] Story's students wanted preparation for practice, not legal theory.

Perhaps a second reason for Story's decision not to attempt to write a multivolume comprehensive commentary on the model of Blackstone or Kent was the pressure of time and the realization that the field was adequately supplied already. American editions of Blackstone were rife, complete with American case annotations, and Chancellor Kent's *Commentaries* were still relatively new.[106] For Story to attempt the time-consuming task of authoring such a comprehensive work de novo would have been foolish.

Although these reasons may explain why Story chose not to attempt to write in the established legal literary genres, they do not adequately explain how he came to be the "father" of the legal textbook. One commentator has suggested that the immediate reason for Story's adoption of this format was the influence of Nathan Dane and his *General Abridgement and Digest of American Law*, published in 1823.[107] Although it is reasonable to ascribe some influence to Dane and his work, the *General Abridgement* is substantively different in form from the *Commentaries* and thus it seems likely that other factors were active.[108] Yet another possibility is that Story was influenced in his choice of format by the development of the textbook-writing tradition in England. Sir William Jones published his *Essay on the Law of Bailments* in 1791.[109] Stewart Kyd published his *Treatise on the Law of Bills of Exchange* in 1790, and John Powell published a series of monographs between 1785 and 1790, including his *Treatise on the Law of Mortgages* in 1785 and his *Essay Upon the Law of Contracts and Agreements* in 1790.[110] Nevertheless, during the latter part of the eighteenth century and early part of the nineteenth century, the textbook form was still unusual in Anglo-American legal literature and was itself derivative from another tradition.

The textbook form was standard throughout the seventeenth and eighteenth centuries in Continental legal literature. The civilians mainly produced monographs. Digests and abridgments were alien to the Romanist tradition as it had developed in early modern Europe. Comprehensive works on the models of Gaius's and Justinian's *Institutes*, of course, were common relatively early in the modern period.[111]

Civilians began to author textbooks that systematically expounded a specialized area, often drawn from the institutional categories. During the century preceding Story's efforts, a veritable flood of such civilian monographs appeared. It seems clear that Story was aware of many of these civilian treatises, for instance the works of Pothier, and was directly encouraged in his choice of format by them. Thus at a fundamental level, civil law had a significant influence on Story's writings. Indeed, Story himself, in the first of the *Commentaries*, dealing with bailments, makes this formal influence clear. He says:

> There is a remarkable difference in the manner of treating juridical subjects, between the foreign and English jurists. The former almost universally, discuss every subject with an elaborate, theoretical fullness and accuracy, and ascent to the elementary principles of each particular branch of the science. The latter, with a few exceptions, write Practical Treatises, which contain little more than a collection of principles laid down in the adjudged cases, with scarcely an attempt to follow them out into collateral consequences.[112]

This statement raises a second issue in regard to the philosophical background of Story's *Commentaries*: the question of systematization and theoretical elaboration. The problem of the seeming chaos of the common law which so disturbed John Austin was not lost on Story. Story recognized that treatments of particular legal subjects had, for the most part, been untheoretical and unsystematic, little more than elaborate indexes to cases. Like Austin, Story felt the need for greater systematization. Systematization of the law was the key to developing an American legal science. Story, as a proponent of a national law and a national, unifying legal system, favored systematization for it, above all, would make centralization possible. Furthermore, systematization and the placing of law on a "scientific," analytic foundation were necessary to the development and maintenance of law as a learned profession. To the extent that these efforts could counter the increasing clamor by the Jacksonians for a popularization of law and the abandonment of law as a profession, Story's sympathy with systematization also carried political significance.[113]

Most Anglo-American legal literature during and before Story's period made little attempt to sort out the law in an analytic fashion. This was especially true in the United States. There can be no favorable comparison, in the matter of system, for example, between Chancellor Kent's *Commentaries on American Law* and Blackstone's *Commentaries on the Laws of England*. Regardless of whether one agrees with Blackstone's system of categories, it cannot be disputed that Blackstone spent much time and thought on the problem of the proper arrangement and categorization of law and was influenced by Roman and civilian ideas. Kent's *Commentaries* are an altogether different matter. Kent's work is divided into sixty-eight "lectures" and six "parts." These six parts are (1) "of the law of nations," (2) "of the government and constitutional jurisprudence of the United States," (3) "of the various sources of the municipal law of the several states," (4) "of the law concerning the rights of persons," (5) "of the law concerning personal property," and (6) "of the law concerning real property." Although these broad categories display a rudimentary system, they are based not on any theoretically elaborated system of categories, rules, and principles, but rather on the broad divisions of common law jurisprudence.

Story's *Commentaries* on particular subjects do not provide a systematic comprehensive overview on the model of Blackstone or Austin. They do, however, differ from Kent's *Commentaries* in that they show a definite concern with systematization and attempt to strike a balance between what Story appears to have viewed as an excessive concern with theory shown by the civilians and too great a focus on practice shown by most earlier Anglo-American legal works.[114] For instance, in the first of the series, the *Commentaries on the Law of Bailments*, Story begins the text with an exposition of the three categories of bailments and goes on to discuss the various subcategories, based on civil law, of deposits, mandates, loans for use, pledges, hire of things, hire of services, hire of custody, and both common carriers and carriers of persons. Indeed, each of the *Commentaries*, dealing with private law subjects, begins with a general definition of the subject and an attempt to establish a system of analysis. In this, Story is much in keeping with the civilian tradition and is far removed from earlier English concerns with the various writs and forms of action. Even more to the point, like the civilians he follows in the *Commentaries*, Story's text consists of a narrative treatment of the rules and principles of the law under consideration with illustrations from other legal systems. For the most part, cases are not discussed in the text but are relegated to the footnotes. Case law does not, in the *Commentaries*, dictate form. On the contrary, case law is used primarily to illustrate principles established as propositions in the "scientific" manner. In this regard, therefore, Story's work has much in common with the more comprehensive analytic works of Blackstone and Austin.

That case citations are almost exclusively confined to footnotes in many of Story's *Commentaries* and that the text gives a principled narrative with analysis should not be undervalued. Although there were English-language textbooks before Story's, his textbooks, on this specific point, are different. For instance, John Powell in his *Treatise on the Law of Mortgages* did clearly produce a monograph. The text of that monograph, however, is case-centered. The discussion, within the categories set out by Powell, proceeds according to the leading case authorities. In effect, this textbook form still bears many of the traces of the digest form of literature and thus tends less toward abstract theoretical evaluation and analysis. Much the same can be said of Sir William Jones's *Essay in the Law of Bailments*. Within the various categories of bailment described by Jones (and borrowed from the civilians) the text centers on cases, *Southcote's case, Coggs v. Bernard, Lane and Cotton's case*. Story's treatment of bailments in his 1832 *Commentaries*, in contrast, makes the cases subservient to the rules, even the leading case of *Coggs v. Bernard*.[115] Here again, this additional step away from the digest tradition toward the more abstracted, theoretical, "scientific" exposition more closely resembles contemporary civilian works than anything else. In effect, Story's *Commentaries* are more "scientific" than are those of his predecessors, in large part, perhaps, because of his civilian models.

Story's Use of Substantive Roman and Civil Law in the Commentaries

Although it is well-known that Story used Roman and civil law in his judicial decisions and in his written works, the extent to which he used it and the ways in which he used it remain less well explored. As seen above, John Austin drew on Roman and civil law primarily as a philosophical and linguistic source for his own efforts at systematization.[116] Austin was a creative user of Roman and civil law. Story was also a creative user, but in a different and, perhaps, less interesting way.

It is common to compare Story's use of Roman and civil law in his *Commentaries* to the way Lord Mansfield, one of Story's idols, used it in his decisions. George Sharswood, in his law lectures at the University of Pennsylvania in the 1850s, described Mansfield's use as follows: "This splendid monument of human wisdom, was to him a well-filled store-house of reasoning, from which a ready supply of principles and of rules, might always be drawn to guide him in the decision of cases unprovided for by our own jurisprudence."[117] Story, like Mansfield, used Roman and civil law as a source for filling gaps in the common law. Roman and civil law represented an old and complex system tried by history and containing solutions to problems not before dealt with by the traditional common law sources. Both Story and Mansfield knew that the opportunity for importing civil law concepts into the common law was great, especially in commercial law and admiralty. Mansfield was highly original in his acts of importation.[118] His numerous attempts to undermine the murky common law doctrine of consideration and replace it with the civilian notion of *causa* gave rise to much commentary and controversy.[119] Story, it will be seen, was generally less willing to attempt to replace common law doctrines and rules with Roman and civilian counterparts. On the contrary, in substantive areas Story's efforts went in a different direction. In many cases, where there simply was no common law rule, Story, like Mansfield, would draw on civilian sources for inspiration. Where a common law rule existed, however, Story would cite civilian sources analogically, either to contrast the civilian approach if it was substantially different or to confirm the universal appropriateness of the common law rule in its agreement with civilian learning. Several examples drawn from Story's writings will illustrate this point.

Story's *Commentaries on the Law of Bailments* provides an excellent illustration of the way in which he used civil and Roman law. Its full title is *Commentaries on the Law of Bailments with Illustrations from the Civil and the Foreign Law*. This was Story's first textbook, which he prepared as Dane Professor at Harvard, and was designed for the use of both law students and practicing lawyers. Story had as common law models Sir William Jones's *Essay on the Law of Bailments*, first published at London in 1781, and the section on bailments in Chancellor Kent's *Commentaries*.[120]

Sir William Jones's *Essay on the Law of Bailments* is a fascinating book. It opens with an abstract analysis of the historical rise of commerce, of the importance of inland navigation, and of the wisdom of Roman law and the barbarous beginnings of the English common law and moves to the development of mercantile law in England. Having begun in this philosophical manner, Jones goes on to explain the purpose of the work:

> I propose to begin with treating the subject analytically, and, having traced every part of it up to the first principles of natural reason, shall proceed, historically, to show with what perfect harmony those principles are recognized and established by other nations, especially the ROMANS, as well as by our ENGLISH courts, when their decisions are properly understood and clearly distinguished; after which I shall resume synthetically the whole learning of bailments, and such rules as, in my humble apprehension, will prevent any further perplexity on this interesting title, except in cases very peculiarly circumstanced.[121]

Following this declaration, Jones goes on first to discuss the law of bailments in the ancient world, especially in Rome. Then, in the main part of the text, he discusses the development of the law of bailments in England and concludes with several comparative sections on the laws of the northern nations, laws of the ancient Britons and of the Indians, and, finally, a synthesis of the law, attempting to establish definitions, rules, propositions, exceptions, and general corollaries.[122]

In his discussion of the English law of bailments, Jones works within five categories borrowed from Lord Holt, who derived them from Roman law: deposits, mandates, loans for use, pledges, and hiring. The latter he subdivides into three: hiring of a thing, hiring of work, and hiring of carriage.[123] Although this section is devoted to an exposition of English law, in fact much of the discussion derives from Roman and civilian sources. To take a specific case, Jones begins his discussion of the law of deposit with *Bonion's Case* (1315).[124] This case, an action brought for *detinue*, concerned the deposit of a locked chest filled with jewels, subsequently stolen by thieves. The question at issue seems to have been whether the bailee should be responsible for the contents of a *locked* chest.[125] Jones's analysis of the case first cites Lord Holt's opinion, then Coke's opinion, and then moves on to a discussion of Roman juristic opinions on the same subject.[126] Based on these precedents, Jones gives his own opinion on the subject. Jones's use of the Roman juristic opinions in this discussion is significant. In effect, Jones considers the Roman rules as authoritative as the common law rules, requiring the same degree of analysis and no further justification. For Jones's argument, both the common law and the civil law citations provide precedent of equal value. Jones does not attempt to contrast the common law rules with the Roman rules or to compare the different approaches critically.

Chancellor Kent discusses the law of bailments in Lecture XL of his *Commentaries*. He follows Jones in his categorization of bailments and in his discussion of *Bonion's Case*.[127] The form of Kent's argument is slightly different, however. First, he states the facts of the case and cites Lord Holt's opinion. Then he states that Roman law "was the same as to the responsibility of a depositary." Where Jones extensively cites conflicting opinions among the Roman jurists, Kent uses the Roman citations (derived from Jones) solely as illustrative of the rationality of the English rule and does not go further. Kent's discussion of this point is far briefer and more superficial than Jones's and his use of Roman law even less critical.

Story's *Commentaries on the Law of Bailments* are far more extensive than the efforts of either Kent or Jones. He begins his textbook with a general discussion of the whole law and then moves on to specific categories: deposits, mandates, gratuitous loans, pledges, and hire. This last category, hire, is further broken down into subcategories, including hire of things, hire of labor, hire of custody, carriage of goods, postmasters, innkeepers, and common carriers. In short, Story uses the same basic categories as do Lord Holt and Sir William Jones. His structure of the analysis within these categories, however, is different from that of Jones or Kent. He juxtaposes Roman law with common law and approaches Roman opinion on a different footing. Within each category Story states the various rules and elaborates upon them. He then goes on to state the common law rule but then discusses only the civil law rule in detail. Thus Story analyzes *Bonion's Case* as follows. First, Story poses the abstract hypothetical as to whether a bailee is responsible for the loss of the contents of a closed package which were unknown to him. He next cites, generally, Roman juristic speculation on the subject, drawn entirely from Jones. Then he cites and discusses *Bonion's Case*. Finally he states the common law rule: "That the depositary is bound to reasonable care, proportioned, indeed, to the nature and value of the article, and the danger of loss, and the measure of that care being slight diligence, the result is, that he is generally liable for gross negligence only." Story then goes on to discuss exceptions to this general rule, and it is here that another major difference between Story and Jones emerges. Story rejects the Roman rule that a depositary "is liable for losses where he has made an officious offer," that is, is liable for negligence as well as fraud, whereas Jones accepted it uncritically.[128]

Story thus does not treat Roman law as the authority that Jones does. Rather, he treats Roman law as an alien system, composed of rules and principles that should be used if they comport with common law notions and ideas of justice and fairness, not because of any inherent authority or superior rationality. It is especially notable that Story rejects the civilian rule (the Roman rule was adopted both by Pothier and Domat) in this context, for he was well aware that the common law of bailments as a whole derived, in large part, from Roman and civil law. Thus, in spite of this "genetic" connection, Story still felt that the Roman and civil law lacked any authority other than that of rationality. Where he agreed with the Roman and civilian rule he accepted it, but otherwise he did not. In this case, Story judged the Roman and civilian rule to be too harsh and contrary to the spirit of the common law and so rejected it.[129]

It is also important, however, in comparing Story's approach to that of Jones, not to lose sight of the fact that Story's labors were entirely secondary as to the use of the Roman sources and very much dependent on Jones, even for the later civilian writings. Thus Story's originality did not lie in the discovery of Roman and civilian sources but rather in the way he used these sources. As illustrated by this discussion of *Bonion's Case* and the law of bailments, Story looked to Roman law for comparison and contrast but felt no compulsion to accept Roman and civilian rules unless they were acceptable to his common law reasoning. Story looked at the Roman and civilian sources quite consciously as a common lawyer looking for useful material, but he accepted foreign notions only when he found them persuasive. Roman and civil law for Story had no magical quality. When it was useful and in keeping with the common law, he would adopt it. If contrary to his notions of what the common law should be, he rejected it outright.

The discussion above illustrates one of the principal ways in which Story discussed Roman and civil law in his various *Commentaries*. It testifies also to the critical eye with which Story examined foreign legal materials. Unlike his predecessors and those lawyers in the natural law tradition who looked to Roman law as a virtual depository of *ratio scripta*, Story was willing to reject Roman and civil law if he felt that the principles underlying a particular substantive rule were inappropriate for the American common law.[130]

Yet this critical attitude toward Roman and civil law does not frequently manifest itself in the *Commentaries*. Rather, the vast majority of citations to Roman and civil law in the series of *Commentaries* serve a purely illustrative and confirmatory function.[131] In most cases, when Story cites a Roman or civil law substantive doctrine, he does so to show that the American or Anglo-American rule is paralleled by the civilian rule. Again, examples drawn from the various *Commentaries* can serve to illustrate this aspect of Story's work.

In the *Commentaries on the Law of Bailments*, for instance, Story devotes several pages to a discussion of the right of a pledgee to use goods pledged to him for his own purposes. The general rule at common law, according to Story, was established by Lord Holt in *Coggs v. Bernard* and is to the effect that if the pawned goods will be harmed by use, they cannot properly be used by the pledgee. If, however, the goods will be no worse for wear, it would seem that he might use them, but, in fact, notes Story, they may not be so used if use exposes them to any "unnecessary and extraordinary perils." Story then goes on to discuss Roman and French law, which he states "do not . . . seem materially to differ from the common law." From this, he proceeds to a discussion of Louisiana law under the *Code of 1825*, which is the same.[132] The various foreign rules are simply stated without analysis or criticism because they agree with the common law.

In the *Commentaries on the Law of Agency*, to give another example, Story discusses the inability of an individual *sui juris* to take upon himself an incompatible duty, that is, to become an agent in a transaction in which his personal interest is adverse to that of his principal. Immediately after setting out the common law doctrine, Story comments: "The Civil law recognized in the fullest manner the same doctrine."[133]

A third way in which Story used Roman and civil law was interstitially. Perhaps the best illustration of the way in which Story adopted Roman and civil law principles when no common law substantive rule existed is to be found in his *Commentaries on the Conflict of Laws Foreign and Domestic*.[134] Kurt Nadelmann in his seminal article "Joseph Story's Contribution to American Conflicts Laws," emphasized this interstitial nature of much of Story's importation of civilian doctrine in the conflicts field.[135] As Nadelmann stressed, the area of conflicts of law was not barren in the United States before Story published his *Commentaries*. There had been scores of cases in the various states as well as two treatises published in the 1820s by Jabez Henry and Samuel Livermore.[136] Nevertheless, as Story noted in his preface to the *Commentaries*: "The materials are loose and scattered and are to be gathered from many sources, not only uninviting, but absolutely repulsive to the mere Student of the Common Law."[137] In his *Commentaries on the Conflict of Laws*, Story attempted to set out these various materials, both common law and civilian, and where no common law rule existed, to state the civilian doctrine as authority. Thereby, Story imported civilian ideas into American law.

It is remarkable that nowhere in Story's various *Commentaries* is there any serious attempt to supplant common law rules with civilian or Roman doctrine. Unlike Austin or even Sir William Jones, it would appear that Story generally was unwilling to reject a common law rule outright, even if a Roman or civilian rule had greater cogency.[138] In his discussion of whether a bailee should be held liable for theft of the bailed goods, Story took strong issue with the Roman and civil law doctrine accepted by Sir William Jones that the bailee would be liable because theft is evidence of gross neglect on the part of the bailee. Story attacked Jones's treatment on significant grounds:

Exclusively of this dictum, the sole reliance of Sir William Jones is on the text of the Roman law and the commentaries of the civilians. Even if the true purport of the Roman law, (as well as the commentaries of the civilians thereon,) were not open to controversy, and susceptible of various explanations, the application thereof, *as an authority in the common law, is not admitted.* (Emphasis added.)[139]

Mindful of this unwillingness to suggest that a civilian or Roman rule might actually replace an inferior common law rule, we must ask why Story cited Roman and civilian doctrines at all. Obviously, Story found Roman and civil law interesting. Yet, in a very real sense, it was a mere garnish on his exposition of common law.[140] In Story's jurisprudence, the common law tradition was preeminent.

Story and Austin: Two Early Nineteenth-Century Perspectives on the Use of Roman and Civil Law

The preceding sections of this chapter attempt to analyze in some detail the influence of Roman and civil law on John Austin and Joseph Story. Several interesting conclusions emerge from this analysis. First, it is undeniable that both Story and Austin made use of Roman and civilian legal materials in their scholarly work. Yet there were important differences.

Neither Austin nor Story had a profound knowledge of Roman and civil law in all its complexity. Austin's was derived from several years' reading in the basic Roman institutional writings and from his time in Germany spent studying the later civilian institutional authors. Story's was derived, apparently, from private study, primarily in the civil-law-influenced English legists such as Jones, Mansfield, and Holt, in the French civilian treatise literature by authors such as Pothier and Domat, in the Scots civilians, and in early modern civil law texts such as those of Voet, Vinnius, and Heineccius. Story appears to have been virtually ignorant of German legal scholarship. Neither Austin nor Story gives evidence of much depth of learning in the Roman primary sources.

The different civilian traditions from which Austin and Story drew their knowledge of Roman and civil law may have influenced their use of these alien legal systems. One could argue that the overwhelming preoccupation of the German civilians with system and order, with abstraction of rules and principles, influenced Austin in his opinion that the common law was chaotic. Yet to do so is to ignore both the domestic English tradition of Finch, Hale, and Blackstone and the importance of Bentham and the utilitarian codification movement upon Austin's work. Perhaps it would be more correct to say that the German preoccupation with legal systemization was a happy circumstance of which Austin could take full advantage to suit his own purposes. Similarly, one might argue that Story chose to use Roman and civil law precisely because he realized that their systems provided substantive rules in areas not adequately elaborated at common law, as had Holt and Mansfield. Yet, here again, this would overlook both a domestic tradition of interest in the civil and Roman law before the beginning of Story's scholarly career, as well as the fact that much of Story's use of Roman and civilian doctrine was confirmatory and merely illustrative of the universal validity of common law rules. It would seem, therefore, that it is far too simple to say that either Story or Austin used Roman and civil law simply because it was there and because they were familiar with it.

Perhaps one way to approach an explanation of Austin's and Story's use of foreign law is by posing a basic question. To what extent were Roman and civil law *central* to the work of each? If one can answer this question and contrast the answers it will, perhaps, become more clear how and why each valued Roman and civil law.

For Austin, it should be obvious that Roman law, Roman institutional ideas, and Roman legal vocabulary were absolutely central to the main course of the *Lectures*. It is not without some significance that Austin questioned the necessity of appointing someone to the chair of Roman law at London after his own appointment to the chair of jurisprudence. For Austin, Roman law was scientific law, and scientific law was what jurisprudence was all about. By adopting civilian systematic ideas and Roman legal vocabulary, Austin was able to reject forcefully any claim for the necessity to understand law in its historical context. Thus not only could he reject any argument that the unsystematic and chaotic nature of the common law was an inevitable by-product of historical development impossible to change by radical reform, but he was also able to develop a principled attack on Savigny's writings against codification.[141] For Austin, Roman institutional legal ideas were quintessentially disembodied, historical abstractions and, as such, were perfect for developing an ideal, even "Platonic" jurisprudence unsullied by the inconsistencies of life. Roman law, as Austin understood it, was the legal reductionist's dream. One can suggest, indeed, that without Roman and civil law, Austin's *Lectures* could not have been written. Thus, why did Austin choose to make Roman and civilian institutional legal ideas central to his work?

The answer to this question is bipartite. In part, one may suggest that Austin adopted Roman and civilian institutional ideas because by his day there had come to be a consensus among English jurists that the uncodified common law simply did not have within it the seeds of an adequate system. By adopting Roman and civilian ideas and vocabulary, Austin could draw upon centuries of experience with systematizing and bringing the law into a logical order. In short, Austin employed Roman and civil law because it was the best model available to him. Indeed, that Austin chose to go to Germany before beginning his lectures at London suggests that he had decided on the necessity of using Roman and civilian legal ideas long before he began composing the *Lectures* and before he had mastered Continental institutional learning. One may thus suggest that Austin was responding to a commonly perceived notion that Roman and civil law were the repositories of an ideal concept of system, available for mining by the enterprising English jurist.

A second reason for Austin's substantial use of Roman and civil law may well have been its political and philosophical significance. It is too easy to forget the political aspects of Roman law, especially in the late eighteenth and early nineteenth centuries. Austin was a political conservative and opponent of the Reform Act of 1832.[142] Although it would be an overstatement to suggest that his desire for systematization of law stemmed from political motives, it is less difficult to suggest that the Roman law held a general political attraction for Austin. Roman and civil law were seen by many as part and parcel of an aristocratic system, one in which the mob held little power. Roman law was the legal system of Cicero and Marcus Aurelius. Mastery of it was difficult. Its logic was complex. It could be used as a tool for conservative reform, to abolish the antiquated aspects of the common law repulsive to Austin, while preserving the rule of law. As such, it could well have seemed ideal to an upper-class barrister and law professor of a conservative political bent.

What about Story? Were Roman and civil law central to his scholarly work? In the main, the answer to this question must be no. The various *Commentaries* show little evidence of Story's knowledge of primary Roman sources. Basically, Story knew English-language works, either translations or original works based on Roman and civil law, and he knew the work of the French civilians well. Nevertheless, civil law is not central to any of the *Commentaries*, except, perhaps, the *Commentaries on the Conflict of Laws*, which are very dependent on the civilian writers by default of common law rules. By and large, however, Story could easily have written the other *Commentaries*, on bailments, bills of exchange, promissory notes, agency, and partnership, without ever mentioning Roman and civil law. Citations to Roman law built on the discussions of earlier writers, Jones on bailments, for instance, or Livermore on agency, so that such references to civil and Roman law might be seen partly as traditional as well as a reply to these earlier authors. But generally, the majority of Story's citations of Roman and civil law are superfluous to his argument, merely pleasant excursions into esoteric learning. In his scholarly writings, at least—excluding his judicial opinions—Story treated Roman and civil law as supplementary and not as central, as "icing on the cake."

Why, then, did Story use so much Roman and civil law in his scholarship? If it was not central, as it was to Austin's work, why bother? One could answer this question in several ways. First, it has been suggested, based on the prefaces to the early *Commentaries*, that Story adopted this method of writing because he held the Dane Professorship and because Nathan Dane in his *Abridgement* had included much French material as authoritative.[143] This answer is too simple. One could also take a biographical view, as did Nadelmann, and suggest that Story's early admiralty work as a lawyer and judge convinced him that Roman and civil law were important and worthy of attention.[144] After all, the *Commentaries* are schoolbooks, and Story clearly did believe that a little civilian learning was not a dangerous thing. Indeed, in a letter to Chancellor Kent, Story wrote: "I could not well see how I could avoid introducing it [civil law] without leaving future accounts in ignorance of important sources of information, and even without bringing up the knowledge of the learned in the Common law some views of principles which had carried continental jurists in an opposite light."[145] Obviously, the inclusion of learned esoterica from the Roman and civil law helped to give Story's works a feeling of erudition. Thus Story, like John Adams before him, may have used Roman law to make himself appear to be learned. Further, learning in the early nineteenth century continued to be premised on the Greek and Roman classics. By adding Roman materials, Story may also very consciously have attempted to elevate the study of law to a university level, away from practical apprenticeship in a law office. Certainly, for the Dane Professor at Harvard, such an attitude would have been natural.

It is also important to recognize the importance of the political dimension of Roman and civil law to Story's treatises. Story, like Austin, was a political conservative. According to Kent Newmyer, Story showed distinct traces of traditional whiggism in his writings and in his personal relations.[146] He was firmly opposed to the "mobocracy" that the Jacksonians and their supporters seemed to threaten. In this context Roman and civil law had a definite appeal on two levels. First, as may well have been the case with Austin, Story could easily have seen Roman and civil law as the repositories of such Ciceronian concepts as republican virtue and enlightened, but not excessively democratic, government.[147] Such a legal philosophy, of course, would have been appealing as a means of combating the threat of Jacksonian democracy.[148]

Equally appealing to Story, perhaps, was the political utility of systematic ideas from Roman and civil law. Story, like Austin, favored legal codification, but of a non-Benthamite form. He did not support radical Benthamite philosophical codification but was a proponent of what has been called moderate codification. Story believed that limited codification, as in the making of digests of law, would make the law more manageable, as well as unified. Story favored codification as a means of improving the law, not as part of a movement to make every man his own lawyer.[149] Thus both the French and Roman codificatory efforts were ideal models for Story.[150] Perhaps he chose, in part, to illustrate his common law treatises with Roman and civil law examples not so much to convince his readers of the rightness of civilian and Roman doctrines as to draw their attention to these systems as a whole.

On the Utility of the Civil Law for the Common Lawyer

It is the conventional wisdom that Roman and civil law played little part in the formation and development of the Anglo-American legal tradition. Some few scholars, mainly civilians, have argued the other extreme, that Roman and civil law were immensely influential.[151] Neither view is totally correct, and it would seem that a compromise position is warranted. This chapter, through a detailed analysis of the work of Austin and Story, illustrates the two categories of borrowing that existed. On the one hand, as exemplified by Austin, Roman law was viewed as an ideal system that could act as an "ordering principle." This borrowing sought to impose Roman and civilian notions on the common law and to rework the common law, even to its very terminology, in the image of an alien system. The other tradition, exemplified by Story, saw in the Roman and civil law an opportunity to supplement the Anglo-American tradition and to confirm parallel Anglo-American rules but rejected any notion of a radical reworking of our native tradition into an alien image.

It is tempting to characterize the efforts of Story and Austin as early essays in comparative law and to praise them for that reason alone. Again, this is far too simplistic an approach. Rudolf Schlesinger has suggested that true "comparison" must be distinguished from mere "juxtaposition."[152] Furthermore, comparative legal scholarship must attempt to evaluate critically at least two different legal traditions and ought to approach the source materials for such a comparison without predisposition or prejudice. By these standards, neither Austin nor Story should properly be called a comparativist in the modern sense. Austin's interest in comparison was peripheral, and his approach to both common law and civil law was colored by his search for order and system. Story, too, was not truly a comparativist. His efforts, in Schlesinger's words, were, to a large extent, mere juxtaposition of legal rules with little attempt at synthesis. Nevertheless, though neither Austin nor Story was a comparativist in the modern sense, their use of Roman and civil law is significant, for it reveals much about the development of common law scholarship in the early nineteenth century. And, of course, their histories are but the beginning of the story.

2

Roman and Civil Law in the Anglo-American World Before 1850

In 1870, an essayist began his review of the *Writings of Hugh Swinton Legaré* by lamenting: "The great names of the South are dying out. For want of an adequate record, men, whose genius the whole country honored in their lifetime, are beginning to sink into obscurity."[1]

In the first half of the nineteenth century, there flourished a brilliant and distinctive legal culture in the southern United States. While the northern tradition tended to center around concepts of practical virtue and was relatively narrowly focused on the more technical aspects of law, in the South lawyers were also men of broad culture, following more in the path, perhaps, of Thomas Jefferson, the great polymath, than Theophilus Parsons, the brilliant but intellectually ascetic Massachusetts judge.[2]

The South led the way, for instance, in legal education. George Wythe at the College of William and Mary was the first full-time law professor in the United States.[3] His model was followed at the University of Virginia and the University of Georgia. Law schools were established and continued successfully at Transylvania University in Lexington, Kentucky, and at Tulane in New Orleans, among others.[4] Southern lawyers were founders of and contributors to major literary journals such as the *Southern Review* and the *Southern Literary Messenger*.[5] Several built great libraries and became patrons of the arts and of letters.[6] They studied not only in the South but in the North at Harvard, for instance, and abroad in England, Scotland, and on the European continent.[7] Brilliant legal centers existed at Charleston and in New Orleans.[8] And the political questions of the day, such as nullification and secession, called the best legal minds into the fields of constitutional law and political theory. Thus it is particularly unfortunate that as the antebellum southern tradition died out and the historiography of the period became obsessed with analyzing the influence of slavery, the full vitality and breadth of this tradition have been utterly forgotten.[9]

It has been common to speak of American legal development in virtually complete isolation from the intellectual traditions of Europe during the nineteenth century.[10] It is as if the extensive contacts between the Founding Fathers of the American republic and the great lawyers, philosophers, and statesmen of Enlightenment Europe were simply broken off and forgotten after 1800.

To take this narrow historiographical position is to ignore completely the extensive interaction between civil law and common law ideas in the United States during the nineteenth century in the works of American common law jurists and to ignore, as well, the extensive contacts between American and European scholars and jurists.[11] Interest in Continental legal scholarship and practice was vigorous throughout the early nineteenth century. In the first chapter I discussed the impact of Roman and civil law ideas on the most important of the northeastern American jurists, Joseph Story and his circle. But the influence of Continental legal learning was notable in the antebellum South as well. European scholarship was an important part of the southern legal tradition, just as European literature formed a major part of the southern literary public's reading matter.[12] Southern lawyers trained abroad and were in close contact with Europeans. Roman and civil law scholarship reached a high level among southern lawyers and jurists in the common law jurisdictions of the South during the antebellum period in, for example, Virginia and South Carolina, as well as in those with civil law traditions such as Louisiana and Texas.

One circle of civilians that has received very little attention is that which grew up around Charleston and Columbia, South Carolina. This group, in particular, stands as an example of the highest intellectual attainments reached by antebellum American lawyers. They rivaled their northern colleagues, Story, Kent, and DuPonceau, in both knowledge and influence. The three principal members of this circle were Francis Lieber, Hugh Swinton Legaré, and James Murdock Walker.[13] All were South Carolinians, two by birth, one by adoption. Hugh Swinton Legaré was born in Charleston in 1797; James Walker was born in Charleston in 1813; Francis Lieber was born in Berlin in 1798 but emigrated first to the northeastern United States in 1827 and then to Columbia, South Carolina, in 1835. Legaré and Walker were practicing lawyers as well as government servants. Walker was a South Carolina state legislator; Legaré served as American chargé d'affaires in Belgium, as well as United States attorney general and secretary of state pro tem in 1842–43. Lieber held the chair of constitutional history at South Carolina College in Columbia for two decades. In 1857 he left South Carolina for Columbia University School of Law in New York and there held the second chair in law under Theodore Dwight.[14]

Walker, Lieber, and Legaré were all prolific authors. Walker wrote three books: *An Inquiry into the Use and Authority of Roman Jurisprudence in the Law Concerning Real Estate; The Theory of the Common Law* (which is actually a study in comparative legal history and a disquisition on the relationship between Roman law and common law); and *Tract on Government* (which he published anonymously).[15] Lieber, too, wrote several books, including his *Legal and Political Hermeneutics*, the *Manual of Political Ethics*, and *Civil Liberty*.[16] *Legal and Political Hermeneutics*, the most prominent of his works, has been characterized by the late Arthur Schiller as the first American attempt to establish a set of "canons" of legal interpretation.[17] Although not explicitly a civilian or Romanist work, Lieber's text drew principally on Roman legal sources and the principles of the new German school of biblical criticism for its inspiration and its models in developing hermeneutic rules. Legaré authored no books, but he was a co-founder of and a frequent contributor to the *Southern Review* as well as an occasional contributor to its forerunner, the *North American Review*, both of which were widely read literary magazines on the model of such European journals as the *Edinburgh Review* and contained substantial amounts of legal material.[18] All three men were passionately involved in their writing not only with Roman and civil law but also with classical and European culture.

Lieber, the German émigré, never abandoned his connections with Germany, even though he fully embraced his new country.[19] His correspondence reveals a wide circle of scholarly and personal friendships with both leading European and American jurists. This circle included American lawyers such as Kent and Story and Europeans such as the Swiss J. K. Bluntschli and the German C. J. A. Mittermaier. Lieber's wide professional and social acquaintance may be attributable in part to his peripatetic career. He began by journeying from Germany to Italy in the household of Gottfried Niebuhr, the classical historian, and, after a brief stay in England, found his way to Boston for several years, where he founded a swimming school, then to Philadelphia, where he worked on penology and prison reform, and, finally, to Columbia, South Carolina, where he took up a professorship.[20] In part, too, his wide acquaintance undoubtedly derived from his efforts to cultivate powerful and important men such as Story, Kent, and Mittermaier so as to further his professional career. Lieber had the advantage both of his German university training and extensive travels and his willingness to pursue those he felt could aid him professionally.[21]

Indeed, Lieber served as an intermediary for European legal culture in two related ways. First, of course, through the nearly half-century of his career in the United States, Lieber incorporated Roman and civil law ideas into his writing and teaching and provided a corpus of work that helped to popularize this incorporation. Second, Lieber acted as a personal intermediary among German and American jurists. For instance, he introduced Joseph Story to Carl Joseph Anton Mittermaier at a crucial time in both their careers. Story had just taken the Dane Professorship and was embarked on the ambitious project of writing his several *Commentaries* on various topics in American law. Mittermaier and Lieber helped Story to acquire current German scholarship on these topics (such as conflicts of laws) and ensured that Story's writings would become known on the European continent. Reciprocally, Story aided Mittermaier in his major project at this time, publication of the *Kritische Zeitschrift für Rechtswissenschaft und Gesetzgebung des*

Auslandes. Story contributed a specially written article on American law to Mittermaier's new journal and joined its board of editors.[22] In all of this, Lieber's role as an intermediary was crucial.

Legaré's birth and early education were wholly domestic, but after graduation from South Carolina College, he resolved to study abroad. Later correspondence indicates that his initial desire to go to Germany to study law was thwarted by the then unstable political situation on the Continent. Instead, in 1818 Legaré matriculated as a student at Edinburgh University in the Department of Civil Law.[23] At this time the Edinburgh faculty boasted two professors who would have been of interest to a young American law student. David Irving was professor of civil law and offered two courses on civilian subjects.[24] The first was an introductory course in Roman law based on the text of Justinian's *Institutes*.[25] The second, the more advanced course, analyzed Justinian's *Digest* and jurists' law.[26] Both courses consisted of lectures based, in large part, on the work of Heineccius, a leading eighteenth-century German commentator.[27] Also then lecturing at Edinburgh in the philosophy faculty was Dugald Stewart, the first volume of whose *Elements of the Philosophy of the Human Mind* had appeared in 1792.[28] Stewart was a student of James Reid and Adam Ferguson, and his philosophical work was firmly in the tradition of the Scottish Enlightenment.[29] Therefore, much of it was concerned with law as one of the "human sciences" and a philosophical approach to law and morality.

The year at Edinburgh had a major impact on Legaré. It was apparently during this year that he first acquired his love of Roman and civil law. As his sister wrote:

> Now, in its wide and regular principles, the accumulation of such long-applied learning and ability, it rose upon his sight as a great and noble science, capable of being brought to enlighten, as had never yet been done, the narrower and more dogmatic methods of our inherited or native jurisprudence. Its exacter and more elegant vehicle and authors, and its close connection with his favorite bodies of literature and history served also, no doubt, greatly to allure him. It became henceforth, therefore, one of his regular studies, especially as mixing so much with another—that

of law, natural and national; and finally grew (as we shall see) to be one of his chief attainments, with a view to a very lofty and bold juridical purpose.[30]

Legaré's stay in Edinburgh was not to be his only foray abroad, however. He returned to the Continent in 1832, after having achieved professional success at the South Carolina Bar, to become United States chargé d'affaires in Brussels. In spite of ill health and a constant shortage of money, he found the time, the energy, and the funds to travel widely on the Continent.[31] He traveled especially in Germany, to seek out books and to meet and study with Friedrich Carl von Savigny, desiring to learn as much as he could about Savigny's "historical school," to which he later claimed allegiance.[32]

James Murdock Walker was born in Charleston in 1813.[33] His father was a Scotsman, his mother a native of Charleston. He was educated at Charleston and then at South Carolina College in Columbia from which he graduated in 1830. After college he returned to Charleston, where he studied law with Mitchell King, a leading practitioner and doyen of the Charleston Bar, and was called to the Bar in 1834. Apparently, he had a successful practice and also concurrently served several terms in the state legislature. Although his professional and social life was centered in Charleston, both by birth and parentage and because of the extremely cosmopolitan nature of Charleston itself during this period, he was exposed to a substantial dose of Continental and classical culture and learning, which shows clearly in his written works.[34]

Of course, exposure to European culture does not automatically give rise to an interest in civil law, nor does it make those who are so exposed into experts on Roman and civil law. Lieber, Legaré, and Walker, nevertheless, all showed not only a high regard for Continental legal learning in their writings but also substantial expertise in this field. To author books and articles such as theirs, they not only needed some training in civilian and Roman legal scholarship, as Legaré, for instance, obtained in Edinburgh, but they also needed language skills and access to substantial library holdings on Roman and civil law.

Of the three men, Lieber seems to have been the best endowed linguistically, speaking not only English but German and French and reading the classical languages.[35] Legaré apparently did not learn German until 1833, but after that he also learned French and the classical languages.[36] Walker's background is the most obscure, although he clearly read Latin. Thus all three could read some classical and European sources, and in the antebellum South, they were available.

Many American law libraries (and some general libraries) in the first half of the nineteenth century had substantial holdings in civil law and Roman law. For instance, Harvard had an excellent collection through the generosity of one of its alumni, Samuel Livermore.[37] Livermore's library formed the nucleus of Joseph Story's working collection when he was writing his *Commentaries*. Here, again, the breadth of the southern legal and literary tradition as contained in Livermore's library was to play an important role nationally. Books on Roman and civil law were not difficult to find in the antebellum South. In South Carolina, two libraries, in particular, were rich in these holdings and were used by the "Civilian Circle" of Lieber, Legaré, and Walker.

The library of South Carolina College was not large, but its collection was cosmopolitan and well chosen, including some of the most important books on Roman, civil, and natural law. Among the civil law holdings were introductory texts such as Jean Domat's *Les loix civiles dans leur ordre naturel* and Thomas Wood's *Institutes of the Civil Law*. There was a copy of Arthur Browne's lectures on the civil law as well. Hugo Grotius, Pufendorf, Thomas Rutherforth, Georg F. Martens, and J. J. Burlamaqui were all represented in the natural law section. The library had copies, also, of John Louis Delolme and Flowers on the French constitution, Cesare Beccaria on criminal law, and A. B. Goguet on the *Origin of Laws*. The library had in addition a copy of Edward Gibbon's *Decline and Fall of the Roman Empire*, the forty-fourth chapter of which was a standard introductory text for Roman law studies during the early nineteenth century, both in the United States and on the Continent.[38] Naturally, the library had an extensive collection of Cicero's works, both in the original Latin and in English translation. Cicero, like Gibbon, was seen as a principal literary source for Roman law and legal oratory in the nineteenth century.[39] The college library at Columbia was available to all three men. Furthermore, both Walker and Legaré had access to the Charleston Bar library, which, though a working lawyer's library, also apparently had civil law holdings. For instance, Walker used the Bar library's copy of Duck's *De usu et authori-*

tate juris civlis Romanorum per domina principum Christianorum, a leading Anglo-Romanist treatise, in writing his 1850 monograph on the Roman law of real property.[40] All three also had their own private libraries to consult. Of these, the best known to us, from its privately printed catalog, is Legaré's. The catalog lists 143 Latin titles, 77 Greek titles, 53 French titles, 61 German titles, 9 Italian titles, 36 English titles, as well as Italian, French, Spanish, Hebrew, and Portuguese dictionaries and reference works. The vast majority of the non-English books—excluding Greek—are Roman and civilian legal texts. The remainder tend to be editions of classical authors and commentaries thereon. Among these titles were not only most of the major editions of primary Roman law texts from the seventeenth and eighteenth centuries, representing the humanist legal-textual tradition, but also all of the major humanist Roman legal commentators on the Continent from Cujas to Heineccius to Savigny. Legaré's library was also very strong in the modern civilians and Pandectists and included the works of Pothier, Cooper, Barbeyrac, Hugo, Jakob Grimm, K. F. Eichhorn, and Heinrich Dirksen.[41] Legaré's civil law collection was better than that in the Library of Congress, as judged by its 1812 catalog,[42] and than the Livermore library, which was donated to Harvard, used by Joseph Story in writing his *Commentaries*, and which became the foundation of the Harvard Law School libraries. Although Legaré owned fewer civilian volumes than Harvard did in 1834, Legaré's library was undoubtedly second only to Harvard's at that time.[43] In short, Legaré's library went far beyond the norm for both private and public law libraries during this period and provided a perfect base from which to work.

But the background, training, and resources available to Lieber, Legaré, and Walker do not reveal the extent to which their "Circle" was so significant. To understand its importance, it is necessary to analyze their writings and document the extent to which they were known to the literate public.

Lieber's main "Romanist" work is his *Legal and Political Hermeneutics*, first published in book form at Boston in 1839. The book is an attempt to systematize and rationalize the confused doctrine regarding proper interpretive principles to be applied in reading legal documents. The text is notable for several of its features. First, it is systematic. Lieber attempts to develop legal interpretation into a science based on broadly applicable hermeneutic rules. At the time he was writing, hermeneutic method among the common lawyers was in a primitive state. Commonly accepted rules of interpretation for specific types of legal texts such as wills existed, but no serious attempts had been made to establish universally applicable rules of interpretation. Lieber set himself to this task in the *Hermeneutics*. He analyzes the types of verbal ambiguities a reader may encounter, classifies them according to cause, and then establishes principles for their resolution. To draw a specific example of Lieber's use of Roman and civilian sources, one might, for instance, note Lieber's discussion of the proper interpretation to be placed upon a statement made in contradistinction to a superior authority external to the text in question. Lieber argues that such a statement made contrary to a higher authority must be interpreted as legally null and void. It can have no validity *ab initio* because it is, by definition, impermissible. In supporting this proposition, which follows the general logic of interpretation, Lieber looks to two Roman legal passages for support and confirmation, the first from Justinian's *Code*, the second from an argument of Papinian contained in Book 50 of Justinian's *Digest*.[44] Even more interesting, Lieber goes on to connect this hermeneutic principle based on Roman law to the American practice of judicial review of legislation raising constitutional issues.[45] In short, Lieber not only used Roman legal principles to illustrate his own hermeneutic rules but analyzed American legal principles in light thereof. In fact, the *Legal and Political Hermeneutics* demonstrates throughout not only Lieber's extensive knowledge of Roman and civilian sources but also his ability to employ principles contained in these systems to analyze Anglo-American law. This aspect of his work is particularly significant, for it meant that the *Legal and Political Hermeneutics* could be extremely useful to working lawyers and jurists and not just to scholars and antiquaries. Lieber's approach to Roman and civil law in the *Hermeneutics* is neither antiquarian nor historical. Rather, Lieber used examples from these legal systems for comparative and illustrative purposes. Since he was attempting to develop a *universally* useful method of interpretation and construction applicable to all legal texts, the ability to show that a particular principle of interpretation or construction was valid not only for Anglo-American law but also for Roman and civil law was crucial. In effect, by showing that a particular principle of interpretation was accepted as valid in several legal systems, Lieber was able to confirm precisely that universal aspect of his hermeneutical method which he aimed for. Thus, for instance, Lieber cited not only Roman and civil law but also, in one instance, Chinese law, as described in George Staunton's *Penal Code of China*.[46] In using Roman and civil law as a basis for comparison Lieber put himself within a solid tradition. Story, for instance, also drew from these sources for comparison.[47] Story, however, used the Roman and civil law sources to demonstrate the validity of common law substantive rules or to supplement the common law when a particular substantive law rule was lacking.[48] Lieber used the Roman and civil law materials in a rather different way. He used them to affirm the validity of a particular Anglo-American rule but went further. He attempted to show that the particular rules of interpretation are almost like natural law rules, underlying *all* legal hermeneutics regardless of the system being examined. Story used the comparative material experientially; another system, the Roman, uses a particular rule and, therefore, that rule has the imprimatur of history and experience. Lieber's use of the comparative material is less historical, less like Story before him and Sir Henry Maine after him, and more in keeping with the natural law tradition.

In addition to the *Hermeneutics*, Lieber also wrote extensively on political theory, international law, and the laws of war.[49] In these areas, too, especially in his writings on international law, Lieber showed himself knowledgeable in Roman law.[50] This was unavoidable because international law until the late nineteenth century was firmly grounded in the natural law tradition, which itself, through the writings of scholars such as Pufendorf and Grotius, was heavily dependent on the Roman legal tradition.[51] Here, again, we see Lieber introducing Continental legal materials into domestic American jurisprudence. Of course, Lieber was far from a pioneer in doing so. Traditionally, several specific legal areas had required any practitioner to have some acquaintance with Roman and civil law materials. Admiralty, considered a subtopic of the "law of nature and nations," the nineteenth-century version of international law, required such knowledge.[52] Lieber, in his lectures on international law, displayed a wide-ranging knowledge of the early modern writers on the law of nature and nations as well as a more than passing acquaintance with the Roman sources on which these writings depended. In this way, then, Lieber not only demonstrated his own expertise in the area but also helped to further its incorporation into the mainstream of American legal thought.

Hugh Legaré's expertise as a Romanist shows most clearly in an essay he wrote for the *Southern Review* entitled "The Origin, History and Influence of Roman Legislation," although it is clearly present in other essays as well, such as his reviews of Kent's *Commentaries* and Chancellor d'Agusseau's works and his article on the concept of codification.[53] The long essay on Roman legislation is, in form, a review of five books: Hugo's *Lehrbuch eines civilistischen Cursus*, Story's *Commentaries on the Conflict of Laws*, Christian Haubold's *Institutiones Juris Romani Privati Historico-Dogmaticarum Lineamenta*, A. W. Heffter's edition of Gaius's *Institutes* (based on Angelo Mai's publication of the newly discovered Verona Manuscript of the *Institutes*), and Heinrich Schräder's new edition of the *Corpus Juris Civilis*.[54] The review is a stunning tour de force of contemporary civilian learning. Legaré shows a breadth and profundity of civilian and Roman scholarship the match for which it is difficult to find in the antebellum period, even among such learned contemporaries as Story, Livingston, and DuPonceau. Ranging from a discussion of the history of early Rome and the problems of reconstructing the earliest Roman code, the *Twelve Tables*, through to an analysis of the impact of the new philology pioneered by Richard Bentley and the German school on nineteenth-century editions of the principal Roman law texts, each page reveals enormous learning and a highly developed sensitivity to the sources. The essay ultimately dwells on two specific points, however: the health of Roman law studies both in Europe and the United States, and the utility of Roman law both to the modern civilian and to the American lawyer. Regarding the first point, Legaré focuses on a statement of Henry Hallam, a noted nineteenth-century British historian, who argued that knowledge of and interest in Roman law was fading into obscurity.[55] Hallam was an exceptionally popular and prolific author of the period. He was especially well-known for his *Constitutional History of England*.[56] In another work, his *History of Europe During the Middle Ages*, Hallam commented on the end of the Roman legal tradition.[57] Legaré was enraged at this seeming calumny aimed at the great nineteenth-century civilians and leaped to the rescue. He cites Hugo, Savigny, Niebhur, Eichhorn, Dirksen, and Schräder as examples of the continuing strength of Romanist studies on the Continent:

> At no former period was there ever more ardor and activity displayed in the study of the civil law on the continent of Europe than at this very time. . . . The great jurisconsults of the present day to equal zeal add more knowledge, that is, more exact and available knowledge, a penetration more refined and distinguishing, and, above all, views of the construction of society, and of the principles, the spirit, and the influence of legislation, incomparably more profound, comprehensive, and practical.[58]

Certainly, Legaré's virtuoso displays of Romanist and civilian learning in print placed him within the ranks of those he cited against Hallam. Indeed, at the time of his death in 1843, amid the busy schedule of a lawyer and statesman, Legaré was at work translating into English one of the major seventeenth-century systematic civilian treatises, that of Heineccius.[59]

On the second point, the universal utility of substantive Roman law, Legaré's comments are even more interesting and significant. In this essay Legaré poses the question: "Was there anything in the original character of the Roman law, that fitted it to become thus universally applicable, or by what causes, and through what process, was it ultimately so?" Legaré gave a two-part answer. First, it was clear to him that Roman law had indeed become universally applicable in the Western legal tradition. He noted that "infinitely the largest and most important portion of it—that relating to *meum* and *tuum*—is suitable not only to other countries, but to all other countries—that it is as applicable at Boston as at Paris, and has served equally to guide the legislation of Napoleon and to enlighten the judgment of Story."[60]

At another point in this essay Legaré elaborates further on this theme. In effect, Legaré attributed the widespread utility of Roman and civil law to their systematic and rational natures. It was this philosophical aspect of Roman and civil law that so appealed to Legaré. For instance, he cites a leading textbook writer of the day, Charles Fearne, whose treatise on property law was, by Legaré's period, one of the classics of English land law.[61] Indeed, Legaré admits that it was "generally considered . . . one of the most lucid and satisfactory treatises in the library of an English lawyer." Yet, for Legaré, Fearne's book was unsatisfactory; it is too complex, unsystematic, and "prolix." To Legaré, Fearne is like other English textbook writers. He "carefully collects all the decided cases" and "critically distinguishes the circumstances that ought to affect their authority as law." They provide "safe guides" for "counselors or their clients." They do not provide, however, "a scientific distribution of their subject, of genus or species, class or category." They do not provide usable principles, for "the principle of a rule is seldom stated as a theorem." As a result, when particular facts of a newly arising case "in which the file affords no precedent" come up, the judge is compelled to look elsewhere, for these textbooks give no assistance.[62]

To this sorry state of Anglo-American affairs, Legaré contrasts civilian and civilian-inspired texts. He praises Gaius, the Roman jurist, for his *elegantia juris*. He praises Pothier, the French civilian, as well. And, significantly, he also praises Mr. Justice Story *as a civilian*. He commends the reader to compare Story's *Commentaries on Equity* to Thomas Maddock's *Chancery*, the one a paragon of system and rationality, the other firmly in the traditional, and unsystematic, mold.[63]

Professor Peter Stein has noted that Legaré saw Roman law, especially the Roman notion of *ius gentium*, as representative of what every advanced legal system would develop into.[64] Thus Legaré would appear to have seen Roman law as a model and source for substantive principles as well as a disembodied system that had reached a high point of historical development of much value to all lawyers and legislators as a quarry for substantive law. For Legaré, the Roman legal tradition represented century upon century of legal development. Roman and civilian jurists, according to Legaré, drew "their materials from a longer and more diversified experience than the English lawyers."[65] The civilians had encountered substantive law questions not yet raised in Anglo-American jurisprudence. He cites, for instance, the problem of apportioning rights of use between two states separated by a river. Such a question had long ago been raised in the Romanist tradition and was discussed in Berthold G. Struve's *Corpus Juris Germanici*.[66] In Legaré's opinion, when such matters arose in Anglo-American jurisprudence, the civilian and Roman sources ought to be searched, rather than attempting to fashion solutions de novo wholly within the insular common law tradition.[67] More than his contemporaries, perhaps, even those like Joseph Story who were Romanists themselves, Legaré was willing to embrace Roman and civilian legal method and substantive principles as a fundamental basis for Anglo-American law. More than most of his contemporaries, as well, he had the intellectual background and temperament to do so successfully.

One ought not make a mistake here, however. Although Legaré admired Roman law both for its systematic and philosophical elegance and for the richness of its substantive law tradition, he did not advocate a wholesale reception of Roman or civil law in the United States as a replacement for common law. On the contrary, Legaré, like Story, was an accomplished common lawyer who was quite willing to criticize Roman or civilian rules and prefer common law rules.[68] Indeed, though much of his *Southern Review* essay on Kent's *Commentaries* may be read as a paean to the civil law, in his later essay for the same journal on codification, he was willing to dispense with a civilian or Roman notion as ill-considered and antithetical to the common law spirit.[69] Legaré, like virtually all of the Anglo-American jurists of the period from 1800 to 1860, wanted to enrich the common law through selective use of Roman and civil law sources and enjoyed the study of the more philosophically sophisticated Roman and civilian systems but never wanted to see the civil law triumph over the common law in the Anglo-American world.

The personal history of James Murdock Walker is the most obscure of the three men discussed herein, but his writings tell us much about his mind, if not about him as a man. He published three books, all of which dwell substantially on Roman law and show a high level of expertise in the subject. One book, the *Inquiry into the Use and Authority of Roman Jurisprudence in the Law Concerning Real Estate*, published in 1850, is explicitly a work on substantive Roman law. Two others, *A Theory of the Common Law*, published at Boston in 1852, and the *Tract on Government*, published anonymously at Boston in 1853, have Roman law as their underpinnings. In the *Inquiry* Walker set himself the task of examining the origins of common law property rules, especially the law of remainders, and the relation of these common law rules to the Roman law. The *Inquiry* is one of the earliest American contributions to the debate among legal historians as to whether substantive Roman law was ever received into the Anglo-American tradition.[70] Walker's argument is directed specifically to then contemporary legal historians, such as the Englishman John Reeves who, in his *History of English Law*, argued that Roman law had had no influence on the development of the common law, even in the period before the reign of Edward II.[71] In this, his first, short book, Walker attempted to refute Reeves's theories. He noted of them "that this opinion is not only unfounded in fact, but that it has also had detrimental effects upon the cultivation of the law as a science."[72] It was Walker's opinion—common among those who argued that some form of reception of Roman rules *had* taken place—that the denial that a reception had occurred permitted common law lawyers and judges to refuse to use Roman or civilian rules even on a selective basis because their use—in this antireception view—would be alien to the common law tradition. In effect, Walker argued that the legal historical argument was of more than scholarly concern, for it was being used to justify contemporary refusals to reform the common law through the use of Roman and civilian ideas.

Walker's second book, the *Theory of the Common Law*, has, unfortunately, been ignored by virtually all legal historians, even those interested in Roman and civil law. This neglect is sad, though understandable, because the book presents a complex and lengthy (but fascinating) continuation of Walker's investigations begun in the *Inquiry* and carries them into contemporary jurisprudence. It is, in form, an attempt to explicate "the science of law," to analyze those "rules of human conduct which are universally recognized as obligatory."[73] As such, it is very similar to the contemporary work of the English legal philosopher John Austin in his *Lectures on Jurisprudence*.[74] Like Austin, Walker argued that Roman and civil law could be properly used as the basis for a scientific examination of common law jurisprudence. In so doing he echoed not only Austin but his countryman Legaré. Walker says:

> An indispensable instrument in the investigation of all scientific truth is method. Science cannot exist without it. Now our juridical writers altogether neglect it. . . . It is in this respect that the Roman has so great an advantage over the Common law. The universal error of our juridical writers is in supposing that, even in

those countries over which the Civil Law presides, it is valued chiefly for its doctrines. The reverse is the truth. . . . The legal literature of no other people [the Romans] can show a casuistry so thoroughly spiritual, where the matter of fact only seems designed to corporealize and exhibit the spirit.[75]

Building on this insight, Walker undertook to organize the common law of real property as outlined in the *Theory* on the lines of Roman law. In fact, the book is largely an attack on Fearne's *Remainders*, the leading property law treatise of its period and a work which Legaré, too, had condemned.[76] Walker's book is an attempt to "Romanize" the common law of property into a coherent and rational system. In doing so, Walker displays a wide-ranging knowledge of both the Roman and civilian primary sources and the commentators thereon. Finally, undoubtedly under the influence of his Romanist reading, Walker displays an intolerance toward the writ system and common law formulas and a bias in favor of "scientific legal principles." He says:

It is manifest that formulas do not commend themselves to the natural reason of mankind, and therefore cannot become the property of humanity. They are the mere husks of the law. . . . If the law be merely an unconnected series of decisions and statutes, its use may remain, though its dignity as a science be lost. Reason must yield its supremacy to memory, and the *cantor formularum* is the greatest of lawyers.[77]

In taking this position against the mindless use of writs and in favor of "scientific jurisprudence," Walker took his place next to Daniel Mayes of Transylvania College as a precursor of the Langdellian reform movement of the 1870s.[78]

The picture that emerges from this brief history of Lieber, Legaré, and Walker is one of a circle of talented and learned lawyers centered around Charleston and Columbia, South Carolina, interested in and writing about Roman and civil law.

The final question I will address in this chapter concerns the effect that such Roman and civilian learning had on other American lawyers of the period and legal development thereafter. In doing so, I recognize the difficulty of determining intellectual influence, if one is searching for an absolute showing of a causal connection between two events. Instead of attempting to make a *post hoc, ergo propter hoc* argument, I will try to show only that the efforts of Lieber, Legaré, and Walker were neither unknown to contemporaries nor accomplished in a vacuum with no connection to the larger society. Finally, I will conclude by suggesting that these three Roman lawyers of the Old South were not the only members of their profession involved in such Romanist and civilian studies.

Lieber's works had a wide distribution in his lifetime. His works on political theory and on international law were well-known. Indeed, during the Civil War he became an adviser to the Union on military law.[79] Unfortunately, it would seem that the *Legal and Political Hermeneutics* probably was one of his least-known works.[80] Nevertheless, it was far from unknown. Certainly Lieber's *Hermeneutics* was known to his wide circle of friends and scholarly acquaintants. The book was dedicated to Chancellor Kent. Lieber himself gave a copy to Justice Joseph Story. Other notable lawyers and editors of his acquaintance were Peter DuPonceau, himself a noted Romanist,[81] Edward Everett, the editor of the *North American Review*, Edward Livingston, the force behind the *Louisiana Code of 1825*, Rufus Choate, Charles Sumner, and a host of other leaders of the American Bar.[82] All, presumably, read the work. Lieber was not above self-promotion either. In October 1840, for instance, he sent a copy of the *Hermeneutics* to C. J. A. Mittermaier, apparently in the hopes that this German jurist would review it for a learned journal, as he had done with Justice Story's *Commentaries on the Conflict of Laws* in the *Kritische Zeitschrift*.[83] It was, in fact, reviewed favorably in several widely published journals. Indeed, in 1840, after the publication of the *Legal and Political Hermeneutics*, Lieber wrote to his wife of his hope that he might soon obtain a chair in international law at another (presumably northern) university.[84] Lieber's short volume, so dependent on Continental thinking, appears to have been well-known, therefore, to many important contemporary lawyers and politicians and thus undoubtedly had some influence. Indeed, the *Hermeneutics* sold well enough to justify revision and reprinting. A revised edition was planned in the early 1860s but failed to materialize because of the death of the reviser. Finally, in 1880, a posthumous revised edition was published.[85] Certainly the *Hermeneutics* found its way into many American law libraries of the period. A copy was even listed as being in the collection of the California State Library at Sacramento in the 1857 catalog issued by that institution.[86] Furthermore, it was cited in court. Indeed, twice the United States Supreme Court looked to Lieber's book for guidance. Robert Cover has characterized the *Hermeneutics* as the most coherent single exposition of the legal establishment's view of the interpretative process to be found in the antebellum period.[87] Considering the book's foreign law content and comparative approach, that is saying a great deal about the spread of Roman and civil law ideas during this period and about Lieber's role in that process.

Legaré's articles in the *Southern Review* may well have had an even greater diffusion than did Lieber's book. Legaré's intent in his *Southern Review* articles was to provide information for educating gentlemen. One of the preeminent interests, if not preoccupations, of the antebellum southern gentleman was classical civilization.[88] The best part of classical civilization, Legaré thought, was its legal system. The extent to which essays on classical civilization, so well done by Legaré, influenced the professional behavior both of lawyers and nonlawyers, however, is hard to estimate precisely. Stephen Botein has collected a good deal of evidence, for instance, about the importance of Cicero as a role model during this period.[89] Perry Miller and Robert Ferguson have suggested that classical literature influenced contemporary legal oratorical styles in both the courts and the legislatures.[90] Certainly Legaré himself avowed that he followed a Roman model in his practice. When asked about his success at the Bar, he responded: "In general, sir, I practice upon the old Roman plan; and, like Cicero's, my clients pay me what they like—that is, often nothing at all."[91] And, of course, Legaré's essays were read by jurists. For instance, in a letter of October 13, 1839, Francis Lieber wrote of reading Legaré's "excellent article on Roman law" and James Murdock Walker, in his *Inquiry*, bracketed Legaré with Kent and Story as a leading American jurist.[92]

Nor was Legaré's role in diffusing Roman legal knowledge limited to his writings. Whereas Lieber used Roman and civil law texts for comparative and illustrative purposes in his writings and lectures, Legaré used these sources as legal authorities not only in his writings but also in his court appearances. As attorney general in 1842, Legaré represented the United States before the Supreme Court twelve times. The majority of these cases involved disputed land grants in territories formerly under French or Spanish rule, thus the legal issues involved were often Roman or civilian in origin. Of the three men discussed herein, Legaré was most able, seemingly, to incorporate Roman and civilian principles directly into American law. Both men, of course, thereby helped to spread knowledge of Roman and civil law and both also used Roman and civil law to try to reform some aspects of the Anglo-American legal tradition. Legaré's arguments before the Supreme Court in those twelve cases apparently helped to do so, at least in a small way. Certainly they impressed one justice. In a lecture reported in the *Boston Daily Advertiser* in 1843, Justice Story recalled Legaré for his law students. He said:

> I had looked to see him accomplish what he was so well fitted to do—what I know was the darling object of his pure attention—to engraft the civil law upon the jurisprudence of this country, and thereby to expand the common law to greater usefulness and a wider adaptation to the progress of society . . . he . . . devoted himself . . . to the study of the civil law, with a view to make it subservient to the great object of his life—the expansion of the common law, and the forcing into it the enlarged and liberal principles and just morality of the Roman jurisprudence. This object he seemed about to accomplish; for his arguments before the Supreme Court were crowded with the principles of the Roman law, wrought into the texture of the common law with great success. In every sentence that I heard, I was struck with this union of the two systems.[93]

An essayist writing in the *Southern Review* in 1870 echoed Justice Story's comments. Legaré, he said, wanted to achieve "the gradual infusion of a large portion of the spirit and philosophy of the Civil law, and even of its forms and process, into the more common system of jurisprudence."[94]

James Murdock Walker's influence is the most difficult to assess because we know so little about him and his books are infrequently mentioned in contemporary sources. We may presume that *A Theory of the Common Law*, simply by virtue of its publication by Little, Brown at Boston, had more diffusion than his privately printed *Inquiry*. Neither book seems to have been widely reviewed or noticed, however. The *Inquiry*, nonetheless, was the subject of a substantial review in the *Southern Quarterly Review* in 1851. The reviewer was greatly impressed with the book and recommended it to his readers. He praised Walker in glowing terms:

> It must appear, from what has been said, that in the present absence of English translations of works on the civil law, he renders a valuable service to the cause of jurisprudence, who, like Mr. Walker, devotes himself to the labour of tracing the analogies of the older and new systems, and importing a knowledge of the truthful doctrines of the former.[95]

There is also one extremely interesting aspect of Walker's other book, the *Tract on Government*, published anonymously in 1853, that merits mention. The *Tract* is a work on political theory rather than law specifically, but like both the *Inquiry* and the *Theory*, the *Tract* bases much of its argument on Roman models. Most interesting about the *Tract* is that it takes the position that the dissolution of the Union, argued for so fervently by the South Carolina secessionists, would be disastrous. Indeed, if one looks at the political stance of all three men, Lieber, Legaré, and Walker, all were allied with J. L. Petigru, the leading antisecessionist member of the Charleston Bar.[96] Could their knowledge of Roman law and Roman history have had some effect on their politics? Could Walker's political position against secession in the *Tract* reflect this influence of Roman models? Could their knowledge of the dolorous effects of civil war on the Roman Republic have made them so staunchly defend the American Republic? This is, indeed, an interesting point for speculation.

In concluding this survey of the South Carolina circle of Romanists, it is necessary to make it clear that although Francis Lieber, Hugh Swinton Legaré, and James Murdock Walker were notable Romanists in the antebellum South, they were far from alone in their interests. Indeed, quite the contrary was true. The southern literary magazines of the antebellum period frequently contained articles on Roman and civil law and often contained reviews of foreign books on these subjects as well. Obviously, the classical world appealed to the southern gentleman. Lawyers in the South were, quintessentially, gentlemen. Thus it is not surprising that we find articles on Roman and civil law sprinkled through the pages of the *Southern Literary Messenger* and the *Southern Quarterly Review*, next to reviews of fiction, notes on science, and poems such as "To My Own Little Girl" and "Moses Smiting the Rock."[97] And though most of these notices and reviews concerning Roman and civil law are brief and somewhat superficial, several approach a level of expertise, if not equal to Lieber's or Legaré's, or even Walker's, respectable nonetheless. For instance, in the *Southern Literary Messenger* for 1842 there is a long article by "a lawyer of North Carolina" on the civil law. In many respects this article is reminiscent of Legaré's essays in the *Southern Review*. It, too, begins with a discussion of Hallam and attempts to disprove his theories. This article, moreover, criticized the common law for its lack of a principled foundation and system:

> Though the Common Law may arrogate to itself all that is beautiful and perfect in reason, its advocates may ransack philosophy, in order to find an established principle applicable to every rule therein expressed; yet to the contemplator of that venerable structure, it too often appears, when surveying the patchwork resorted to, to prevent conveyances in mortmain, and the many unexpected resources which the Statute of Uses introduced, that very much of this law is the result of accident. So complicated is the stern and inflexible system, that the introduction of a new regulation has often conflicted with standing rules of laws; and the application of a remedy has been perverted by the finesse of ingenious men, to the creation of still sorer evils than those it was intended to correct.[98]

And like Legaré, the anonymous "lawyer of North Carolina" held that the principles of Roman law were of universal validity and that Montesquieu's dictum that laws "are peculiarly adapted to the particular nations which gave them birth" was totally inapplicable here:

From the mouth of the Tiber to that of the Mississippi, the Civil law may be traced through multifarious nations of various governments, exercising over the whole its healthful and genial influence. It is as admirably adapted to those nations, where the mandate of the King is heard and obeyed with fear and trembling, as to those where all other authority is drowned in the voice of the people. Instead of being exclusively and inseparably connected with a city whose glory is fast fading from the earth, the Roman Law has become blended with the fate of many people; and its existence is coupled with the existence of nations that are yet in the vigor of youth. What revolution in the social organization of the world will be sufficiently great to exterminate a law that is so generally disseminated, and so admirably adapted to the necessities of the human race.[99]

Indeed, so far had Roman and civil law studies made their way into the southern legal consciousness during the antebellum period that they are found, too, in a plan for an ideal "legal university" published in the 1837 volume of the *Southern Literary Messenger*.[100] It must be remembered that in 1837 university-affiliated law schools were rarities. Harvard and Transylvania were among the few.[101] But it was also a time of experimentation in legal education. Benjamin Butler, then the attorney general of the United States, was just beginning his attempt to start a new law school in New York City.[102] Thus this 1837 essay was both reflective of its time's views and experimental in its proposals. The essay begins with a critique of the then common form of legal education, apprenticeship in a law office. It moves on to discuss the proposal for the establishment of a "law university."[103] The faculty of the university would consist of professors of logic, rhetoric, moral philosophy, history and historical jurisprudence, and civil law, as well as the various common law subjects.[104] The justification for having a professor of civil law (and instruction in that subject) is particularly revealing. Civil law, according to an anonymous essayist, is

as regards contract (a comprehensive title in the law) . . . "fons et principum," and which though not law here by enactment, involved and elucidates the principles of justice so fully, so clearly, so justly, and has furnished so large a portion of the basis of the law of all civilized nations, that he who is well skilled in its teachings shall have little more of general principles to learn.[105]

Thus Lieber, Legaré, and Walker should be viewed as but a sampling of lawyers who represented and embodied the significance of the Roman and civil law tradition in the legal culture of the antebellum South. One could as easily have discussed other important southern lawyers who possessed both interest and expertise in Roman and civil law during this period. One might have mentioned Chancellor George Wythe of Virginia, for instance, whose writings and decisions are replete with Roman law, as Hamilton Bryson has demonstrated.[106] Or one might mention William Cooper, a Tennessee lawyer who was instrumental in the codification of Tennessee law, in fact becoming chief justice of the Tennessee Supreme Court, who traveled widely on the Continent in the 1860s, studied equity in London, and wrote on Roman law in the *Southern Review*. Or one might mention Benjamin Porter, born in Charleston in 1808, who became the supreme court reporter for the state of Alabama and succeeded where Legaré failed in translating the works of the German Romanist Heineccius into English. Or, finally, one might mention Brigadier General Albert Pike of the army of the Confederate States of America, commissioner for Indian affairs for the Confederacy, who, amid the grapeshot of Civil War battles, is reported to have translated into English the entirety of the *Corpus Juris Civilis* as a means of relaxation.

In conclusion, one may make several observations about Roman and civil law and their influence on antebellum southern lawyers and legal scholars. First, the southern ideal of the lawyer as a classically educated gentleman aided in Roman and civil law's acceptance into the southern legal tradition. Similarly, the attraction of Continental literature and philosophy—especially German—naturally inclined the best southern legal scholars toward Roman and civil law, a process that was aided by the frequency with which such southerners traveled on the Continent or brought Continental scholars to the South. The popularity of literary magazines in the South during this period further aided this process, for they provided an outlet for southern lawyers' literary efforts, often focused on European or Roman legal subjects. Of course,

Roman and civil law also were attractive to southerners for intellectual reasons. Roman law was the law of a great republic, and the republican tradition was then strong in the South. Roman and civil law were seen in both the South and the North as more systematic and philosophically sophisticated than the common law. Roman and civil law also could provide historically tested substantive rules when such were needed. And, naturally, Roman and civil law appeared particularly appropriate for study in the South, even in common law jurisdictions, because several of the southern states, Louisiana, Arkansas, Florida, and Texas, had either once been or still remained under civilian-based legal systems. Thus it was that the tradition of Roman and civil law studies flourished in the antebellum South until the Civil War destroyed this tradition along with so many others.

3

Roman Law, Comparative Law, and the Historical School of Jurisprudence in England and America After 1850

MAINE, CUSHING, HAMMOND, AND POMEROY

It has become conventional to see the middle of the nineteenth century as the point at which Roman law studies in England and the United States ceased to have any vitality.[1] In England, Austin's point of view and the movement toward systematization, sparked by Roman law studies, were in decline. Roman law continued to be taught by civilians for civilians, but, so the conventional wisdom goes, without any great success or intellectual content.[2] In the United States, the common law was triumphant and no longer seen to be vying with the civil law for legal ascendancy. The southern intellectual tradition in law and literature was first weakened by the exigencies of the Civil War and then virtually destroyed both by the decimation of the flower of the southern intelligentsia during the war and by the postwar period of Reconstruction. In the East, law and legal studies, too, reeled under the impact of the Civil War. In the law schools, the first period of the great teachers who took an interest in Roman law, such as Kent and Story, was ended, while the next period of intellectual ferment under Langdell, James Barr Ames, and their disciples, we are told, was yet to begin. In sum, traditional history of legal scholarship leaves little room for Roman and civil law in the Anglo-American tradition during this period. In fact, however, interest in Roman and civil law continued to thrive in both England and the United States from 1850 to 1880, albeit from different motives and oriented in somewhat different directions than in the earlier period. There was also a geographic shift westward. If, during the first half of the nineteenth century, Roman and civil law studies were primarily tied to the newly formed law schools and to the search for a systematic jurisprudence, as well as to a highly intellectualized and abstracted vision of the law and legal practice,[3] during the third quarter of the century these studies came to have been more broadly based and intimately tied to the growth of a new historical school of jurisprudence both within the law schools and without and to a newly arising interest in comparative law studies on both sides of the Atlantic.

In the development of this post-1850 Anglo-American interest in Roman law, one intellectual influence stands out beyond all others. That is the corpus of work produced in the first half of the nineteenth century by the German scholar and jurist Friedrich Carl von Savigny.[4] Savigny was the greatest of all German legal historians writing in the nineteenth century except, perhaps, for Theodor Mommsen, fifty years later.[5] Beginning with his 1818 anticodification pamphlet, *Vom Beruf unserer Zeit für Rechtswissenschaft und Gesetzgebung*, and coming to full flower in his *Geschichte des römischen Rechts im Mittelalter* and *System des heutigen römischen Rechts*, Savigny set forth a then novel theory of law and legal development.[6] For Savigny, law was a cultural and social manifestation of a nation (*Volk*), inseparable from the unique historical circumstances within which it had evolved. Positive, that is, man-made law, in Savigny's view, could not be understood except within its historical milieu. Borrowing from then current theories of linguistic and ethnological development and transmission, Savigny argued that attempts to isolate the study of law from broader cultural and historical studies were doomed to failure, for law could be explained only by historical means. Thus for Savigny and his disciples, to understand law, one is forced to understand a nation's history. "Good" law is law that arises from a nation's historical existence and reflects its unique qualities. The sources of law are not to be found in logic or theology but in the everyday life of a people.[7]

Savigny's impact on legal theory and the study of law in England and the United States cannot be overemphasized.[8] Already in the first part of the century he had gained adherents in both England and the

United States. Hugh Swinton Legaré had declared himself a follower of Savigny in the 1830s.[9] In England George Long placed his *Discourses*, delivered at the Inns of Court in the late 1840s, in the path outlined by Savigny, and the Scotsman David Irving praised Savigny and the historical schools in his *Introduction to the Study of the Civil Law*. James Reddie, another learned Scot, discussed Savigny as the ultimate representative of legal scholarship in his *Historical Notices of the Roman Law*.[10] Savigny's *Vom Beruf* was early on translated into English as was the first volume of the *Geschichte des Römischen Rechts im Mittelalter*, and copies were to be found in both English and American libraries. For many of his followers it was as if a clear beam of lucidity had at last dispelled the obscurity caused by his Pandectist predecessors and contemporaries, as the axiomatic tradition exemplified by Christian Wolff, Heineccius, and Anton Thibaut had turned many common lawyers opposed to systematization away from Roman law studies.[11] Savigny's historical theories shifted the focus of theoretical legal inquiry away both from the natural law tradition and from the worst excesses of the systematizers onto the importance of placing law and legislation in its national, historical context, thus providing a new, independent reason to study Roman law. To understand law was to know its history. Hence, knowing Roman law became a prerequisite to understanding other, later legal systems both because Roman law underlaid them to varying degrees and because, as Sir Henry Sumner Maine and his followers argued, the history of Roman law could, by comparison, illuminate the history of the common law.

The impact of Savigny's theories on the study of Roman and civil law was, therefore, especially profound. Now, Roman law ceased to be viewed by jurists who followed Savigny's teachings as *ratio scripta*, an emanation of omnipresent, metahistorical principles, but rather came to be seen as a legal system that had developed and evolved as Roman society itself had developed and evolved.[12] It was, of course, still seen by many as a principled system, but not metahistorical. For the first time, jurists and scholars of Roman law could see their subject from the historical perspective, beginning with the *leges regiae* and the *Twelve Tables* and continuing to the Byzantine codifications and medieval epitomes.[13] This is not to suggest that Savigny and his followers reduced

Roman law solely to an antiquarian or academic subject, though they laid the grounds for this later development; rather, they created the context within which Roman and civil law could become the basis for the historical and comparative study of *all* legal systems, including the common law. Indeed, though Savigny would argue against a "modern" Roman law (as envisaged, for instance, by Rudolf von Jhering), he saw Roman law as a great teacher that would permit modern lawyers and legislators to aid the development of their own uniquely nationalist legal systems. Implicit, too, in Savigny's view of law was the notion of the interrelationship between the need for legal change and the inevitability of societal development. It was this relationship, in fact, that provided the seeds for the new focus of Roman law study both in England and in the United States, for Roman law was to become the basis of comparative law studies.

Henry Sumner Maine

Without question, the most important English figure in the Anglo-American development of the historical approach to Roman and civil law during this period was Sir Henry Sumner Maine. Maine was born in 1822 into a prosperous family.[14] He graduated from Pembroke College, Cambridge, in 1844 and in 1845 became a fellow of Trinity Hall, Cambridge, a foundation that specialized in training lawyers. In 1847 Maine became Regius Professor of Civil Law in Cambridge. At that time, civil law studies at Cambridge were in severe decline and, according to testimony given before the 1846 Select Committee on Legal Education, the Regius Chair had become little more than "an ill-paying sinecure."[15] Nevertheless, it is to this period that Maine's henceforth abiding interest in Roman law may date. In 1852 Maine left Cambridge to become the first reader in Roman law and jurisprudence at the Inns of Court. In 1862 he became the legal member of the Council of India.[16] In 1869 he became Corpus Professor of Jurisprudence at Oxford, and he returned in 1877 to Trinity Hall, Cambridge, as its master. In 1887 he was named Whewell Professor of International Law at Cambridge but died the following year.

Maine's professional success, so in contrast to Austin's failure a half-century before, was accompanied by an outpouring of books and articles. His first and, in many respects most important, work, *Ancient Law*, was published in 1861 and continues to be in print today.[17] It was in many respects a work of his youth. It was followed by *Village Communities, Dissertations on Early Law and Custom, Popular Government*, and his Whewell lectures, the *Lectures on International Law*.[18] From the publication of his first book, it was clear that Maine had acquired substantial expertise in Roman law, and it is thus to this book that one should turn first.

Ancient Law is a curious book. Unlike Austin's *Lectures* it almost totally lacks any scholarly apparatus.[19] It has few footnotes and rarely cites sources. It is, clearly, a popular book, designed not for specialists or for students but for educated laymen. It is not a teaching book or a book for scholars. It is, rather, a polemic for comparative law study and, in many ways, for law reform. More interesting is its arrangement. Austin's treatment of Roman and civil law was clearly systematic and influenced both by the traditional arrangement and divisions of Justinian's *Institutes* and by the axiomatic structure adopted by later commentators such as the German Pandectists.[20] Maine's arrangement of his subject in *Ancient Law* is wholly chronological. The book begins with a survey of ancient codes and then moves on to a discussion of legal fictions. It next proceeds to a discussion of the distinctions between municipal law and the law of nature and the differences between law and equity. From there it moves to a further examination of natural law and a discussion of natural law theorists. Chapter 5, however, marks a shift of focus. This chapter begins with the two legal theories that Maine believed to rival the historical approach and to be misconceived: the utilitarian approach of Bentham and the philosophical approach of Montesquieu. Drawing upon his central criticism, that each theory was essentially ahistorical, and, therefore, of little practical value, Maine in this central chapter attempts to lay a foundation for his future substantive categorical chapters by drawing an idealized picture of primitive society and the "simplest social forms in a state as near as possible to their rudimentary condition." Thus he begins with the Germans of Tacitus's *Germania* and moves to the ancient Near East of the Bible. From there he progresses to a discussion of the role of law in primitive society in general, political theory as applied to such societies, and the importance of *patria potestas*, kinship, marriage, and slavery. He concludes the chapter with his famous observation that societies move from status to contract.[21] In Chapters 6 through 10, Maine describes the development of specific fields of private law, beginning with testamentary succession, proceeding through property and contract, and ending with delict and crime. For all of these chapters, Roman law is both the touchstone and the central paradigm upon which Maine's historical theories hang.

Clearly, this arrangement of the book is far from the institutional tradition of the division of the law into persons, things, and actions and between public and private law.[22] There is one close parallel, however, that has been little noticed by later commentators. In the substantive part of the book, Chapters 5 through 10, Maine begins by discussing the family and status. As William Gardiner Hammond pointed out, it is precisely this area which the original Roman jurists, including Gaius, undoubtedly believed to constitute the "law of persons."[23] Thus even in his arrangement of *Ancient Law* Maine was influenced by Roman models.

Maine's arrangement of *Ancient Law*, although not institutional, is easily comprehensible and reveals much about the sources of his interest in Roman law. The first four chapters are, in a sense, methodological prolegomena. They describe those "mechanisms" of the law which Maine believed to be critical to legal development: codification and legislation, the use of legal fictions, and the development of equity jurisdiction.[24] To Maine each of these mechanisms is a means by which the legal process moves, by which legal change is made possible. So these first chapters describe, in general terms, how Maine believed legal systems could and would develop and change. Substantive law is discussed in these chapters, but only to illustrate these mechanisms of development. The last of these first four chapters, which discusses the development of natural law theory, is the most polemic, for in it Maine shows what can happen if the mechanisms of change he had discussed earlier are stymied by metahistorical theories and devices, in this case the notion of an eternal law, never changing and inadaptable to historical circumstances.[25] Here, presumably, Maine tossed the gauntlet to Austin and his disciples. In the fifth chapter, Maine sets the stage for the rest of the work. Here, once the mechanisms of change are understood, Maine goes back to the historical groundpoint: primitive society. He must start here for he could not show the process of change unless he first established a standard against which all development can be measured. The final five chapters do precisely this. Roman law, throughout these chapters, provides for Maine both a baseline and a historical case study.

Maine's purposes in *Ancient Law* were several. First, he wanted to show the primary mechanisms of legal change. Second, he wanted to illustrate the progress of that change paradigmatically. It is his motivation for this latter, this obsession with legal development, that is the key to his use of Roman law in his books. Maine was not an antiquarian. Nor was he moved by some adulatory enthusiasm for all things classical. Indeed, *Ancient Law* mixes discussion of Roman law with Indian law as well as Germanic and Scandinavian law.[26] To understand *Ancient Law* properly, it is necessary to recognize that it is essentially a seminal work in legal history and comparative law aimed at illuminating the present and, indeed, influencing the present rather than the past. It is not an attempt to delineate the principles of Roman law. The reader does not gain the knowledge of Roman law from Maine's masterpiece available from the more mundane works of his countrymen John Taylor or Samuel Hallifax or those of his transatlantic colleague Luther S. Cushing.[27] Maine's work is also decidedly and deliberately not history in its traditional sense. Roman legal history is not as well set out in *Ancient Law* as it is, for instance, in Gibbon's forty-fourth chapter or Hugo's textbook.[28] Rather, *Ancient Law* is a work of legal ethnography designed to provide a comparative view of the development of particular private law institutions for a modernist purpose. Roman law occupies a prominent place in this study precisely because its institutions were not only well documented but could be traced through a long and well-documented historical period, thus exposing the intimate connections therein between social change and legal change. Nevertheless, it is fair to say that though Maine was a far worse Romanist than his predecessor Savigny, he was a far more creative Romanist than his successor James Bryce. In Maine's view, this comparative ethnological approach permits the reader to gain insight not only into the relationship between social and legal change generally but also into the development of modern law, both retrospectively and prospectively. Maine believed that although particular details of legal development in various societies must differ because of different historical circumstances, he also believed that societies developed in broadly similar fashion. Thus if one could understand the mechanisms of change in Roman law as well as the full impact of those mechanisms over the life of Roman society, then one could also understand the mechanisms of English or Indian society and determine the appropriateness of any particular legal act or reform guided by this understanding and insight.[29] In this Maine closely followed Savigny, his German guide, and foreshadowed twentieth-century comparativists, such as Rudolf Schlesinger, who believe that there are certain "common cores" to all legal systems.[30] Indeed, it is interesting that Maine adopted a view toward codification very similar to that espoused by Savigny in his 1818 pamphlet.[31]

Maine's view on codification was expounded in an important article published six years before *Ancient Law*. This seminal article is entitled "Roman Law and Legal Education."[32] It was a topic of great significance to Maine at this period in his life because his professional appointment was in that subject, although he never fully adopted the academic life. In this essay, Maine sets forth not only the justification for including Roman law in the legal curriculum, a position already set forth by the Austinians in 1846 before the Parliamentary Select Committee,[33] but also, in effect, establishes a program for his subsequent work. Maine rejects out of hand the simplistic historical argument that English lawyers needed to study Roman law because Roman law underlay modern English law, a position that had been championed in England by such accepted earlier scholars as John Selden and Arthur Duck.[34] Maine accepts Roman influence on English law, but argues that "a system like the laws of Rome, distinguished above all others for its symmetry and its close correspondence with fundamental rules, would be effectually metamorphosed by a very slight distortion of its parts, or by the omission of one or two governing principles."[35]

Thus, according to Maine, under the impact of English society, even Roman law would lose its purity and be transformed into something different, uniquely English, in response to the exigencies of English culture and history. That was no reason, however, to abandon the study of Roman law, in Maine's view. On the contrary, he argued, there was a far better reason to study the Roman legal system:

> It is not because our own jurisprudence and that of Rome were once alike that they ought to be studied together; it is because they *will be* alike. It is because all laws, however dissimilar in their infancy, tend to resemble each other in their maturity; and because we in England are slowly, and perhaps unconsciously or unwillingly, but still steadily and certainly accustoming ourselves to the same modes of legal thought and to the same conceptions of legal principle to which the Roman jurisconsults had attained after centuries of accumulated experience and unwearied cultivation.[36]

This, of course, is Maine's statement of why he thought comparative jurisprudence was so important. And, of course, this view is wholly consistent with the study of legal history and Roman law. It is also wholly consistent with the interests of a practical lawyer and reformer, a role Maine embraced. Maine commented, in *Village Communities*, that "if not the only function, the chief function of comparative jurisprudence is to facilitate legislation and the practical improvement of law."[37]

For Maine, therefore, the primary importance of Roman law is not as a source of substantive legal principles, as it was for Joseph Story, or as an inspiration and model for systematization, as it was for Austin and his followers. Rather, Roman law provides a mirror of experience for the legislator and reformer with an interest in comparative-historical sources. A study of Roman law—and its later development as civil law—permits observation at close quarters of the ways in which a complex imperialistic and commercial society had dealt with legal problems and legal change.

The implications of this argument for the study of Roman law in the latter half of the nineteenth century are substantial. Since, under this view, one studies Roman law principally to understand the relation of law to society, one must study the law in context. Thus the only useful way to study Roman law would be in conjunction with the study of Roman history. Indeed, the preferable method would be to study Roman law in what Frederick Pollock later called the "parallel comparison," that is, comparison to English law or Hindu law at a comparable stage of historical development.[38] At the same time, those aspects of Roman law and Roman history one would choose to study would be dictated by modern legal and political concerns because, ultimately, the purpose of the study is not "pure" history but a better understanding of modern law. For Maine and his followers, therefore, the study of Roman law as a systematic and abstract subject, consisting of principles logically deduced from each other with no relation to history or society, would have been useless for this purpose.

Although Maine's principal use of Roman law was for purposes of comparative jurisprudence, he also recognized that its study provided additional benefits. In the essay on Roman law and legal education he follows Austin in regarding Roman legal terminology as far superior to that of English common law and endorses Austin's view that adoption of Roman law terms would help to improve English legal reasoning.[39] In this view he echoes his predecessors such as Austin and foreshadows his successors such as Bryce.

In the essay, Maine connects the superiority of Roman legal terminology and reasoning to two specific topics that were of great interest to him. He explains first that Roman legal ideas and terms underlie international law so that any English lawyer interested in this subject must master at least the rudiments of Roman law.[40] This was not a particularly new or innovative insight. As early as 1656, Robert Wiseman, a noted English civilian, argued for the study of civil law in England in his *Excellencie of the Civil Law*, on the grounds that it was the basis for legal relations between sovereign states and the law of the sea.[41] Furthermore, Maine, like many of his predecessors, praises the Romans for the sophistication they showed in both legislation and codification and suggests that Roman legal ideas and terms would be useful to the English in these activities.[42]

Maine supported Roman law as a part of the English legal curriculum for two additional reasons. First, he believed that Roman law and the modes of reasoning and discourse native to it were of great importance in the development of moral philosophy both in England and on the Continent. Thus, Maine argues, it would be impossible to understand the English tradition of moral philosophy properly unless one had some acquaintance with Roman law and juristic writings.[43] This notion is particularly interesting because much of the basis for nineteenth-century English moral philosophy is found in the philosophy of the Scottish Enlightenment, which itself was much influenced by civilian studies.[44] Maine, like his contemporaries, placed great emphasis on the significance of moral philosophy as a subject of academic study, for moral philosophy was believed to be integral to proper legislation. Therefore, Maine believed Roman law to be significant for those who would take part in the legislative process.

The second additional use for studying Roman law that Maine propounds has a very modern cast. Maine argues that Roman law is the foundation of European civil law and that to understand present-day civil law it is necessary to understand Roman law. Further, he asserts, it was, indeed, becoming a lingua franca of law and lawyers throughout the world, and even in England lawyers must be cognizant of this universal language or be left behind: "The idle labour which the most dexterous practitioner is compelled to bestow on the simplest questions of foreign law is the measure of the usefulness of the knowledge which would be conferred by an Institutional course of Roman jurisprudence."[45] Here, again, there are echoes, perhaps, of earlier English jurists such as Wiseman in the belief that English jurists cannot remain isolated and aloof from their Continental brethren but must study Roman law so they are at least superficially conversant with European legal systems.

It becomes clear, therefore, that Maine did not so much argue for the abandonment of the uses to which Roman law had been put by the English under the influence of Austin and earlier lawyers interested in Roman and civil law than for adding to these uses a new and intellectually seductive purpose. Now, not only could the study of Roman law in England be justified by recourse to the argument that Roman legal language and its concepts were superior to and a necessary supplement to the common law but also by pointing out that, since all societies tended to develop along roughly parallel paths and law tended to develop in connection with society, by knowing how Roman law developed and how certain legal ideas worked at a particular stage of social development, one could predict how English law itself ought to and might develop. In short, by making Roman law and legal history the basis for his comparative jurisprudence, Maine made it especially and newly relevant to contemporary law studies and continued to emphasize its relevance to modern legal development and legal reform, thereby helping to bolster its continued inclusion in the English legal curriculum and continuing interest in it among English lawyers.[46]

Luther Stearns Cushing and Roman and Civil Law in America at Mid-Century

Luther Stearns Cushing was one of the most celebrated lawyers and jurists of his day in the United States. He was also, to a very large extent, a transitional figure, the last flowering of the pre–Civil War broadly liberal intellectual tradition in law in the Northeast. Born in Massachusetts in 1803, he took his LL.B. from Harvard in 1826. In addition to his law practice, he became clerk of the Massachusetts House of Representatives in 1832, a judge of the Court of Common Pleas in 1844, and official reporter of the Massachusetts Supreme Judicial Court in 1848. In 1848–49 and again in 1850–51, he lectured on Roman law at the Harvard Law School.[47] In addition to his professional pursuits, he was a hardworking scholar and translator. His interest in Roman and civil law resulted in published translations of Domat's *Civil Laws in Their Natural Order*, Savigny's *Law of Possession*, Pothier's *Treatise on the Contract of Sale*, and Mittermaier's *Effects of Drunkenness on Criminal Responsibility* as well as his Harvard lectures published under the title *An Introduction to the Study of the Roman Law*. He was also a prolific author on American law, his most famous work being his *Manual of Parliamentary Practice*.[48] In addition, Cushing wrote for the *American Jurist and Law Magazine* and, from 1838 to 1843, was its principal editor. He also served on the editorial board of the German *Kritische Zeitschrift*, a journal of comparative law.[49] He was, thus, both a contemporary of Story when he was a young man and a successor to Story in later life. Unfortunately, Cushing's considerable contribution to American jurisprudence has been all but forgotten today. The extensive published corpus of his work, however, makes it possible to reconstruct Cushing's views and extraordinary legal expertise, especially in Roman and civil law.

Without question, the most interesting of Cushing's works from this perspective is his *Introduction to the Study of the Roman Law*. It is one of the first native American handbooks of Roman law. It shows both the orientation and the great extent of Cushing's Roman and civilian learning. The *Introduction* was derived from his Harvard lectures and enriched by the intimate knowledge of Savigny, Domat, and Pothier which he had gained through translating their works into English. The first striking aspect of the volume is its arrangement and its content. It is very much historical and totally alien to the Continental Pandectist tradition and, thus, quite different from the work of Story, Follen, or Austin. Aside from a final chapter, almost an afterword, on the law of bailments, there is virtually no discussion of substantive private law in the book. Although the object of the book as stated in the preface is to impart knowledge "of the science of Roman law . . . which most readily enables the student to engage, at once, in the study of its principles,"[50] no substantive private law principles are, in fact, discussed. Instead, Cushing's book is very much a preliminary introduction to the subject seen as a philosophical and historical study designed to acquaint students with the basic philosophy and sources of Roman law before they might embark on a study of the substantive law. It is, thus, what is generally called an "external history" of Roman law and stands in the tradition of Schomberg's *Historical and Chronological View of Roman Law* rather than Taylor's *Elements*.[51] To a large degree, Cushing's book is also a polemic on the importance of the study of Roman law for American lawyers and law students. Cushing's rationale for Roman law study differs both from those of his American predecessors, such as Legaré or Story, and those of his English contemporaries, such as Maine or J. G. Phillimore.

First, and, perhaps most significant, Cushing rejects the idea that Roman law is *ratio scripta* or even that the art of legal philosophy reached its summit in the writings of the Roman jurists. On the contrary, though Cushing readily admits to the excellence of Roman juristic thought as a ground for the study of "general jurisprudence," he is also quick to point out to his readers that the Anglo-American tradition was of equal greatness:

> Admirable, however, as is the method of the great jurists of Rome, their writings are not to be placed above the legal arguments of the great lawyers of more modern times. The eminent judges of England and America, in this respect, have at least shown themselves to be the equals of their Roman predecessors; while, in the amount and variety of their labors, and in the importance of the questions submitted to them, *the moderns throw the ancients entirely into the shade.*[52]

By far the greatest significance of Roman law study for Cushing, however, is its practical utility for the modern lawyer. First, he points out, many of the general jurisprudential ideas of the Anglo-American common law tradition are "incorporated" into the common law, as they are into the laws of the European nations. Second, many specific legal rules and institutions of England and the United States are, in Cushing's opinion, derived from Roman law. He cites as examples the law of wills, administrations, trusts, successors, and special pleading. In an interesting passage, Cushing also seems to express sentiments similar to those of Maine on the parallelism of legal development in different countries at the same stage of society: "If the last-named system [special pleading] did not derive its origin from the Roman law, then it would seem, that the same system, in substance, must have been the growth of different ages, and of different codes of laws."[53]

Cushing also points out, in a manner reminiscent of Story, that American lawyers need to understand civil law because a number of American jurisdictions have civilian systems: "The foundations of the legal institutions of several of the United States, as Louisiana, Florida, Texas, California, are laid directly in the Roman law. Throughout the vast regions of country embraced within the limits of these states, and which will, ere long, be covered with an enterprising and industrious population, the Roman law prevails in the same manner and to the same extent that the common law does in the other states."[54]

Even apart from instances of parallel development such as in the case of special pleading and the clearly civilian systems of the South and Southwest, Cushing also believed that Roman law was a source of *ius commune* in American common law jurisdictions when common law rules on a specific topic were lacking. The case he cites for illustration is particularly interesting:

> The Roman law has been much more widely extended in modern than the Roman empire ever was in ancient times. Its diffusion, from the middle ages to the present day, has taken place upon the simple principle, equally operative at this moment, that wherever, and whenever, and as to whatever, there was any want of its principles, for the regulation of human affairs, its authority has been at once recognized, admitted, and applied. An example of the introduction and application of the principles of the Roman law occurs with reference to the institution of domestic slavery in this country. Wherever that relation has been introduced, it has been followed and regulated, in the absence of other legislation, by the principles of the Roman law.[55]

Regardless of whether the Roman law of slavery was, indeed, adopted in the antebellum South—about which there is a continuing controversy[56]—obviously Cushing believed this to be the case. He might just as easily have cited, of course, the growing body of law relating to conflicts of law, which, in the path outlined by Livermore and Story, used substantive Roman law rules as a source for American law.[57] Indeed, at the end of the *Lectures*, Cushing includes a full chapter on the law of bailments as an illustration of the degree to which Anglo-American law depended upon Roman and civil law and the importance of its study for American law. This illustration, however, goes further than simply acknowledging the influence of Roman and civil law.[58] It is a remarkable essay in intellectual history and comparative law.

Cushing begins this final chapter with a disquisition on the Norman French origins of the term *bailment* and moves on to a close discussion of the leading English case of *Coggs v. Bernard* and the opinion of Lord Holt in this case, which depended on Henry de Bracton and Roman law.[59] He then makes passing reference to Blackstone's treatment of the subject and proceeds to analyze Sir William Jones's handling of the question of standards of care in his *Essay*.[60] He contrasts Jones's analysis with that of the leading Continental humanist civilian jurists including Hugo Donellus, Christian Thomasius, Jacobus Gothofredus, Heineccius, and Pothier.[61] As a result of this comparison of Continental Roman law scholarship with that contained in Jones's *Essay*, Cushing concludes that Jones's contribution to English law was flawed.

> The system of the three degrees of neglect or fault, which was in vogue on the continent of Europe, at the middle of the last century, and at that time taught by the commentators on the Roman law, as the fair result of its doctrines, was introduced into the common law of England and of this country, in which it still prevails, by the sole authority of Sir William Jones, by the publication of his essay and on the law of bailments.

> This system, it appears, has been since abrogated in France by the new civil code, and is now generally abandoned in Germany, as the result of a more careful study, and a sounder criticism, of the sources of the Roman law.

> The establishment of this system in the common law, as the doctrine and on the authority of the Roman law, when it was in fact not taught there, but was the mistaken inference therefrom of the writers on the subject, furnishes an apt example of one of the principal objections—the then imperfect state of legal science,—of the German historical school, to the plan of codification proposed by Thibaut.[62]

This fascinating example of Cushing's legal historical and critical skills also raises the issue of the influence of Savigny's work on Cushing. Cushing, much like Maine a decade later, was obviously aware of and influenced by the work of Savigny and his followers. He was not, however, a slavish adherent of the historical school. Although the *Lectures* betray a generally positive appreciation of the work of Savigny and his followers, it is not an uncritical appreciation. Cushing also recognized the value of the systematizing efforts of the Pandectists, scholars such as Ferdinand Mackeldey[63] and Thibaut, whom Savigny opposed:[64]

> The labors of the historical school have established an entirely new and distinct era in the study of the Roman jurisprudence; and

though these writers cannot be said to have thrown their predecessors into the shade, it seems to be generally admitted, that almost every branch of the Roman law has received some important modifications at their hands, and that a knowledge of their
writings, to some extent, at least, is essentially necessary to its
acquisition.[65]

A final comparison between Cushing and Maine is worthwhile.
Cushing's *Lectures* show a sophisticated level of scholarship and an
extensive knowledge of the Continental sources and juristic writings both of the humanistic period and of the nineteenth century. Indeed, Cushing's *Lectures* are, on the whole, more accurate in their de-
lineation of points of Roman law than are Maine's works. There may
be several possible explanations for this. Although both Maine and
Cushing were early users of the historical comparative approach,
Cushing's comparisons tend to be narrowly focused on Roman law
and Anglo-American common law and thus to fall more closely within
the tradition pioneered by Story earlier in the century (although
Story's comparisons were, generally, ahistorical). Maine's comparisons
are more broadly based, encompassing not only Roman and Anglo-
American law but also Hindu law and the laws of the early Germanic
kingdoms and other non-Western systems. Cushing and Story used
the comparative method narrowly as a critical tool for evaluating
specific substantive legal rules. Maine used it far more broadly to develop a vision of law as a whole and to understand law as an extended
social phenomenon—developmentally. Thus Maine's work has a far
wider scope and objective than does Cushing's and, for this reason,
perhaps, shows a more superficial scholarly technique. Nevertheless,
Cushing and Maine shared several important views; both saw the need
to study Roman and common law historically and also saw Roman law
as of *practical* value to the practicing lawyer and legislator. Maine saw
Roman law as a basis for law reform; Cushing, too, saw Roman law as a
source for contemporary legal activity.

In short, if one were to attempt to put Cushing himself into historical perspective, one would be forced to see him as more traditional
than Maine with views hearkening somewhat back to Story and echo-

ing, in part, those of Austin and not, by a broad sweep of vision, as initiating the type of new movement in legal-historical and comparative law studies in the United States that was begun in England by Maine ten years later. Nevertheless, both men saw direct value in Roman law to the practicing common lawyer. Finally, although both writers were influenced by Savigny and both adopted a historical-comparative approach, an espousal of the comparative approach was not the major thrust of his work, as it was of Maine's. Thus Cushing's efforts, though perhaps more technically accurate than Maine's, were not so innovative or, perhaps, so political and reformist as Maine's and, therefore, perhaps, have not been so well remembered.

William Gardiner Hammond and the Western Jurist

One of the most remarkable American lawyers, jurists, and legal educators of the second half of the nineteenth century was William Gardiner Hammond.[66] He was born in Rhode Island and educated at Amherst College. Even as a young student his interests were wide-ranging, including both literature and classical languages. He read Gibbon's *Decline and Fall* as well as the *Domesday Book* as a youth and at Amherst was editor of the college literary magazine. His interest in law developed early. Before attending college, he had become acquainted with Justinian's *Digest*, and while an undergraduate, he was fortunate enough to attend a trial in a nearby town pitting Daniel Webster against Rufus Choate.[67] After graduation he entered the law offices of Samuel Johnson in Brooklyn, New York, to read the law and subsequently joined the New York Bar. In the mid-1850s, however, Hammond's health faltered so he traveled to Europe for an extensive stay to recuperate.

Once on the Continent, Hammond made his way to Heidelberg, where he perfected his German and acquired what was to be a lifelong interest in Roman and civil law. His stay in Heidelberg was cut short by financial reverses in the crash of 1857 and he returned to the United States. His health, however, was still not good, and in 1860 he moved to Iowa, where he worked as a railroad engineer as well as a lawyer. At this time he began his scholarly publications with a volume of Iowa reports and, in 1867, became editor of the then leading western law journal, the *Western Jurist*.[68] He also became associated with the new law school at Des Moines.[69] In 1869, when this school became part of the University of Iowa at Iowa City, Hammond became its first chancellor.[70] He remained at Iowa until 1881. During this period, he published his edition of T. C. Sandars's *Institutes of Justinian*.[71] This edition contained a long and erudite essay by Hammond on civil law schemes of classification, which was separately published in 1876 under the title *System of Legal Classification of Hale and Blackstone in Its Relation to the Civil Law*.[72] He also published in 1880 his edition of Francis Lieber's *Legal and Political Hermeneutics*[73] and a large number of important legal history and comparative law articles in the *Western Jurist*. In 1881, Hammond left Iowa to become dean of the law school at Washington University in St. Louis, where he continued to write on legal history, comparative law, and legal education and published his edition of Blackstone's *Commentaries*.[74]

Hammond left behind a large corpus of work on civil law and comparative law and legal history both in his articles and in his editions. These published writings show the extent of his learning in civil law, and they show as well the role a leading American civilian assigned to civil law studies in the third quarter of the nineteenth century.

Hammond, like Cushing and Maine, was well aware of Savigny's writings, and their influence is to be found throughout his published work. There is no question that Hammond's approach to Roman and civil law was much colored by Savigny's historical approach. The extent of this influence and the perspective adopted by Hammond toward Roman and civil law are, perhaps, best expressed in a lecture he delivered in his course Civil Law and Its Utility in American Practice, which was published in the June 1870 issue of the *Western Jurist*.[75] That the course was taught at all is significant. Throughout his tenure at Iowa, Hammond taught courses on civil law and comparative law, evidencing his belief that these topics were a fit subject of instruction for a western law school. In this lecture, Hammond stated the grounds for his belief.

Interestingly, Hammond began his introductory lecture by hearkening back to John Adams's studies in civil law and by deploring the decline in interest that had subsequently occurred.[76] For Hammond the study of civil law was intimately connected to the kind of broad, jurisprudential education that a university law school was designed to provide.[77] Thus in this lecture we hear strong echoes of Daniel Mayes's earlier address at Transylvania and of Blackstone's *Discourse*, both of which argued for a broad philosophical educational system for lawyers, and echoes, also, of W. A. Hunter's and James Bryce's later writings. Hammond regarded the study of civil law with its comparative aspect as a needed antidote to the technicalities and narrow perspective of the common law and its practice: "The surest way to eminence in our own law is not to confine one's self entirely to its technicalities. If the knowledge of the Civil law has not declined absolutely since the 18th century, it yet has comparatively, and in the proportion it bears to our own jurisprudence." The law schools provided the means of furthering this aim:

> These [law] schools make it at least *possible* to revive the study of *civil law*, and so far as can be judged from the opinions expressed by leading jurists, and by bodies like the Am. S.S. Ass'n., it seems *probable* that in a very short time we shall learn to regard a legal education as incomplete, if it does not enable the student to make some uses of the treasures of jurisprudence garnered up in the *corp. ju. civ.*[78]

Hammond's purpose in teaching civil law to American law students went beyond its possible contribution as an aid to the study of jurisprudence. He saw it, further, as an "exemplification of all the principles which make law a historical science, in the history of the Civil law." Hammond believed that the history of the civil law provided a perfect example of legal development, which he saw broadly as an important "portion of the life of humanity." But Hammond did not view history as significant solely for its own sake. Rather, like Maine, Hammond saw the historical approach as intimately connected to comparative studies and the two as related means of casting light upon the operations of our own common law system and as tools of reform as well. Hammond's lecture is clear on these points. He stated outright that his object was "not to make you civilians" but, instead, to "try and point out . . . the most striking points of resemblance and of difference between our system and theirs, and the chief uses which may be made of the civil law in studying and practicing our own."[79]

This comparatist theme is more fully elaborated in one of the most interesting of Hammond's publications in the *Western Jurist*, his review of Maine's *Ancient Law*, published in the second volume for February 1868.[80] It is an exceptionally interesting essay, for it is not wholly congratulatory, as were most contemporary reviews.[81] On the contrary, though Hammond praises Maine's efforts and lauds his attempt to develop a general history of early law, he is also critical of flaws in Maine's work.

First, of course, Hammond praises *Ancient Law* as marking "the commencement of a new age of legal studies" and as answering "the need of a new method of study" so that law could be treated as a science rather than merely as an art, "the art of reaching a practical conclusion on practical questions, without consideration of the fundamental principles involved," that is, as a series of technicalities rather than as a broad jurisprudence.[82] In this, of course, he saw *Ancient Law* in much the same light as he viewed Roman and civil law studies, as a broadening experience for narrowly trained common lawyers. Yet Hammond criticized *Ancient Law* for failing to live up to its promise, for concentrating primarily on Roman law, with a smattering of Hindu and Germanic law. Where, Hammond wanted to know, was Greek law and the laws of other ancient societies? For Hammond, the real problem with Maine's *Ancient Law* was that it did not go far enough in the comparativist direction.

These essays on civil law and on Maine's *Ancient Law* help to put Hammond's view of Roman and civil law studies in perspective. It is, obviously, openly historical and comparativist. There is no trace of the veneration accorded to Roman law by Hammond's American predecessors such as Legaré or Story. Nor is there any hint that Hammond believed Roman law to be some form of immanent *ratio scripta*. Rather, Hammond saw Roman and civil law as artifacts, prime material for use for his own purposes. These purposes, unlike Story's, were not to provide substantive rules with which to supplement American law; by the second half of the nineteenth century this was unnecessary. Rather, Hammond's principal purpose for studying Roman law was to have a convenient case study for his comparative jurisprudence. Thus Hammond criticized Maine for failing to take the opportunity to provide material on other legal cultures, to broaden the comparativist's sample.

This historical-comparativist perspective is also brought out in Hammond's long introductory essay to his American edition of Sandars's edition of Justinian's *Institutes*. The task Hammond set for himself in this work was quite specific: he attempted to analyze common law categories, especially as developed by Hale and Blackstone, and contrast these to the highly sophisticated system of categories developed by civilian authors. In this endeavor, Hammond's approach most closely resembles that of Joseph Story fifty years before. In the course of this essay Hammond provides a remarkable survey of the jurisprudential work not only of Hale and Blackstone but also of such more modern figures as Austin and members of the German Pandectist movement. He also deftly compares the advantages and disadvantages of the highly ordered and systematic civilian approach in historical perspective to the seemingly chaotic and ad hoc common law method that had grown up over the centuries. Even more interesting is the very balanced approach to this comparison evidenced in the essay. Hammond notices the positive and negative aspects of both systems and in the course of his analysis stakes out a middle ground as preferable. To an extent, therefore, especially in matters of abstract jurisprudence, Hammond's work in this aspect does show a strong resemblance to Story's of half a century earlier, but with a historical component added and with more emphasis on the broadly educational function of comparison and less regard to formulating new substantive rules for everyday use.

This historical-comparativist approach in Hammond's writings is found also in articles by other authors published in the *Western Jurist* during Hammond's tenure as editor. The issues of the *Western Jurist* published in the 1860s and 1870s provide a strong refutation to Peter Stein's contention that interest in Roman law disappeared in the United States by the mid-1850s.[83] In addition to Hammond's articles, the *Western Jurist* published major articles on Roman and civil law or on subjects involving substantial analysis of civil law rules.[84] One of the most interesting of these is a reprint of an article by W. A. Hunter, an

English teacher of Roman law, first published in the *Law Magazine and Review* in England and titled "The Place of Roman Law in Legal Education," a piece that evidences what was to become the dominant English theory of the place of Roman law in common law education.[85]

Hunter begins his article, which was first presented as an introductory lecture to the Roman law class at University College, London, in 1874, with a firm repudiation of theories that Roman law had had a direct effect on English law and notes that "manifestly, therefore, the Roman law cannot rank in importance with common law. He goes on to argue, however, for the historical and comparative value of Roman law studies, echoing the sentiments of Maine, Hammond, and Bryce:

> It is instructive to observe the English and Roman law, when they seek the same objects by like means; but it is even more instructive to observe how they adapt themselves to the wants of two distinct civilizations. We are thus taught in a manner never to be forgotten, that law plays, although an important, still a subordinate part in the structure of civilized society. We learn that great as is its influence on the moral feelings and institutions of a people, it is the handmaid, and not the mistress of the sciences of morals and legislation.

He states further:

> These subjects have a great interest, not merely from an historical point of view, but from a more practical one. It shows the flexibility with which law must adapt itself to the ever varying conditions of life. According as social demands change, so must law change too. The adjustment of these two things is the work of the legislator, and it is well for us to study that work in examples far away from the circle of our personal interests and prejudice, with impartial indifference.[86]

It is not at all difficult to understand how Hammond would have been attracted to the historical-comparativist bent of Hunter's essay. Here, again, is a clear exposition of the value of Roman law to comparativist studies and of the perspective to be gained through such studies. Here, too, is shown a proper appreciation for the historical study of a legal system. All in all, Hunter's essay undoubtedly struck a sympathetic chord in Hammond's psyche.

If one were to attempt to formulate some broad characterization of William Hammond's approach to Roman and civil law it would have to be that it was both scholarly and comparativist. Obviously, Hammond was a good scholar of Roman and civil law, although he was perhaps not as learned as, for instance, Hugh Legaré. But he was also not an amateur. He amassed a library of some three hundred volumes on Roman and civil law, and he wrote extensively and lectured on it during his tenure at Iowa.[87] Nevertheless, Roman and civil law was certainly not his predominant scholarly interest. Indeed, after 1880, his focus shifted away from Roman and civil law. While he edited Sandars's *Justinian* he also edited Blackstone's *Commentaries*. He wrote on the history of English and American law just as he wrote on the history of Roman and civil law. While he was editor of the *Western Jurist*, he published articles on various legal systems.[88] In short, Hammond may be best understood, perhaps, as a forerunner of John Henry Wigmore's "world legal historian," a scholar who valued all legal systems equally for what light a comparison among them could shed on each of them individually. Regardless of this approach, however, Hammond was a moving force in keeping Roman and civil law studies alive in the United States in the 1860s and 1870s.

John Norton Pomeroy

It may appear incongruous to include John Norton Pomeroy in a study of English and American civilians and comparativists. Pomeroy is best known for his works on remedies, constitutional law, and equity jurisprudence.[89] Yet it is precisely because Pomeroy was not specifically a civilian that makes his interest in Roman and civil law studies all the more important.

John Norton Pomeroy was born in Rochester, New York, in April 1828. His father was a lawyer and judge, and his family on both sides were longtime New Englanders. His early education was typical for the time and was capped by his attendance at Hamilton College. From there he went to Lebanon, Ohio, where he read law in the offices of Thomas Corwin and taught at a secondary school. After three years he returned to Rochester and was admitted to the New York Bar in 1851. For ten years he practiced law there. In 1861 he moved to New York City, but finding himself a failure at the law there, he resorted again to schoolteaching. During this period of professional failure he wrote his first major book, the *Introduction to Municipal Law*, first published in 1864.[90] This book made his career. Within a year he was appointed a law professor in New York, where he remained until 1878, when he took up the Chair of Municipal Law at Hastings Law College in San Francisco. He held this chair until his death in 1885.

In no way could one suggest that Pomeroy was a devoted aficionado of Roman and civil law. He was, however, a firm believer in the historical approach to law. In his inaugural address at Hastings he proclaimed: "In the first place, I most profoundly believe that the law must be studied historically."[91] Nevertheless, Pomeroy was far from an antiquarian. For him, history was the handmaiden of actual practice, for it provided students and lawyers with the broad perspective necessary to the well-trained lawyer. Thus Pomeroy valued Roman and civil law as historically significant legal systems, an acquaintance with which would enrich a common lawyer's understanding of his own system.

Certainly, though Pomeroy cannot be characterized as a Roman or civil law scholar, even on the model of Hammond, he had more than a passing acquaintance with the subject. This knowledge is shown not only in several articles he published in popular periodicals during the 1860s and 1870s but also in his—in many ways—underappreciated first book, the *Introduction to Municipal Law*. He also knew the literature of Roman and civil law. According to his son, his library contained a fair number of Continental law books, and in his own writings he specifically mentions the works of Savigny, Hugo, Mackeldy, J. F. T. Ortolan, and Niebuhr, among others.[92]

To understand and evaluate Pomeroy's knowledge of and interest in Roman and civil law, one must turn to his 1864 *Introduction*. This book was not intended as a substitute for Kent or Blackstone or for a university legal education. Instead, it was designed to introduce the American legal system to university undergraduates and intelligent laymen, as well as to provide supplementary reading for law students. Its organization is broadly historical, beginning with basic concepts and categories, unwritten laws, and the law-fact distinction. It then moves on to a discussion of the history of the English and American judiciary and next to the sources of Anglo-American law. The third part of this section deals with Roman law and with the medieval maritime laws. From here the book proceeds to a consideration of various areas of substantive law, concentrating on the Anglo-American tradition but also straying beyond, for instance, to a discussion of French marriage laws.[93] Certainly, it is noteworthy that well over one hundred pages in a basic American law textbook of the third quarter of the nineteenth century are devoted to Roman law.[94]

Throughout the *Introduction*, Pomeroy takes both a historical and a comparative view of his subject and, for him, as for Hammond, the Roman legal system provides an excellent case study:

> The Roman law affords the most complete and instructive example of the rise, full development, decline, and death of a system of national jurisprudence. The value of the example consists in the illustration which it furnishes of the normal method of legal growth, and also in the excellence of the legislation itself which was the final product of the maturity of the Roman organizing power.[95]

Throughout the book, Pomeroy's analysis depends on this insight. For each substantive topic in Anglo-American law, Pomeroy provides a short historical sketch as well as a brief comparative note of Roman or civilian practice. In each case the purpose of both the historical sketch and the comparative note is the same: to place the present-day Anglo-American rule in a broad philosophical context so as to permit the reader to evaluate its utility and philosophical justification. Thus, again, Pomeroy's historical-comparative use of Roman law is similar to Hammond's and Maine's but is not oriented toward the actual adoption of foreign substantive law or concepts as was the approach of earlier scholars such as Story or Legaré. For Pomeroy, as for Hammond, a scientific approach to law required a broad philosophical outlook. Foreign systems of law examined comparatively could provide such a broad context. Roman law was both substantively the most sophisticated and the best documented of such systems. Therefore, the study of Roman law was not only justifiable pedagogically but was, in fact, necessary. Furthermore, Pomeroy believed, like Maine, that different legal systems, even though historically distinct, often evolve in extremely similar ways. Thus, to his mind, the study of Roman law could directly contribute to the study of English and American law and so his comparative approach was useful to contemporary lawyers and law students.

A good example of Pomeroy's approach to this comparative study of parallel development is found in his treatment of the means of bringing a dispute to trial laid out in the *Introduction*. This discussion, central to Pomeroy's analysis of general legal procedure, begins with his observation on the broad stages such legal forms undergo:

> After the first steps are taken . . . but before the legal ideas have yielded to the influence of general ethical principles, the procedure is distinguished by a strict adherence to forms, often in the highest degree arbitrary. At more advanced stages this arbitrary character and technical nicety of legal actions gradually, gives way; the substance, the merits of the dispute,—are more regarded by the courts; the deviations from prescribed formularies are passed over. Finally, when the jurisprudence has attained a position where the greatest possible weight is given to considerations of abstract right, and the last to those merely historical and institutional . . . the judicial procedure will have retained only so much of form as is indispensable to the orderly and speedy administration of justice.

The enunciation of this broad historical principle is followed first by a historical analysis of Roman trial procedure beginning with the formulary period and extending to the later empire. Pomeroy concludes this survey by noting:

> I have dwelt thus at considerable length upon this portion of Roman legal history, because it serves to illustrate in a striking manner that of England. When we come to view the progress of jurisprudence in the latter country, we shall discover the same causes at work, in an identical manner, the judges yielding to the demands of the times and the wants of suitors, inventing new

forms of legal remedy, and thus suffering the law to flow on into new and ever widening channels.[96]

He goes on to discuss the Anglo-American development, constantly comparing it to analogous Roman developments.

One might make two final remarks about the significance of Pomeroy's use of Roman law. First, of course, it is very similar to the work of Hammond and Maine and firmly within the historical-comparative school, so influenced by Savigny. For all of these jurists, Roman law was the perfect source for illustrative and philosophically broadening comparisons. By finding historical parallels and comparing the legal responses among different cultures to similar societal forces as a nation developed, all sought to illuminate the dark corners of common law jurisprudence. Equally important in regard to Pomeroy is that he was not, by any means, a Romanist or civilian, nor did he have European training or extensive European contacts. Instead, he was very much an American law professor but one, who, in the spirit of his times, had been influenced by Savigny and the historical school and who regarded some knowledge of Roman law as a necessary adjunct for the common lawyer, seeing in Roman law a perfect fund of historical *exempla*. Thus Pomeroy may stand out as a model of how even the nonspecialist American law professor might study and write about Roman and civil law in the 1860s and 1870s and find a contemporary value in their Roman and civil law studies.

Roman and Civil Law in the First Generation After 1850

It should by now be clear that far from disappearing after 1850, Roman and civil law studies found a new lease on life in England and in the United States. To be sure, they were no longer pursued primarily as a source for new substantive rules by which the common law could be supplemented, nor were they held up as the model of technical and philosophical clarity by which common law could be reformed. Luther Stearns Cushing, writing and lecturing just at the turn of mid-century, represents, perhaps, the last figure for whom such concerns carried great weight, and even he had moved far from the Austin-Story model.

Equally, the study of Roman law as a genteel, if not gentlemanly, pursuit represented to a degree in Story's and H. S. Legaré's works had also disappeared. Instead, Roman law achieved a new importance in the period after 1850 as part of the newly arising disciplines of legal history and comparative law and was nurtured in the rapidly expanding university law schools by law professors such as Hammond and Pomeroy who were bent upon escaping the narrow technicalities of the law and teaching in the new scientific model developed a generation before by men such as Daniel Mayes and just on the verge of being popularized by contemporaries such as C. C. Langdell.[97] In this way the writings of Maine, Cushing, Hammond, and Pomeroy foreshadowed the development of Roman and civil law studies in England and the United States in the last generation of the nineteenth century, which, indeed, began, as so many generations do, just as the earlier was coming to an end.

4

The Domestication of Roman Law in the Anglo-American World After 1850

In many respects the period after 1875 was the crucible in which the modern Anglo-American legal system was forged. The period from 1875 to 1920 saw the growth of the modern law firm, the establishment of the Langdell model of legal education, and the beginning of the shift away from the concerns of the nineteenth century (such as codification) to the concerns of the twentieth (such as procedural reform).[1] It was also a period in which the study of and interest in Roman and civil law was finally and fully domesticated. No longer were these systems seen as viable alternatives to the Anglo-American common law, as they had been a century before. Nor were they seen any longer as necessary sources for the supplementation of the common law. After a century (in the United States) of case law and statutory activity, the problem was too much law, not too little. The concern with systematization of law, too, was now less in evidence either in England or the United States, and Roman models were less necessary. During this period, instead, Roman and civil law continued to provide the basis for historical-comparative law studies and teaching in both the United States and England, as they had begun to do in the quarter-century before under the guidance of Sir Henry Maine and William Gardiner Hammond. They also continued to be seen as representing a high level of juristic sophistication and thus as a useful part of elementary juris-prudential training. By and large, during this period the position of Roman and civil law studies in the Anglo-American world was consolidated but also diminished. It was diminished because these subjects, and especially Roman law (rather than modern civil law), quickly came to be seen almost solely as academic subjects and, indeed, in many cases subjects best suited for undergraduate study or, at most, as the basis for the theoretical rather than practical side of professional law studies.[2] Their study provided a useful comparative perspective on present-day problems encountered in the technicalities of the common law of contracts or torts, for example, and thus one finds common law scholars such as Samuel Williston using Roman and civilian law sources in this way, but in a merely ancillary capacity.[3] Roman and civil law studies also came to be seen as an important part of the increasingly widespread interest in legal history, fueled by the work of the immediately preceding generation of legal scholars such as Sir Henry Sumner Maine and William Gardiner Hammond. We find, for instance, learned discussions of Roman and civil law in the work of English-speaking European and Roman legal historians and also in that of common law historians such as F. W. Maitland and Oliver Wendell Holmes.[4] To an extent this latter interest occurred because one of the legal historical problems that greatly exercised many of the common lawyers during this period was the question of whether Roman law had been received into the common law during the Middle Ages and Renaissance.[5] Finally, it was also during the late nineteenth century that Roman law, especially, came to appeal to lawyers who had antiquarian interest in the history of law.[6] It was "charming."

What is most significant about this domestication of Roman and civil law in the common law countries, however, is that in the process of being domesticated, they came for the first time to be seen by many as subjects isolated from common law legal subjects. Other than as comparative material, Roman and civil law were divorced, both in the academic curriculum and in the minds of most jurists, from modern legal concerns. The vital interplay among Roman, civilian, and common law ideas in the development of doctrine that had been argued for and, to some extent, had taken place earlier in the century was much diminished. Instead, the academic movement that had originated with Maine in the 1860s in England and had been championed by Hammond in the United States in the 1870s came to fruition at the end of the century. Roman and civil law became acceptable subjects for study but were of far less practical concern to modern jurists.

Roman Law as a Subject of Academic Study

Although the position of Roman and civil law studies was, in some ways, diminished by their almost complete "academicization" and isolation in this period, it was also, in large part, consolidated by this same process. Once these subjects had received the imprimatur of legal academe and had become widely accepted as legitimate subjects of scholarly inquiry, their position was safe and their continued study in both England and the United States was assured, unless somehow they later lost this acceptance. Indeed, one particular change in the nature of legal education in the United States especially helped to assure their survival. This, of course, was the growth of a professional academic cadre in the law schools.[7] Until the late nineteenth century, from the Civil War on, law teachers were also law practitioners or judges.[8] During the last three decades of the century, however, the Harvard Law School championed the cause of the full-time law teacher and scholar who devoted himself exclusively to academic pursuits, a model that rapidly became standard throughout the United States and England.[9] With the rise of a professional class of law teachers who were expected to write books and articles, Roman and civil law became good subjects for fulfilling such professional expectations.[10]

With this domestication of Roman and civil law studies there came also a veritable outpouring of books and articles, both in England and the United States, about Roman law and especially about teaching Roman law. Many of these works are rather pedestrian and are simply short summaries of the main points of Roman law for use by college undergraduates or the interested law student, in effect, Roman law in a nutshell. Others of the genre, however, such as the *Introduction to Roman Law* published by James Hadley and based on his Yale College lecture course, are more sophisticated.[11] Hadley's book, for instance, begins with a history of Roman law as a legal system, both before and after Justinian. It was designed to provide historians and classicists with a working knowledge of Roman law.

One of the most notable features of many of these more sophisticated analyses of Roman law is their incorporation of the historical premises championed by the German and Anglo-American followers of Savigny and Hugo, such as Maine and Hammond.[12] We see now an appreciation for the periodization of Roman and European legal history that is either absent or barely noticeable in the works of preceding generations. Of course, lawyers and historians were well aware of the various periods of Roman history before the late nineteenth century; Gibbon's history firmly established these in the late eighteenth century.[13] During the early part of the nineteenth century, however, as discussed in previous chapters, while there was still some real attempt at creating a *modern* Roman law and incorporating Roman and civilian ideas into the common law, there was no practical relevance to whether a rule was republican, classical, or postclassical. Story, for instance, was interested in the substance of the rule and its inherent worth, not its historical development. These earlier scholars were most interested in the rules themselves and the fact that they were derived from a different system. The dating of a particular law and the tracing of the evolution of a particular rule were unimportant to these men. With the rise of the historical school under Savigny, Hugo, Maine, and Hammond, however, and the academicization of the study of Roman and civil law in England and the United States, the historical development of Roman and civil law became more important because these researches were often motivated primarily by historical rather than strictly legal questions. Contributing also to this phenomenon was the increasing participation in the field by teachers of undergraduate history and classics without legal training, men such as James Hadley, whose interests were wholly impractical in the professional sense and thus divorced even from those of men such as J. N. Pomeroy, who, of course, had written for undergraduates as well.[14]

This new academic factor, however, introduced a set of new concerns that had not been particularly interesting to most lawyers. When Luther Stearns Cushing and Charles Follen taught Roman law at Harvard, their main concern was to teach the basic rules of Roman law to law students who might then use these rules as comparative data when involved in modern, common law concerns and who might, thereby, better understand their own legal tradition. Even Maine and Hammond wrote primarily for lawyers and law reformers and were not ivory-tower academics.[15] When men like Hadley taught Roman law to undergraduates, they were attempting to provide a context for their students' reading in classical literary texts and for their understanding of ancient history. The students were not required to think about Roman and civil law as legal subjects like lawyers, but rather as literary and historical aids. The books of this genre reflect this approach.

Of course, there were some who saw a connection between the undergraduate and professional curricula in the United States. In 1905 a symposium was held in Michigan to discuss the continuing inclusion of the teaching of Latin and Greek in the American undergraduate curriculum. It was particularly interesting as regards the teaching of Roman law, for it included a discussion of the importance of teaching the classics as a preprofessional subject for would-be lawyers. Some of the participants argued in effect that classics (including Roman law) provided a perfect prelaw curriculum. In the course of the discussion several practicing lawyers argued that Latin was particularly well suited as a prelaw subject, especially if the study of the language included the elementary legal literature (including Justinian's *Institutes*). The reasons for such inclusion, several stated, were that a study of Roman law helped students to develop a feeling for precise legal terminology and a study of Roman law and terminology would help students later when they came to study the common law because the civil law and its terms had been engrafted upon many common law subjects such as chancery or the laws of descent and inheritance.[16]

Indeed, for university professors during this period who began to study Roman and civil law as subjects primarily to answer historical and literary questions, the absence of modern professional concerns could, in some respects, be liberating. To this extent, the study of Roman law, especially, became "pure," rather like the study of pure mathematics or theoretical physics or ancient history. Thus for instance, the growing German concerns with such highly technical and wholly impractical subjects as the study of interpolations in Roman legal texts came to preoccupy some Americans as well.[17]

One of the most interesting, albeit peculiar, literary subgenres of

Roman legal study in the Anglo-American world arose in this period from this new sense of liberation. A few scholars of Roman law were beginning to develop something of a sense of humor about their subject, for one finds rather bad poetry being written about Roman law. For instance, a Roman law tutor at Oxford penned some doggerel on the subject of his teaching.[18] The most famous example, however, is a long epic poem authored by Joseph Story's son William Wetmore Story.[19] Story was trained as a lawyer, taught at Harvard Law School, and wrote the standard mid-nineteenth-century treatise on contract law.[20] There is little indication that he was much interested in Roman and civil law in his academic period, although his biographer, Henry James, indicates that Story and his wife were guests of Savigny in the late 1850s. Story, however, soon gave up the law and moved to Rome, where he became a sculptor.[21]

It was during his Roman period that he composed the epic *A Roman Lawyer in Jerusalem.*" [22] The poem is typical of late nineteenth-century epics—lugubrious and rather boring—but it highlights the new integration of Roman law into the general cultural context of English-speaking lawyers. It is hard to imagine an English or American lawyer or law teacher of the early nineteenth century writing a poem on this topic. Roman and civil law were far too serious professional subjects. Indeed, many southern lawyers of the antebellum period were poets as well as lawyers.[23] The pages of southern literary journals are littered with their efforts. But Roman and civil law were not everyday, household subjects to be reduced to metrical form. By the later part of the century, however, even this had begun to change.

While Roman law gained acceptance in the undergraduate curriculum, it also came to be widely accepted both in U.S. law schools and in English universities as part of the new professional law curricula that had been instituted around mid-century. During these decades a number of teachers of Roman law published articles explaining how Roman law fit into the newly conceived university legal course. W. A. Hunter, who lectured on Roman law at University College, London, for instance, published an early article in the *Law Magazine and Review* titled "The Place of Roman Law in Legal Education," based on a lecture he gave in 1874. Indeed, so popular was this article that it was published in the *Western Jurist* in the United States by William Hammond.[24]

Hunter's piece is particularly interesting and reminiscent of Maine's lecture on a similar topic as well as Hammond's attitudes, but it is also very representative of the predominant English view of the place of Roman and civil law in the legal curriculum for several decades after its publication. Hunter rejects outright the centrality of Roman law for a practical lawyer's education (he suggests that the study of the modern civil law system may be more important). In contrast to its practical value, Hunter believed that the principal reason for teaching Roman law to English law students was that it was an excellent part of their "preliminary education" for it helped them to develop a "scientific" approach to the law. He explains that "what I mean by scientific knowledge of law is a knowledge of the uses and purposes and values of the rules of law as distinguished from a mere acquaintance with the rules as rules." Roman law, according to Hunter, was the perfect vehicle to teach such an appreciation of law as more than mere rules. Roman law was not only a storehouse of legal ingenuity, but it also provided a comparative basis for evaluating and understanding common law rules. He goes on to explain that it is precisely in those areas where the differences are greatest between the two systems that a student may best acquire a deeper understanding of both systems. He uses the Roman system of *manus* marriage and the common law of marriage to illustrate how this may be done.[25]

In stressing the value of Roman law for deepening the student's understanding of common law, Hunter took a position close to that of Sir Henry Sumner Maine, which is not at all surprising. But Hunter goes beyond discussing the comparative approach and the concomitant value of the study of Roman law. He also values Roman law as a means of teaching students about law in general, what we would now call jurisprudence. First, he points out that whereas the common law and its study must, of necessity, from the very nature of the common law, be fragmentary and disjointed, Roman law may be presented to the student as a complete system that may be mastered in toto because of its relatively "small bulk."[26] Indeed, here Hunter echoes the sentiments of his early nineteenth-century predecessors who appreciated Roman law for its systematic qualities. Hunter does not, however, as his predecessors such as Austin did, take the next step and argue that Roman law ought to be used as the basis for systematizing common law, but he does recognize that the systematic aspects of Roman law lend themselves to teaching basic legal ideas to law students.

Indeed, Hunter's early views on Roman law as the perfect vehicle for teaching general jurisprudence are echoed in a curious but highly enlightening lecture delivered in Germany in the 1880s by Erwin Grueber, who was then a reader in Roman law at Oxford.[27] Grueber was a German who emigrated to Oxford to improve his professional position. He authored a standard edition of *Digest* 9.2 with commentary, which was used at English universities in the basic Roman law course.[28] On a visit back to Germany, Grueber was asked to lecture on the place of Roman law in English legal education. In this lecture he echoed many of Hunter's sentiments. He took it for granted that Roman law was and would continue to be a part of the basic law curriculum—which modern civil law was not. In so doing he also made it clear that whereas in the German universities Roman law was studied as a subject which young lawyers must learn for practice purposes, in England Roman law was taught, in effect, as a course in legal philosophy and general jurisprudence. It was a means of teaching young students how to think like lawyers and was thus complementary to the teaching of common law subjects.

What one finds, therefore, in English law teaching in this period is the use of Roman law as the basis for teaching general jurisprudence and legal method and for developing in law students an appreciation for the evolution of legal rules and the social context within which legal rules must be understood.[29] Of course, here, as in the study of Roman law for purely historical and literary purposes, the hand of Savigny, Maine, and the historical school is in evidence. And, again, Roman law is isolated from modern practice. Indeed, this may help to explain the growing split between the study of Roman law and modern civil law during this period. Modern civil law was seen as a part of comparative law and even trade law, for a working knowledge of French or German jurisprudence would be directly useful to the practicing lawyer in a way Roman law was not.

It is possible to get a unique perspective on the role of Roman law in English legal education through an examination of two lectures given by James Bryce, the Regius Professor of Civil Law at Oxford from 1871 until 1894 and one of the leading Romanists in England.[30] Both

Bryce's inaugural lecture and his valedictory lecture have been preserved, and both address this question.[31]

In his inaugural, Bryce states many of the same themes outlined by Hunter in London several years later and foreshadowed by Maine and Hammond. Training in Roman law provided students who planned on becoming common lawyers with significant advantages even though, as Bryce readily acknowledged, it had played little role in the development of the English common law. First, Bryce echoed Maine and others like Hunter who believed that Roman law was the best source of comparison a common lawyer could hope for. He, too, like Hunter, stressed the value of the differences more than the similarities in imparting to the student the best understanding of the common law. Most important to Bryce, however, was the value of Roman law as a training ground for the young legal mind. He makes a particularly interesting and subtle argument on this point. He states categorically that the common law is not inferior to the Roman or civil law, but he admits that the common law, because of the unique circumstances of its development, has become a chaotic conglomeration of case law and statute that is difficult for a beginner to master. He suggests that the student who first attempts to learn the common law for eventual practice will often be stymied in his studies by the difficulty of mastering the sources. This would cause the student to be unable to learn at the same time the general ideas inherent in all legal systems and the methods and qualities of mind that ought to be devoted to all legal problems.[32] The Roman law, in contrast, Bryce believed to be systematic and manageable in the form in which it had come down to his generation. Thus his recommendation was similar to Hunter's: let the English law student cut his teeth on Roman law and acquire the skills necessary to master the common law.

Twenty-three years later Bryce returned to the theme of his inaugural in his valedictory address. He reaffirmed that in his experience Roman law was rarely of substantive use. He could recall one instance in which he had been able to quote Justinian's *Digest*. But twenty-three years of teaching had convinced him that as a means of teaching general jurisprudence to beginning law students and as a source of comparative material for understanding the common law, Roman law was unsurpassed.[33]

In his valedictory Bryce introduced another, new reason why Roman law should continue to be the object of study and teaching in the English law faculties. He granted that England had yet to produce a Romanist of the stature of Savigny, Jhering, Karl Adolf Vangerow (his own teacher), or Bernhard Windscheid, but he claimed a special aptitude for the English Romanists. He argued that precisely because Roman law was isolated from modern practice in England, English Romanists could cast a detached eye upon their subject and analyze Roman texts in a way the European civilians could not. Here, again, one hears how in its very domestication and isolation from the vitality of law in practice, Roman legal studies gained their liberation. Indeed, Bryce ended his reflections on the importance of Roman law in the English legal curriculum on a note of optimism that Maine could never have sounded: "I cannot doubt, looking not only to the progress of the study in England, but to its rapid and solid growth in the universities of America, that the study of Roman law, once so nearly extinct among us, is now destined to shine with a steady light for generations to come."[34]

Perhaps the best summary expression of the late nineteenth-century English attitude to Roman law as a subject of law teaching is found in a comparison Hunter made at the end of his lecture:

> Roman law thus appears to occupy the place in the course of legal education that pure scientific study does in medical education. It is a preparatory study, familiarizing the mind with the methods and, to a certain extent, with the subject matter of the strictly professional work. It is such studies that dignify a profession; which elevate the mind of professional men, and enable them to take a wide view of their work.[35]

In the United States during this period similar developments in the role of Roman law in law schools were taking place. Several law schools were offering courses in the subject.[36] And they were not just the elite eastern schools. Hammond had begun teaching Roman law at Iowa in the early 1870s. A student at the University of Nebraska law school could study Roman law as part of his law course, as could a student at the Chicago-Kent School of Law.[37] Indeed, Roman law had become so accepted in the legal curriculum that even practicing lawyers had come to believe that it was a normal part of a law student's education. Thus a speaker at an 1885 meeting of the Illinois Bar Association in Springfield, Illinois, included the study of Roman law as part of the basic legal course.[38] Roman law had come to the prairie.

One of the best expositions of the role of Roman law in American law schools during this period is an article published in 1897 by Munroe Smith of the Columbia faculty. Smith, like Hunter and Bryce, acknowledged that mastery of the substance of Roman law would not be of great value to practicing common lawyers. Roman law was rarely cited in American courts by 1897. In some special areas, which were much influenced by Roman and civil law, such as conflicts of laws, Smith saw some value to knowing Roman law, but students could learn this in a course on conflicts and did not necessarily need to study Roman law specifically. Indeed, Smith believed that if the purpose of legal education was primarily to train practicing lawyers, narrowly defined, then Roman law would not be much of an asset to the legal course and could easily be omitted.[39]

But Smith did not believe that legal education should be oriented solely toward the preparation of young men for the exigencies of practice. He suggests that law should be seen not as a trade but as a profession, by which he means that lawyers must recognize that they have a duty to provide social service. This, of course, implies that the lawyer must not only practice law but constantly seek to improve it through his efforts. Consequently, law schools should, in Smith's view, not only teach a trade but prepare their students for reforming the law and, as a result, reforming society. In this context, Smith saw that legal history could be a good teacher and, therefore, the study of Roman law could serve a useful purpose. But Smith acknowledged that a course in English or American legal history might be preferable to one on Roman law because it would be more familiar to law students.[40]

But Smith was not content to limit law to a trade or a profession, for he suggested that law was also a science and must be taught as a science. It was in regard to this third aspect of law and legal education that Smith believed the study of Roman law to be central. For law to be a science, it required *method*. The method he felt to be central to the scientific study of law was the comparative method, and Smith, like Maine, Hunter, Hammond, and Bryce, believed that the Roman legal tradition provided the best counterpoint, on grounds of accessibility and availability, to the study of common law.[41]

Another particularly interesting perspective on the teaching of Roman law in the United States during this period is provided by an article by Rudolph Leonhard, a professor of Roman law at Breslau who was a visiting professor at Columbia during the academic year 1907–8.[42] Leonhard, like his colleague Munroe Smith, promoted the American study of Roman law for its comparative value in understanding the common law better, but he also espoused an early version of the theory that there are "common cores" to all legal systems, both civilian and common law, and that it is through the study of both that students may begin to discover these common concepts. It is also interesting — given the date and the then prevalent isolationist tendencies of the American public—that Leonhard also urged Americans to study Roman law for a nonlegal purpose. He believed that through an understanding of Roman and civil law, Americans might be brought out of their parochialism and gain a greater understanding of their European counterparts.[43] In these two ideas Leonhard was visionary, for they became central to the revival of Roman and civil law studies in the United States after the Second World War.

One of the most interesting differences in the late nineteenth-century English and American theories on the place of Roman law in the law school curriculum is the English belief that Roman law should be used as a means of teaching general jurisprudence, a belief not common in the United States. Certainly, this difference had a major effect on the development of law school curricula in both countries. In England, Roman law became a standard first-year law subject. In the United States it was an upper-level or even a graduate elective. In England, therefore, every law student learned some Roman law whereas in the United States only those who chose to do so enjoyed such instruction. In part, this difference may be seen in the different approaches of Hunter (and Bryce) and Munroe Smith. The Englishmen viewed Roman law as part of a law student's preliminary preparation for the study of common law. The American viewed it, as did the visiting German, as an enrichment of the upper-level common law curriculum.

Roman Law as a Subject of Research and Writing

The revival of Roman law in British and American law faculties was accompanied by an outpouring of books and articles on Roman and civil law. During the last two decades of the nineteenth century and the first two of the twentieth, it was difficult to avoid seeing an article on these subjects if one read the legal literature. For the most part, these articles tended to be either comparative or historical with little written either about the modern use of Roman law in the common law countries or the use of Roman and civil law as a foundation of general jurisprudence. The first topic seems to have been limited to the civil law countries wherein Jhering's influence and the development of *Begriffsjurizprudenz* continued apace.[44] Although Jhering's work was known in the United States—indeed, well-known to scholars such as Roscoe Pound—no realistic attempt was made during this period to reshape Roman law to replace common law.[45] That had stopped a half-century before. The absence of scholarly writing on Roman law as a basis for general jurisprudence may be owing to academics' perceptions that this was more a pedagogical than a scholarly concern.

One can gain some idea of the type of writing on Roman and civil law that was being produced during this period through a brief survey of a representative sample of such articles. To pick a significant sample, one may look at those articles on Roman and civil law published in the *Harvard Law Review*, which began publication in 1887.

Several of the articles published by Harvard were openly historical and antiquarian. John Couch published an article, for instance, on the status of women in early Roman law. Lawrence Lowell published a study on the use of torture as an evidentiary device (which has its origins in Roman law), and John Chipman Gray published a study of the use of precedent in different historical systems of law. C. S. Lobingier wrote an article on the *Code Napoleon*, Peter Hamilton wrote on the

Spanish Civil Code, and Samuel Williston wrote comparative studies on contract law and the law of pledge. In addition, the young Ernst Freund wrote on the new German *BGB*, Walter Neitzel wrote two articles on German civil practice, and S. C. Weil published a series of seminal articles on the history of water law, tracing it back to its Roman origins.[46]

The backgrounds of these various authors are particularly instructive. For the most part they were academics who did not specialize in Roman and civil law studies but, rather, were primarily interested in gaining a comparative perspective on modern common law issues. Two, however, were not academics, and their activities add a unique aspect to the revival of interest in the Roman and civilian texts during this period. Peter Hamilton was a United States district judge in Puerto Rico, and C. S. Lobingier was a United States judge in Shanghai, China. One may speculate that the interest of both was sparked by their daily confrontation with alien legal systems, an inevitable fact of colonial life.

Although the authors of these articles, which appeared in the *Harvard Law Review*, would not have considered themselves to be civilians and were not so considered by others, in this period of the late nineteenth and early twentieth centuries, a number of prominent English and American scholars clearly were expert Roman and civil lawyers. Of these, perhaps the most important were William Warwick Buckland and James Bryce in England and Charles Phineas Sherman and Roscoe Pound in the United States. These four men, all law teachers, were the greatest Romanists and civilians of their period and, with Maine and Hammond, fully established the model for Roman law scholarship that continued for decades.

James Bryce was born in Belfast, Ireland, in May 1838. He studied the classics in Glasgow and at Oxford, rapidly becoming one of the leading scholars of Roman law of his generation. He became a fellow of Oriel College, Oxford, in 1862 and was called to the Bar in 1867. And like Austin before him (although Bryce thought less of Austin than many), he went to Germany to study Roman and civil law. There he was particularly fortunate because he was able to study with one of Germany's greatest Roman lawyers, Vangerow, at Heidelberg.[47] In 1864 he published his first major historical work, *The Holy Roman Empire*, an earlier version of which had won the Arnold Prize at Oxford in 1862.[48] In 1870, at the age of thirty-two, he became the Regius Professor of Civil Law, a chair he held until 1893, when the lure of politics and a place in Gladstone's government forced him to leave academe.

James Bryce was the intellectual as well as the professional heir of Sir Henry Sumner Maine. His own writings on Roman law reflected the theories he propounded on the place of Roman law in English legal education in his 1870 inaugural lecture. Bryce was, perhaps, the greatest comparative lawyer of his day. He carried Maine's work further than anyone else. His best work in comparative law and Roman law is to be found in his two-volume *Studies in History and Jurisprudence*.[49]

Bryce, though apparently expert in the technical details of Roman private law, chose not to write on this subject as did, for instance, his Oxford contemporaries Erwin Grueber and William Markby. Instead, Bryce's researches into Roman law stressed the history of Roman public law and government and detailed comparisons of Roman law and modern systems, primarily the common law in England, the United States, and their colonies. These writings reveal several things about Bryce the Romanist. First, Bryce was the quintessential comparativist; he did not study Roman law for its own sake but rather as a basis for understanding other legal systems against which Roman law could be used as a yardstick. This interest is well illustrated in one of Bryce's most provocative essays, "The Methods of Legal Science."[50] This is a particularly important essay for it focuses both on the role of Roman law in English legal thinking and on the philosophical basis of Roman law itself. It carries forward to a new level of sophistication much of what Maine had written on Roman and comparative law.

The essay begins with a simple question: How was it that the Romans, who never produced a great work of legal philosophy, were able to produce a system held to be philosophical? In response, Bryce provides a thumbnail sketch of modern legal philosophy. He begins by pointing out that, broadly speaking, four methods are generally employed in law and the study of legal science: the metaphysical method, represented by the work of Hegel and Kant; the analytical method, that peculiarly Anglo-American approach championed by Bentham and Austin; the historical approach; and the comparative approach. Bryce dismisses the first two methods. The metaphysical he holds to be too abstract and not really about law but about human nature and the preconditions to a legal system. The second he dismisses as also too abstract and divorced not only from the law in practice but also from the social realities of existence and from the recognition, provided by the historical and comparative methods, that law must change with society. The third and fourth he finds especially helpful and related. The historical approach explains how laws arise and change within their societal contexts viewed over time. The comparative is similar to the historical, for it also shows legal change and evolution, not simply within the context of a single national system and its particular national character but across several systems. Roman law is particularly important to this fourth methodology, for, as Bryce explains, it is the only system, other than the common law, that is sufficiently well-known and fully developed to permit extensive comparison. Further, Bryce points out, Roman law is particularly suited to such comparisons because it is more "philosophical" than the common law. It is more philosophical not because the Roman jurists wrote treatises on general jurisprudence but because the classical jurists' approach to the law was itself more philosophical. By this he means that there is to be found in Roman law a consistency of certain principles (such as *aequitas*) which runs below the surface throughout the law as a whole. Further, Bryce suggests, the Roman jurists wrote better and used more exact language than common law writers.[51] Thus the Roman system provides a better source for examining the utility and fairness of common law rules than any other, with the result that an exact knowledge of Roman law will help to develop a more exact approach to the common law for the common lawyer.

Bryce's approach in this essay is particularly interesting, for it echoes at many points not only Maine's writings but also Austin's, even though Bryce thought that Austin was not a good enough Romanist to write what he wrote. There is one difference, however. Bryce was too good a Roman lawyer to believe, as did Austin, that Roman law was a model of system. He recognized, as Austin did not, that the systematization of Roman law was a product of modern Roman lawyers. Nevertheless, Bryce, like Austin and many of his predecessors, valued Roman law for its terminology, the *elegantia juris* so prized by the classical jurists. Bryce concludes the essay by answering his question in a fascinating manner. He argues that Roman law was a particularly philosophical system because the jurists not only studied philosophy but because they, too, studied comparative law since they were forced to master not only the edicts of the *praetor urbanus* but also those of the *praetor peregrinus*.[52] In this way, the Roman jurists, according to Bryce, were always faced with the results of the comparative approach. In essence, Bryce wrote, the Roman jurists had adopted precisely that method which he, Bryce, believed the English must adopt.

In the essay, Bryce echoed and carried forward many of the ideas he had developed in his inaugural lecture. He also established the program for his own writings on Roman and civil law. Thus in his essay "The Roman Empire and the British Empire in India," Bryce examined the course the two legal systems took in aiding colonization, a theme he addressed again in "The Extension of Roman and English Law Throughout the World." He explored the development of public law at Rome and in the modern world in his essay "Flexible and Rigid Constitutions." He explored legislation in "Methods of Law-Making in Rome and in England" as well as in "The History of Legal Development at Rome and in England." One of his most interesting and technically most accomplished essays explored the development of the law of divorce from classical Roman law through the medieval civil and canon law to nineteenth-century England.[53]

Through all of these essays Bryce reveals himself as a remarkably knowledgeable and open-minded scholar. Wedded neither to the common law nor to the Roman or civil law, Bryce demonstrates in his essays not only a sensitivity for history and a superb knowledge of the Roman sources but also an appreciation for both the Roman law and the common law in their social settings. In this, Bryce is similar to his transatlantic friend Roscoe Pound and to his sometime contemporary but intellectual forebear Henry Maine.

It is useful at this point to place Bryce in his historical context. Bryce's world was quite different from that of Austin and his contemporaries, although their lives overlapped to some degree. Bryce's training in and knowledge of Roman law in particular and legal history in general was far superior to that of his predecessors of a half-century before. The watershed, of course, was Savigny and the development of the historical school and its introduction into England, principally through the work of Sir Henry Sumner Maine. Bryce was able to gain much from his studies with Vangerow and his familiarity with Maine's work that Austin simply did not know. It is, perhaps, too much to say that Bryce could not have accomplished what he did without Maine's *Ancient Law*, published only nine years before Bryce assumed the Regius Chair at Oxford, but there is no question that intellectually Maine was of an earlier generation than Bryce, at least in the matter of Roman and civil law, even though, again, Maine's life and professional career overlapped to a substantial extent with Bryce's. Certainly, Bryce worked in precisely the same field as Maine, although he was probably technically a better Romanist and certainly far more familiar with contemporary civil law, especially in Germany. Bryce himself, however, was something of an anachronism. His work was in the grand historical and comparative tradition begun by Maine and carried on by few scholars after him. Although Bryce was clearly one of the great Romanists of his period, his work was peculiarly Victorian in the breadth of its vision. Though technically far more than competent, Bryce did not spend his career examining the technical details of Roman law, as did, for instance, Theodor Mommsen in Germany or his own contemporary at Cambridge W. W. Buckland. Instead, Bryce consistently throughout his career, in his writings and in his teaching, attempted to relate Roman and civil law to contemporary common law and government and to use his knowledge, if not, like Austin, to reform the common law, than to understand it better. In this, perhaps, he was unique even in his own generation.

In a letter written before he had gotten to know William Warwick Buckland, F. W. Maitland remarked sadly that Cambridge had yet to produce an English civilian on the order of Jhering or the other great German Romanists.[54] Presumably, once he had become acquainted with Buckland, he realized that he no longer had need for such regrets.[55] Buckland was not only a great Romanist but a Romanist on the German model.

Buckland did not set out to become a Roman law scholar. Instead, he was trained as an engineer but, as the result of an accident, redirected his career and took the Law Tripos at Cambridge in 1884. He became a fellow of Gonville and Caius College, Cambridge, in 1889 and was appointed Regius Professor to replace E. C. Clark in 1914.[56] He died in 1946 at the age of eighty-seven. If James Bryce was, indeed, the last of the great Victorian scholars in the tradition established by Maine, Buckland was the first of the great modern English scholars of Roman law. Buckland spent his entire professional career as a teacher of law and as a researcher in Roman law, but his works are entirely different from those of Maine or Bryce. Only one work, his *Roman Law and Common Law*, coauthored with Arnold McNair late in his career, is a comparative study.[57] The others, on the contrary, are detailed examinations of the history and substantive doctrine of Roman law, of the type produced by his successors such as Alan Watson.[58] Furthermore, though Buckland authored a short book on jurisprudence, the thrust of his Romanist work was not directed at Roman law as a basis for general jurisprudence and legal philosophy.[59] In some respects, Buckland's main works, such as his *Equity in Roman Law*, his *Manual of Roman Private Law*, his *Roman Law of Slavery*, and his monumental *Text-Book of Roman Law*, are far more in the tradition of English civilian treatises such as Hallifax's or Phillimore's, though far more historically and analytically sophisticated.[60]

Perhaps the most interesting and most revealing of Buckland's works, however, is his first piece of major scholarship, his *Roman Law of Slavery*. This is not an easy book. It is long; it is highly technical; and its prose style is epigrammatic. Nevertheless, it is an amazingly erudite work, worthy of a Mommsen or a Savigny. In publishing this work in 1908 Buckland established himself as the foremost English Romanist. But the topic itself is particularly important because it is one of the few substantive legal areas that had virtually no comparative value to an English lawyer at the turn of the twentieth century. It is, however, precisely the subject one would expect a scholar to choose if his main interest lay in understanding Roman law from the "inside." Indeed, Buckland explicitly acknowledged this by describing the book as "an attempt to state in systematic form, the most characteristic part of the most characteristic intellectual product of Rome."[61]

In its 723 pages, Buckland's book analyzes the intricacies of the Roman law of slavery with a precision and an eye for detail that one would expect of a former engineer. It also illustrates tendencies in Buckland's work that continued and even grew in later books and articles. First, of course, was his massive erudition. Buckland was a homegrown product.

He never studied or spent substantial time in Germany or on the Continent (although he did spend part of a year in South Africa for health reasons). Nonetheless, his work displays not only a superb knowledge of the primary sources in the various editions but also an exacting knowledge of the best of European scholarship. Yet Buckland did not accept the European scholarly tradition uncritically. He rejected out of hand, for instance, the growing German obsession with *Interpolationskritik*.[62]

Buckland's work on slavery also betrays another important characteristic. Buckland was primarily a doctrinal historian, but he had learned the lessons taught by Maine, Bryce, and Savigny well and did not fail to appreciate the social and historical context of legal rules or the nature and extent of doctrinal development over time. Indeed, Buckland was one of the first English-speaking scholars to appreciate fully the period of juristic development from 180 B.C. to A.D. 250, which we now consider to be the golden age of classical Roman law.

Throughout the entire corpus of Buckland's work, both books and articles, one gets the feeling of immense labor, knowledge, and appreciation of the historical development of the Roman legal system. In his *Roman Law and Common Law*, in addition, one sees that Buckland understood the value of comparative studies and the benefits to be gained from such studies. In his other essay outside of Roman law of the Roman period, his coauthored work on the medieval Roman law glossators, too, one sees his understanding of the development of the civil law tradition in Europe and the ways in which Roman law had helped to establish that tradition, both in its continuities and discontinuities.[63]

It is also interesting and important to notice that many of Buckland's books derived ultimately from his teaching for the Roman law papers which were part of the Law Tripos at Cambridge.[64] This indicates first, of course, the quality of the teaching and the level of sophistication in instruction that had been reached in this part of the legal curriculum. Second, however, one must remember that Roman law held its place in the English legal curriculum as a means of instructing students, primarily first-year students, in general jurisprudence and comparative law. Yet there was obviously a great difference between Bryce, Maine, or Grueber teaching Roman law and Buckland teaching Roman law, for it is obvious that Buckland's internal view of the subject and his extreme historical inclinations must have influenced his teaching in some degree and helped, perhaps, to foster the impression that Roman law was even more divorced from modern-day practice than ever. Thus Buckland's writing and teaching mark a significant milestone in the development of Anglo-American use of Roman law as an educational tool.

Charles Phineas Sherman was born in Massachusetts in 1874.[65] He graduated from Yale College and Yale Law School and took a D.C.L. degree from Yale in 1899. Yale had a long tradition of Roman law teaching. Hadley taught the subject in the college and Albert Sproul Wheeler taught Roman law in the law school.

Sherman's interest and expertise in Roman and civil law seem to date from his period as a graduate student at Yale. Yale had instituted its graduate program in 1876, and the students were trained as comparativists. Candidates for the D.C.L. were required to pass a proficiency examination in Latin and either French or German.[66] Wheeler gave several courses on Roman and civil law, and other faculty taught in these areas as well.[67] For instance, Robert Morris taught a course on the French codes, William Foster taught a course on Savigny's work on obligations, and Simeon Baldwin taught a course on the conflict of laws which included reading the originals of a number of primary and secondary Continental texts.[68] Sherman's D.C.L. thesis, conceived in this learned and cosmopolitan context, was on Roman maritime law.

After receiving his D.C.L., Sherman remained in New Haven as a lawyer and remained as well in close contact with Professor Wheeler. Indeed, it was at Wheeler's instigation that Sherman undertook his first major work, a translation of Fernand Bernard's *First Year of Roman Law*.[69] When Wheeler fell ill in 1905, Sherman was the natural replacement, and he joined the Yale faculty, where he remained for twelve years.

In his lectures at Yale and in his published work Sherman reveals the nature and extent of his interest and expertise in Roman law. At the outset it must be clearly stated that Sherman was a far inferior scholar to such men as Bryce or Buckland or his American contemporaries Pound or Wigmore. But he was also clearly an enthusiast for the subject and was remarkably productive in his published work. Sherman was firmly within the comparative and historical tradition. The topics of his lectures and his writings range over a period of two thousand years. The lectures in one of his courses on Roman law, for instance, covered such topics as property law, the law of marriage and divorce, and the law of persons and adoption, all explored from the very beginnings of Roman law straight to modern civil law rules.[70] Sherman constantly emphasized continuities and parallels in these areas. His vision was broad. It is best represented, perhaps, by the title of one lecture he gave: "Roman law as World Law." For instance, in discussing the Roman concept of legal personality, its beginning and its end, Sherman referred his students to the modern Swiss Codes, which adopted the Roman notion that legal personality begins when birth is complete.[71] Similarly, in discussing the availability of an action for breach of promise, Sherman compared the Roman rules to those of the English common law, as well as to the German, Italian, and Spanish rules.

Perhaps the most representative of Sherman's works is his three-volume *Roman Law in the Modern World*, first published in 1917.[72] These volumes are learned without being analytical. They are an attempt to write a history of the Roman legal tradition from its earliest origins through the Middle Ages and Renaissance and on into the nineteenth century. The first volume is a superficial history of the tradition with little analysis of substantive law. It thus continued the tradition of "external history" and focused on the sources of law, codifications, borrowings, and the like. The second volume is a manual of the substantive Roman law. It is broadly conceived and reasonably well executed. Although again there is little sign of intellectual profundity, it does demonstrate that Sherman had mastered both the primary ancient sources and the modern European commentators thereon. The third volume confirms this latter point, for it is a bibliographical guide to the literature of Roman law and Roman legal history.

A close reading of Sherman's various published books and articles as well as the notes of his lectures suggests that Sherman's attitude to Roman law was very much the same as that of Bryce or Pound and primarily oriented toward the use of Roman law as a source for comparative studies. There is little indication that Sherman wanted to use Roman law as a supplement to modern common law or even as a source for general jurisprudence. But there is also in Sherman's work something quite different. Sherman had more than a trace of the antiquary in his character, and this betrays itself in his writings and, indeed, in his life. He traveled widely in Europe, for instance, always seeking out places of historical import.[73] His works are best characterized as encyclopedic. But one ought not to disparage Sherman and his work too strongly, for he was, in many ways, the most enthusiastic of the proponents of Roman legal studies in the United States, and he taught during his career at several law schools. Finally, though his writings do not exhibit the profundity or scope of vision of Maine's or Bryce's or Pound's precisely because they are so encyclopedic, they are extremely useful to the beginner as well as to the expert; indeed, they continue to be useful today. Thus, if perhaps Sherman cannot be cited as the American Buckland or Jhering, we can still accord to him an important place in the tradition of Roman legal studies in the United States during this period.

Although fairly large numbers of books and articles on Roman and civil law were produced in the United States in the late nineteenth and early twentieth centuries, by and large, they were not great scholarship on the lines of that being done in Italy, France, and Germany, or as good as the work of Buckland, Bryce, Maine, or even Justice Story a half-century before. They tended to be historical but were not methodologically or analytically sophisticated. Some, such as Sherman's, were useful because of their encyclopedic nature. An occasional one, such as the volume of essays on Anglo-Saxon law published in 1876 which attempted to understand the origins of these laws by recourse to a comparison to Roman law, would use the comparative method in the manner of a Maine or a Bryce.[74] Most of the works published during this era were pedestrian, reflecting the mediocrity of their authors as scholars. One man, however, cannot be so classified. Without question, he was the greatest American scholar of Roman and civil law of his period and, indeed, may well have been the greatest such scholar of the twentieth century. That man, of course, who began his career as a Nebraska lawyer and ended it as the longest serving dean of the Harvard Law School, was Roscoe Pound.[75]

As one of the great legal figures of the twentieth century, Roscoe Pound has been the subject of many studies, and it would be both unnecessary and impertinent to attempt to summarize them here. Pound was born in Nebraska in 1870 and, after doing both undergraduate and graduate work in botany at the University of Nebraska, he entered

Harvard Law School in 1889. Upon his graduation he returned to Lincoln, where he practiced law and became politically active. In 1899 he began to teach at the law school at the University of Nebraska, and in 1903 he was chosen as its new dean. Soon thereafter, in 1907, he left Nebraska to join the faculty at Northwestern University, then left Northwestern for Chicago, and finally in 1910 he returned to Harvard Law School, where he remained on the faculty until 1916 and as dean until his retirement in 1936.[76]

It is difficult to determine what it was in Pound's background that drew him to Roman and civil law. According to his biographers, he learned German as a child and, as a student botanist, not only was drawn to the works of German scientists but also minored in Roman law. It is clear that from his earliest years in academe, Pound had chosen a path of teaching and scholarship that always involved him with Roman and civil law as well as with Continental legal philosophy. Indeed, Pound began teaching a course on Roman law in the Latin department at Nebraska in 1895, a course he subsequently transferred to the law school when he joined its faculty.[77]

Much has been written about Roscoe Pound's interest in German legal philosophy, especially the work of men such as Jhering and the school of *Begriffsjurizprudenz*.[78] Certainly Pound's own work in legal philosophy, now largely forgotten (and justly so) except in relation to the realist movement, reflects the cumbersome influence of these late nineteenth-century Germans.[79] But Pound was also deeply interested, especially in his early years, in legal history and, specifically, in the history of Roman and civil law. He also became actively involved in research in comparative law. Indeed, one may fairly classify Pound's work in this area into three broad categories: legal philosophy, the development of the Roman legal tradition into present-day civil law and its use for comparative purposes, and the influence of the Roman and civil law on the laws of the United States.

Pound's interest in and work as an apostle of Continental legal philosophy has been well documented and need not be repeated here.[80] Pound was particularly interested early on in the work of Jhering and his followers on legal philosophy and later became fascinated by the newly emerging sociological movement in jurisprudence championed by younger German jurists. All of these influences show through clearly in Pound's own philosophical writings.

From the perspective of this study, perhaps Pound's most interesting work on Roman and civil law is that which is concerned with the historical development of substantive private law doctrine from classical Roman law up to the modern period. Pound published very little on this subject, with one notable exception. Throughout his career he taught courses on Roman and civil law, and the materials he developed for these courses are still extant. A portion of them was published by the Harvard University Press in 1914, and the remainder are in manuscript form now in the Harvard Law School archives.[81] Although they are teaching materials, they reveal much about Pound the Romanist.

First, these materials reveal to some degree the extent of Pound's knowledge of the Roman and civilian sources. The notes demonstrate that Pound was intimately familiar with the European—especially the German—literature on Roman and civil law. Indeed, it is clear from his personal holdings of pamphlets and reprints as well as books that Pound maintained this knowledge through a transatlantic correspondence and professional network of monumental proportions.[82] Moreover, one offhand comment in the introduction to the 1914 volume, wherein Pound suggests that students with the proper linguistic skills would be better served by reading French or German manuals on Roman law rather than the current English versions, suggests that Pound realized that Anglo-American scholars continued to lag behind their European counterparts.[83]

This 1914 volume also reveals Pound's comparativist perspective inasmuch as it is subtitled *An Introduction to Comparative Law*. It is the texts of the materials themselves, however, that give the clearest indication of Pound's mind. First, they are not limited to the Roman period. On the contrary, within each chapter Pound included selections not only from classical and Justinianic Roman law but also from medieval civil and canon law as well as modern civil law. Pound's choice of sources is both learned and eclectic. He draws frequently from the *Corpus Iuris Civilis* as well as the *Corpus Iuris Canonici*. He draws also from the modern civil codes of France, Germany, Switzerland, and Italy and from handbooks on both modern civil law and ancient

Roman law. The footnotes to the selections are extensive and refer to a multitude of secondary studies. These notes are often comparative in tenor, drawing the reader's attention to other sources both *pro* and *contra*, relating to the point made in the primary text selection.[84]

Perhaps most interesting about Pound's teaching materials, however, is their arrangement and principles of selection. The arrangement is not institutional, except in broad outline. Pound begins with basic jurisprudential notions such as the sources and forms of the law and the proper methods of legal interpretation. He next moves on to a discussion of the nature of juristic acts, including declarations of the will, fraud, duress, and mistake, and proceeds to the exercise and the protection of rights. He then goes on to discussions of the law of persons, property, obligations, and inheritance. While the first and final four parts would have been familiar categories to ancient Roman lawyers and tracked Justinian's *Institutes* in broad outline, the chapters on the nature of juristic acts and on the exercise and protection of rights were clearly based on modern categories, and, indeed, probably reflect the influence of modern German legal scholarship on Pound. This is made particularly clear from the main selections included in these chapters. Pound drew extensively for these upon the works of Ludwig Arndts, Bernhard Windscheid, Heinrich Dernburg, and Jhering, as well as the *Corpus Iuris Civilis*.

This rather novel arrangement tells us about Pound's intentions in his teaching, first, that he used Roman and civil law in ways that are, in some respects, reminiscent of John Austin's and Joseph Story's efforts. He used them as a means of importing philosophically more sophisticated categories into common law discourse. Pound was dissatisfied with common law categories and systematization and looked to the Roman and civil law as sources for cleaning up the common law in much the way John Austin had done. But Pound went further in his attempts to reform the common law by recourse to civil law models, as is demonstrated in the third chapter of the materials on the exercise and vindication of rights.[85]

The vast majority of the materials in this third chapter concern legal procedure as the means of vindicating rights. Throughout the early decades of his career Pound was particularly concerned about procedure and court administration.[86] Indeed, his earliest fame derived in large part from his writings and speeches on the subject of procedural reform in the United States.[87] Thus it is especially interesting to see the extent to which he addressed Roman and civilian procedure. He did so because Roman and civilian procedure was generally far simpler in form and, therefore, more equitable than common law procedure with its emphasis on technical pleading rules. Indeed, it is, perhaps, not too extreme to speculate that Pound's reformist tendencies toward modern common law procedure were inspired and influenced by his study of Roman and civil law.[88] He had, of course, the example of the Roman system of *legis actiones*, which, with its emphasis on technicalities, closely resembled common law pleading and which was abandoned by the Romans as being unfair to litigants. Indeed, in the 1914 materials, Pound included a translation of Book 4, Title 30 from Gaius's *Institutes*, perhaps the best known of the attacks on technical pleading contained in Roman sources.[89] It may well be, therefore, that his own modern efforts drew upon these Roman wellsprings. Thus Pound's use of the Roman and civilian materials hearkens back to Story's efforts to supplement the American common law by reference to Roman and civilian legal sources, as well as to the work of Maine and Bryce. At the same time, it is fundamentally different from the more "purely" historical approach of Buckland or the historical antiquarian researches of Sherman.

It is thus perhaps not surprising that the third area of Roscoe Pound's research interest lay in the history of Roman and civil law in American law. Indeed, it is particularly fitting to conclude this volume with a brief note on its predecessor, Pound's *Formative Era of American Law* and the studies that preceded it. From early in his teaching career Pound taught a course on civil law in America. He authored important articles on the use of French law in the early nineteenth century, on Joseph Story's use of Roman and civilian sources, and on the role of comparative law in the formation of early nineteenth-century American law.[90] In these articles and in his *Formative Era* volume Pound helped to reintroduce American lawyers and legal historians to the influence of Roman and civil law.

Pound's studies concentrate primarily on the revival of interest in Roman and civil law in the eastern United States in Story's period. They are obviously written from a sympathetic viewpoint. They are well done, although Pound did not appreciate the southern tradition in Roman and civil law studies which flourished contemporaneously. The motivation for the studies may be best understood as deriving partly from Pound's own interest in the role that Roman and civil law could play in American law in his own time but also from the then-increasing interest in the question of whether Roman and civil law had been received in the Anglo-American legal tradition. Pound's contributions may be seen as analogous to Lord Justice Thomas Scrutton's earlier Yorke Prize Essay on the influence of the Roman and civil law on English law[91] and as a rebuttal, in part, of Oliver Wendell Holmes's antireception arguments, which formed the basis of his own great historical text, *The Common Law*.[92] Indeed, it should not be forgotten that Pound himself also wrote on the history of the common law, and, therefore, it was natural that his interests in the history of both civil law and common law should intersect in this way.

Roscoe Pound may be fairly viewed as the culmination of the tradition of scholarly interest in Roman and civil law in the United States in the nineteenth century. In some respects, indeed, his work incorporated many of the ideas about the value of Roman and civil law scholarship which had been put forward throughout the century. Pound, like Story and Legaré, saw a use for Roman and civil law as a reforming device and as a supplement to the common law and, like Maine and Hammond, he saw its value as a subject of historical and comparative study. Thus Pound can stand easily as the embodiment of much of this nineteenth-century tradition. It is, therefore, fitting to end this study of this neglected aspect of Anglo-American legal history and the development of common law legal doctrine with him.

Conclusion

The preceding chapters have outlined the ways in which Roman and civil law influenced the thinking of several generations of legal scholars and jurists. They did not attempt to provide a narrative of the actual implementation of specific substantive law rules in the Anglo-American system, nor did they show the ways in which the average lawyer in nineteenth-century Britain or the United States understood or used Roman and civil law.[1] Those issues must await further study. What these chapters did do, however, was to illustrate, through a close examination of the writings of some of the best and most influential British and American jurists, the extent to which Roman and civil law infiltrated their thinking, their writing, and, in some cases, their teaching.

One of the hallmarks of the Anglo-American common law Bar has been an almost perverse pride in the common law's parochialism and insularity.[2] The common law Bar, both judges and practicing lawyers, has made a fetish of the notion that the common law stands alone and apart from the rest of the world's legal systems. It has done so for the most noble of reasons, that is, that the common law is the bulwark of liberty and individuality as opposed to the tyranny that has flourished amid other non-common-law systems, and for the most base of reasons, that is that by being different from the civil law systems, it has maintained its monopoly on legal business. What I have tried to show in this book, however, is that in spite of the rhetoric of parochialism and isolationism so prevalent among common lawyers in the nineteenth and early twentieth centuries, many of the best lawyers were knowledgeable in the Roman and civil law and used that knowledge to further their individual legal activities.

I have not made an attempt in this book to demonstrate the substantive law influence of the Roman and civil law on the development of Anglo-American common law, although such influence was clearly a factor in areas such as commercial law, water law, and others. Instead, in this book I have attempted to show the role of the Roman and civil law systems in the Anglo-American legal world as sources of jurisprudential inspiration, as models of intellectual elegance, and as a comparative basis for law reform efforts.

The role played by Roman and civil law in the thinking of the jurists discussed in earlier chapters changed over the course of the nineteenth century. Peter Stein has suggested that there was a moment in the life of the United States in the nineteenth century parallel to that in the life of England in the sixteenth century when the civil law might well have conquered and displaced the homegrown common law system.[3] If there was such a moment—and I tend to think that there never was—it passed quickly. For most of the century Roman and civil law were destined to play an entirely different role. From the writings of Story and Austin to those of Pound and Buckland, Roman and civil law constituted a backdrop, a constant reference point against which common law thinking might be measured. From the best of the nineteenth-century common law jurists to the worst whom I have discussed, all viewed Roman and civil law as parallel systems worked out to deal with the same societal problems confronting the common lawyers. With the introduction of historical analysis by Hugo, Savigny, and their followers, this parallelism could be refined and individual substantive rules could be analyzed in terms of their origin in the one system and compared to the parallel rule in the other. This gave the common lawyers a comparative benchmark by which to analyze their own thinking. First, Roman and civil law provided models of a systematic legal structure. Second, they provided multiple models of linguistic and terminological precision in the legal sphere. Third, they provided comparative and historical reference points for the comprehension of common law rules. Fourth, because they were foreign and expressed in esoteric languages, Roman and civil law bestowed intellectual and academic prestige upon their common law students. In different periods and in regard to different jurists, the importance of each of these factors as against the others varied, but all remained significant from the beginning to the end of the nineteenth century in both England and the United States.

System

The common law was, until the nineteenth century, anything but systematic. The very nature of its development, the accumulation of the judicial decisions, militated against any systematization. The decisional growth format combined with the rarity of substantive treatises on the various subspecialties within the common law virtually guaranteed that systematization would require some outside influence.[4] There seems, however, to have been throughout the seventeenth and eighteenth centuries a tradition among common law jurists, based on Roman law, and specifically, Justinian's *Institutes*, to attempt to systematize the law.[5] This tradition, although continuous, was not terribly widespread until the end of the eighteenth century. As Alan Watson has brilliantly shown, William Blackstone's *Commentaries of the Law of England*, perhaps the most influential common law treatise ever written, derived its order and structure from the Roman institutional tradition.[6] This Blackstonian institutionalism marked a watershed in the impact of Roman law as a systematizing agent, and after the publication of the *Commentaries*, systematization of the common law, or at least attempts to do so, became far more widespread.

Roman law, or at least Roman law as it was known to the lawyers and jurists of the late eighteenth and early nineteenth centuries, provided the perfect inspiration for common law systematizers. The materials of Roman law best known to these systematizers, men such as Austin or Story or Kent, came in the form of Justinian's *Institutes* and *Digest*, both the result of deliberate and painstaking systematization by jurists in the sixth century, and through the work of the then dominant Pandectists working in France, Holland, and Germany, such as Pothier.[7] To the common lawyer with systematizing tendencies, the late Roman and modern civilian materials provided the perfect source not only of inspiration but of actual conceptional systems. Although there were differences between the common law and the civil and Roman law, these differences tended to be of little importance in terms of broad systematization. The common law of contracts could easily be substituted for the Roman and civil law doctrine of obligation, and the common law tort could easily be substituted for the Roman and civil law category of delict.

Of course, the most interesting question in this example of influence is why the common lawyers of the eighteenth and nineteenth centuries came more and more to look to the systematic models of the civilians. Here, clearly, several factors were at work. First, and too easily trivialized by modern legal historians, was the intellectual attractiveness of the Roman and civilian systems. To many jurists of the late eighteenth and nineteenth centuries, trained in logic, mathematics, and the science of poetic meter, the materials presented to them when they turned to the study of law must have appeared to be horrendously chaotic.[8] The growth of the law depended on the efforts of thousands of judges, each with a great deal of latitude to stretch or even abandon precedent. The literature of the law, other than that firmly within the institutional tradition, tended to be more in the nature of indexes and compilations (often by judicial author or reporter rather than by subject matter). To many such an unsystematic body of knowledge was intellectually abhorrent in the post-Enlightenment era. Thus the Roman institutional models must have seemed like a godsend.

A second reason for the attractiveness of systematization related to the first was the growth of scientific legal education during this period and the need for adequate teaching materials.[9] It is not coincidental that many of the jurists most attracted to the Roman systematic model were also law teachers, men such as Blackstone, Story, Austin, and Kent. In the late eighteenth and early nineteenth centuries, in both England and the United States, university-based legal education for common lawyers was beginning to challenge the older apprenticeship model for dominance.[10] In mounting this challenge, the proponents of university-based legal education realized that they must distinguish their offerings from the more traditional and less expensive apprenticeship. To do this, the early university law teachers adopted the "scientific" model then prevalent in universities and being applied to other academic disciplines.[11] Those who chose the apprenticeship path to admission to the Bar would learn the law through direct observation of legal proceedings and through the study of cases by reading reporters.[12] The proponents of scientific legal education needed to present their materials differently. Unlike the scientific jurists of the Langdellian era, who chose to use cases, albeit arranged in broad subject categories, as the basis for an experimentalist science of law, the late eighteenth- and early nineteenth-century proponents of a scientific, university-based legal education adopted the taxonomic approach then current in the universities to which they belonged. For this purpose, the models of Roman and civilian systematization were both easily at hand and thoroughly suited to the task.

A third reason for the appeal of the Roman and civilian models of systematization was political. In both England and the United States the beginning of the nineteenth century saw the start of a political groundswell of opposition to the common law system. Common law judges were viewed as members of the political and economic elite whose decisions were both arbitrary and supportive of the interests of their class.[13] Increasingly, calls for codification and the shift of law-making power from the allegedly elite judiciary to the more democratic and populist legislature gained currency.[14] The Roman and civil laws provided a model for codification in Justinian's Code as well as Napoleon's. But perhaps more important, the Roman and civilian sources also offered an alternative model of codification which was still able to mitigate the most severe examples of judicial arbitrariness and the complexity and mystery of the common law which made it inaccessible to nonlawyers. This, of course, was the systematic model short of true codification. Systematization of the legal system not only helped to strengthen case-derived rules as precedents but also made the study of legal rules as doctrine accessible to individuals who had not suffered through a long apprenticeship and developed mastery over the chaotic materials used by common lawyers. For the first time during this period, we see the publication of common law books designed for non-lawyers, all of which adopted the categorization and systematization that had been influenced by Roman and civilian models.

Thus systematization brought with it important benefits that were exceptionally attractive to a large number of common law jurists. One could argue that given the intellectual, educational, and political appeal of systematization in the late eighteenth and early nineteenth centuries, it was virtually inevitable that common lawyers would turn to the one available source for inspiration, analogy, and actual concepts and categories: the Roman and civil law.

Precision

One of the most characteristic aspects of the common law before the nineteenth century was the peculiar and formalistic nature of its language and usages. Originally, common lawyers used Law French in their courts and a specialized form of pleading known as the forms of action. Even by the late eighteenth century, when Law French had been systematically rendered obsolete and the forms of action were dying out, the shadow of these two uniquely common law aspects was still long. The language of the common law was highly technical, filled with obsolete words and phrases.[15] Court procedure continued to be torturous and comprehensible only to those long schooled in its intricacies. In both the United States and England, reformists attacked the "mysteries" of the common law and argued for an abolition of the technicalities of language and usage which rendered it remote from common usage and understanding.[16]

A second, more philosophical difficulty with the language and usages of the common law stemmed from their essential nature. Common law language was a product of an often chaotic historical development. The concepts expressed were often obscure and rooted in the shifting precedents of the common law courts. The language of the substantive law, of tort, of contract, of estates, was often so obscure that it impeded the development of a more comprehensible, logical, and systematic set of laws. Thus just as the systematizers and codifiers needed to revamp the conceptualization of the framework of the common law, they needed also to change the very language within which the common law functioned so as to make it philosophically acceptable. Legal philosophers such as John Austin or Francis Lieber were driven to look outside of traditional common law language to find a more precise terminology to express the more precise substantive legal ideas that they were attempting to interject into the Anglo-American context. Perhaps one of the best examples of this effort was Lieber's attempt, in the *Legal and Political Hermeneutics*, to develop a set of canons of interpretation for Anglo-American lawyers.[17] The common law simply lacked such a thing in its language and did not provide the precise distinctions necessary to accomplish this goal. Thus Lieber was forced to look at Roman and civil law ideas (as well as the developing science of biblical criticism) to find a vocabulary to be used for this purpose.

A second telling example comes from John Austin's attempts to systematize the common law in such areas as contracts in his *Lectures on Jurisprudence*. The common law of contracts is deeply rooted in medievalisms, and many of the key concepts, such as consideration, do not lend themselves either to precision or to systematization. Such concepts function in the common law context precisely because they are obscure and, therefore, allow substantial judicial discretion. Austin, in his attempts to provide a systematic understanding of the law and to rid the law of obscurity could not work with such terms and concepts. Thus, forced to look elsewhere, he found the Roman and civil law systems to be paragons of clear language and precise terminology, utterly separate from the obscurity of the language of the Anglo-American common law.

What was it in the Roman and civil law sources that appealed to the eighteenth- and nineteenth-century Anglo-American jurists who used this foreign terminology? Why did they believe that the Latin terms drawn from Roman law were more precise than their own English and Law French? The answer may be complex. In fact, many Roman law terms and phrases are as obscure as their common law counterparts. Anyone who has attempted to understand the Roman and civil law notion of *causa*, the key concept in these systems' substantive law of obligation, will testify that judicial and textual use of *causa* is often just as obscure and variable as the common lawyer's use of consideration.[18] And common lawyers who complain of the obscurity and complexity of the law of perpetuities need only spend a few hours attempting to understand the Roman and civil law concept of *dominium* to realize that the Roman and civil law systems can match the common law point for point in any comparison for obscurity and complexity.

Why, then, did men such as Austin and Lieber deliberately abandon common law terminology for Roman and civilian? The answer, perhaps, is simply that by adopting foreign terminology, in both language and system, common law jurists were able, in effect, to impose upon these foreign terms new and precise definitions that served their purposes. To attempt to redefine traditional common law terms would have been madness and would have met with enormous resistance from common lawyers. To attempt to redefine Roman and civil law terms and to introduce them into the common law would meet with less resistance because the common lawyers would, generally, have been ignorant of the original meaning of these terms.

A second reason for the attractiveness of Roman and civilian legal language was precisely that it was less well-known than common law English and French and was associated with classical learning and university education. Thus the introduction of Latin terminology not only lent an elite air to the study of law but helped to associate legal study with the universities and away from the courts and lawyers' offices. This is particularly important also when viewed in the broader educational context. The use of Latin for the expression of legal ideas had the effect of placing the study of law very much in the company of the study of many scientific subjects such as biology, botany, and medicine, which also used Latin.[19] The introduction of Roman and civilian terminology assisted jurists like Austin and Lieber not only in their attempts to reform the substance of the law and to eliminate jurisprudential obscurity but also to elevate the professional status of the law to strengthen the argument for university legal education. Thus, as was the case with systematization and the use of Roman and civilian models throughout the late eighteenth and nineteenth centuries, the use of Roman and civilian models for terminological purposes helped in the development of the new university-based model for legal education as well.

Comparative Law

The third means by which Roman and civil law sources influenced the thinking of common law jurists during the nineteenth century was as a principal inspiration for and source of comparative materials. From its earliest days, the common law developed insularly, away from but always aware of the very different civilian systems that had developed from the Roman law. In England, civil law coexisted within the common law, being administered in the church courts, the courts-martial, and the admiralty courts.[20] The civilian Bar, though never as large as the common law Bar, was significant, and a number of its members achieved prominence as legal writers and law professors. Indeed, the civil law possessed a monopoly on university-based education in England until the establishment of the Vinerian Chair at Oxford in the latter part of the eighteenth century.[21] A whole genre of literature arose during the sixteenth and seventeenth centuries consisting of "parallels" between the civil law and the common law.[22]

In the late eighteenth and early nineteenth centuries, the two factors that played a significant part in fostering interest in and study of the differences between the social, physical, and geographical conditions that gave rise to the common law in England were not necessarily the same in the United States. In England, for instance, land was scarce and labor freely available, while in the United States, land was abundant but labor was often scarce. The common law was deeply rooted, as Maitland clearly understood, in the feudal structure of the medieval English state.[23] No such structure existed in the United States. Thus in the United States it became increasingly clear, in the nineteenth century especially, that many of the traditional English common law rules were ill-suited to the New World. In their search to fashion new rules for the United States, many American jurists turned to the other great legal system whose monuments could be examined in countless books for inspiration and for help. Inevitably, such a turning to the Roman and civil law gave rise to a tendency to compare the common law to the civil law and to evaluate the two sets of rules against each other. Similarly, when no common law rule could be found, the Roman and civil law were wonderful sources for material.

The second factor that had an equal impact in fostering the growth of comparative law and the use of Roman and civil law materials for this purpose was the rise of mercantile imperialism and colonial empires. In the nineteenth century, the English found themselves possessing a vast overseas empire, for much of which the common law was ill-suited and unknown. The English believed much of the indigenous law to be primitive. Thus in schools and colleges designed to train colonial administrators, such as Haileybury College of the East India Company,[24] though students were well grounded in the common law, much attention was given to the examination of both the indigenous law and the Roman and civil law, using the latter as a paradigm against which the former could be measured. It is not surprising that in Henry Maine's great work on comparative law, references to Indian law are intermixed with references to primitive Roman law and that when Sir William Jones attempted to begin the codification of Indian law he turned to the Roman codes as models.

A third factor in the use of Roman and civil law as a part of comparative law in the nineteenth century in both England and the United States relates to the growing strength of university-based common law education in the latter half of the nineteenth century. Such education was "scientific" and thus required a methodology that was philosophically more sophisticated than traditional rote memorization of precedents and commentary thereon. Hugo and Savigny introduced the historical perspective, integral to which was the realization that laws must be studied within the social, cultural, and historical context from whence they came. Thus the follower of Savigny would need not only to study the history of his own legal system but to look at other legal systems in their own contexts to verify that social and cultural differences did, indeed, lead to differing legal rules.

A final aspect of this phenomenon, seen in the works of men such as Hammond and Grueber, was the belief that the study of the solutions of several legal systems to the same problems would help law students to develop their analytical and critical abilities to enable them to cope better with newly arising problems.[25] In essence, the comparative method was seen as a principal tool for teaching jurisprudence and instructing lawyers in the art of problem solving. Here, again, because Roman and civil law rules often dealt with the same problems as the common law, their attractiveness was strong. Thus, as interest in comparative law grew in the nineteenth century, it inevitably brought with it an increased interest in Roman and civil law among common lawyers because these were the best known and documented of any of the non-common-law legal systems.

Knowledge of Roman and Civil Law as
a Mark of Professional Status

Perhaps the most interesting aspect of the attraction of Roman and civil law to Anglo-American common lawyers during the nineteenth century concerns professional status and prestige. Throughout much of the seventeenth and eighteenth centuries the legal profession did not enjoy high social status. It was a bourgeois occupation, and lawyers were seen more as technicians and, in many cases, criminal sorts and "scalawags" than as professionals on a level with clergymen or landowners. In part, this may have stemmed from the nonuniversity apprenticeship model that dominated legal education and, in part, may have derived from the frequent popular association of lawyers with their lawbreaking clients. Whatever the cause, however, lawyers were rarely viewed as gentlemen, unless they were gentlemen by birth or breeding wholly apart from their training.

The study of Roman and civil law provided common lawyers with status-elevating advantages. First, such study required mastery of Latin, a language that was the preserve of universities and was considered the sine qua non of the "literate" man. In addition, many common lawyers who used civil law also professed some knowledge of French or German (even though this knowledge was rarely extensive), and the sprinkling of foreign quotations in decisions or briefs was seen as a mark of learning and, hence, gentlemanly status.

Examples of this phenomenon from the late eighteenth and early nineteenth centuries are numerous, from Adams's study of Vinnius's *Institutes* to Legaré's comparison of his law practice with that of Cicero.[26] Throughout this period the study of Roman and civil law was often more a case of "show" for status purposes than it was for the acquisition of substantive legal knowledge.

There was also a political aspect to the study and use of Roman law, in the United States in particular. Models of political organization drawn from the republican period were especially popular in the United States during the first half of the nineteenth century. The great lawyers, men like Webster and John C. Calhoun, consciously sought to emulate the great Roman lawyers and statesmen like Cicero. Thus Calhoun would, on occasion, wear the *toga praetextatus* when giving an oration, and Webster liberally sprinkled his courtroom orations with long quotes, in Latin, from the works of Cicero and his contemporaries.[27] Not surprisingly, the study and use of Roman law fit perfectly into this context.

The End of the Moment

I began this concluding chapter with the observation that there was a moment in the Anglo-American legal world when Roman and civil law exercised a particular attraction to jurists and theoreticians, as well as to practicing lawyers. This moment lasted, I suggest, roughly from the late eighteenth until the early twentieth centuries. I believe that I have suggested reasons and adduced examples of why this moment came about and how it manifested itself. What I have left to do, for the sake of completeness and intellectual elegance, is to suggest why it came to an end. I think that the answer to this final question is complex, but it is still worth making a brief attempt at an answer.

First and foremost, the coming of the European war, sparked by German aggression, made many in the Anglo-American world averse to all things Germanic, including their legal system and their scholarship. Many of the personal connections that had strengthened the influence of ideas, if not, in fact, caused them, were destroyed.[28] Few English or American lawyers had much to do with Germany and German *Rechtswissenschaft* after the First World War. The Kaiser Wilhelm Chair at Columbia Law School was abolished.[29] In many fields, including classics, German scholars were shunned by Anglo-American scholars. The English-speaking world simply turned its back on a culture that could tolerate the atrocities of war and encourage the aggression that Germany had displayed. This anti-German feeling was significantly hardened by the rise of the Nationalist Socialist Party in the late 1920s and early 1930s, and it was rare for an American jurist to venture to Germany during this period. Indeed, Roscoe Pound, at this time dean of the Harvard Law School, destroyed his credibility and his career by being too closely associated with Hitler and the Nazis.[30] Certainly, the flow of jurists and scholars was now not from England and the United States to Germany for training, but rather from Germany and her dominions came many who sought refuge and asylum in the United States and England following the Second World War. But most of these émigré scholars preferred to embrace the Anglo-American common law rather than the civilian tradition in which they had grown up and by which they had been betrayed.[31]

A second reason for the loss of attractiveness of Roman and civil law studies in the United States, and in England to a lesser degree, must be attributable to the decline in language skills, particularly Latin and Greek, among lawyers and jurists. The era when Cicero could be studied by law students in Latin as an example of forensic elegance was over by the interwar period. School curricula were moving rapidly away from the classical model of the nineteenth century, and Latin and Greek were being replaced by chemistry, physics, and calculus. The success of the industrial revolution in both England and the United States meant not only a shift in school curricula away from the classics but also a general cultural shift away from Victorian retrospection, which embraced the classical and medieval worlds, to a more prospective approach, embracing a future filled with scientific and technological marvels. Roman law and the civil law systems it had spawned must have seemed very much an antiquarian pursuit. With the decline in the mercantile empires and the concomitant decline in comparative law during this period, no compelling reason remained for a jurist to study Roman and civil law. It is precisely during this period that we see juristic thought turning to the modern models. In the United States, particularly, men such as Karl Llewellyn and Underhill Moore, Jerome Frank, and Robert Maynard Hutchins were looking to the social sciences, not to musty old tomes, for inspiration.[32]

It is easy to bemoan the decline of Roman law studies during this period, even though a few men like Charles Sherman, Roscoe Pound, and W. W. Buckland kept the flame burning weakly in the deepest recesses of the halls of academe. But it is also not difficult to understand why this occurred. Law schools were firm parts of their universities and did not need to prove to their nonlawyer colleagues that they were scholarly. Jurists were increasingly confronted with the challenge of reconciling law and jurisprudence with the difficulties of modernity and technology. And, of course, the Germans had changed their role on the world stage from bringers of culture to bringers of war and desolation. Roman law studies in England and the United States spiraled downward.

In the period after the Second World War there was some revival of interest in Roman and civil law in the Anglo-American world, owing in part to refugee scholars such as Ernst Levy and Adolph Berger, David Daube and Stephan Kuttner.[33] It was also owing in part to a growing recognition that these refugee scholars and their knowledge of different systems could, indeed, help Anglo-American lawyers cope with a global economy. To this very day, this reasoning seems to be responsible for the maintenance of at least some interest in Roman and civil law studies in the United States and England. Roman law continues to be taught at Oxford and Cambridge, and it is taught at several American law schools, including Harvard, Chicago, and Berkeley. Certainly, its attractiveness to law students and lawyers today is nothing compared to a century and a half ago. Nonetheless, the flame continues to burn in the Anglo-American world, and scholars such as Alan Watson, Charles Donahue, Dick Helmholz, and Bruce Frier continue to produce works of scholarship on a high plane. Indeed, the Harvard Law School continues to offer a summer course in Roman law for practicing lawyers, and it continues to find students willing to attend.

What, then, can we conclude? Roman and civil law have always played a role in the development of Anglo-American jurisprudence and practice. There have been moments when the intellectual influence of the Roman law has been high. During the seventeenth century in England, there was one such moment when the greatest of the civilian doctors flourished. In the nineteenth century and the early twentieth century there was another such moment, and the influence of the Roman law was felt strongly again. That moment, too, passed. But who knows? As we enter the twenty-first century, and talk of a new *ius commune* is again abroad in the land, perhaps jurists will again turn to that greatest of all legal systems, Roman law, and its civil law offspring, and a new moment shall come.

The End

IN PIAM MEMORIAM GEOFFREY ELTON MAGISTRI MEI

NOTES

Origins

1. See Frederic William Maitland, *English Law and the Renaissance (The Rede Lecture for 1901)* (1901; rpt. Littleton, Colo.: Fred B. Rothman, 1985).

2. See Peter Stein, "The Attraction of the Civil Law in Post-Revolutionary America," *Virginia Law Review* 52 (1966): 403–34, also published in *The Character and Influence of the Roman Civil Law: Historical Essays* (London: Hambledon Press, 1988), 411–42.

3. See Lawrence M. Friedman, *A History of American Law*, 2d ed. (New York: Simon and Schuster, 1985).

4. See Sir William Searle Holdsworth, *A History of English Law* (1903; rpt. London: Methuen, Sweet and Maxwell, 1938–66), vols. 1–16. See also Stroud Francis Charles Milson, *Studies in the History of the Common Law* (London: Hambledon Press, 1985).

5. Stein, "Attraction of the Civil Law," 411–42.

6. See esp. Matthias Reinmann, ed., *The Reception of Continental Ideas in the Common Law World, 1820–1920*, Comparative Studies in Continental Anglo-American Legal History Bd. 13 (Berlin: Duncker & Humblot, 1993).

7. On the Roman law influence on American water law, see S. C. Weil, "Waters: American Law and French Authority," *Harvard Law Review* 33 (1919): 133; see also Alan Watson, "The Transformation of American Property Law: A Comparative Law Approach," *Georgia Law Review* 24 (Winter 1990): 163.

8. See the forthcoming publication by M. H. Hoeflich, "Ciceronian Ethic and Nineteenth Century American Law."

9. R. H. Helmholz, "Use of the Civil Law in Post-Revolutionary American Jurisprudence," *Tulane Law Review* 66 (1992): 1649.

10. Lawrence M. Friedman and Robert V. Percival, *The Roots of Justice: Crime and Punishment in Alameda County, California, 1870–1910* (Chapel Hill: University of North Carolina Press, 1981).

11. John H. Baker, "English Law and the Renaissance," *Cambridge Law Journal* 44 (1985): 46–61.

12. Helmholz, "Use of the Civil Law."

13. M. H. Hoeflich, "Roman Law in American Legal Culture," *Tulane Law Review* 66 (1992): 1723.

14. Holdsworth, *History*, 12:677–702. See also George D. Squibb, *The High Court of Chivalry: A Study of the Civil Law in England* (Oxford: Clarendon Press, 1959).

15. Holdsworth, *History*, 12:677–702. See also Squibb, *High Court of Chivalry.*

16. Daniel R. Coquillette, *The Civilian Writers of Doctors' Commons, London: Three Centuries of Juristic Innovation in Comparative, Commercial and International Law* (Berlin: Duncker & Humblot, 1988).

17. Sir Robert Wiseman, *The Law of Laws, or The Excellencie of the Civil Law Above All Humane Laws Whatsoever* (London, 1664).

18. Coquillette, *Civilian Writers*, 268–82, 300.

19. M. H. Hoeflich, "The Americanization of British Legal Education in the Nineteenth Century," *Journal of Legal History* 8 (1987): 246–48. See also Holdsworth, *History*, 15:239.

20. Hoeflich, "Americanization of British Legal Education," 247.

21. See, above all, Meyer Reinhold, ed., *The Classic Pages: Classical Reading of the Eighteenth-Century Americans* (University Park: Pennsylvania State University Press, 1975); Meyer Reinhold, *Classica Americana: The Greek and Roman Heritage in the United States* (Detroit: Wayne State University Press, 1984); Carl J. Richard, *The Founders and the Classics: Greece, Rome, and the American Enlightenment* (Cambridge, Mass.: Harvard University Press, 1994); M. N. S. Sellers, *American Republicanism: Roman Ideology in the United States Constitution* (New York: New York University Press, 1994).

22. Hoeflich, "Ciceronian Ethic."

23. Howard Mumford Jones, *O Strange New World* (1952; rpt. New York: Viking Press, 1964). See also Samuel Eliot Morison, *The Intellectual Life of Colonial New England* (1956; rpt. Ithaca, N.Y.: Cornell University Press, 1960); Thomas Goddard Wright, *Literary Culture in Early New England, 1620–1730* (1920; rpt. New York: Russell & Russell, 1966).

24. Noble E. Cunningham, Jr., *In Pursuit of Reason: The Life of Thomas Jefferson* (Baton Rouge: Louisiana State University Press, 1987), 6.

25. Hamilton Bryson, "The Use of Roman Law in Virginia Courts," *American Journal of Legal History* 28 (1984): 135–46.

26. Frank L. Dewey, *Thomas Jefferson, Lawyer* (Charlottesville: University Press of Virginia, 1986), 63, 65–71.

27. On the Batture controversy and Jefferson's role in it, see esp. George Dargo, *Politics and the Clash of Legal Traditions* (Cambridge, Mass.: Harvard University Press, 1975); Gustav Schmidt, "The Batture Question," *Louisiana Law Journal* 1 (1841): 84–151.

28. Daniel R. Coquillette, "Justinian in Braintree: John Adams, Civilian Learning, and Legal Elitism, 1758–1775," in *Law in Colonial Massachusetts, 1630–1800*, ed. Frederick S. Allis, Jr. (Boston: Colonial Society of America, 1984), 359–418; quotation on 373.

29. Dewey, *Jefferson*, 15.

30. Anton-Hermann Chroust, *The Rise of the Legal Profession in America*, 2 vols. (Norman: University of Oklahoma Press, 1965).

31. Stein, "Attraction of the Civil Law," 411–42.

32. M. H. Hoeflich, "Law and Geometry: Legal Science from Leibniz to Langdell," *American Journal of Legal History* 30 (1986): 95–121.

1. Roman and Civil Law in the Anglo-American World Before 1850: John Austin and Joseph Story

1. M. H. Hoeflich, "Roman and Civil Law in American Legal Education and Research Prior to 1930: A Preliminary Survey," *University of Illinois Law Review* (1984): 719.

2. The standard source for Austin's life is his wife's introduction to the 1863 edition of the *Lectures* reprinted in later editions. See also W. L. Morison, *John Austin* (Stanford: Stanford University Press, 1982). The biographical account in the text is drawn from these two sources.

3. On the historical school, see John Reddie, *Historical Notices of the Roman Law and of the Recent Progress of Its Study in Germany* (Edinburgh, 1826); see also G. P. Gooch, *History and Historians in the Nineteenth Century* (London: Longmans, Green, 1913), 42–54, and Max Gutzwiller, *Der Einfluss Savignys auf die Entwicklung des Internationalprivatrechts* (Freiburg, Schweiz: Kommissionsverlag: Gschwend, Tschopp und Co., 1923).

4. On the importance of Austin's work for the subsequent development of English jurisprudence, see Morison, *John Austin*, 148–77, Wilfrid Rumble, *The Thought of John Austin: Jurisprudence, the British Constitution, and Colonial Reform* (London: Athlone Press, 1985); Michael Lobban, *The Common Law and English Jurisprudence, 1760–1850* (Oxford: Oxford University Press,

1991). On Austin's teaching, see Wilfrid Rumble, "Austin in the Classroom," *Journal of Legal History* 17 (April 1996): 17–40; Raymond C. J. Cocks, *Foundations of the Modern Bar* (London: Sweet and Maxwell, 1983).

5. Ibid., 9, 12.

6. Andreas Schwarz, "John Austin and the German Jurisprudence of His Time," *Politica* 1 (1934): 178, 181; see also Enid Campbell, "German Influences in English Legal Education and Jurisprudence in the 19th Century," *University of Western Australia Law Review* 4 (1959): 357. Campbell argues that Austin was thoroughly Germanized by his stay in Bonn and that his passion for order in the law developed therefrom. See also Peter Stein, "Legal Theory and the Reform of Legal Education in Mid-Nineteenth Century England," in *L'Educazione Giundica: Profili Storica*, vol. 2, ed. A. Giuliani and N. Picardi (Perugia: L'Università degli Studi di Perugia, 1977), 238–44.

7. Reddie, *Historical Notices*; see also Gooch, *History*, 42–54, and Gutzwiller, *Der Einfluss*.

8. Schwarz, "John Austin," 186.

9. Ibid., 187.

10. The text of Gaius's *Institutes* was rediscovered at Verona in 1818. On the importance of the *Institutes* to the development of Western law, see D. R. Kelley, "Gaius Noster: Substructures of Western Social Thought," *American Historical Review* 84 (1979): 619.

11. Schwarz, "John Austin," 191–93.

12. John Austin, *Lectures on Jurisprudence*, ed. Robert Campbell, 2 vols. (Jersey City, 1869).

13. M. H. Hoeflich, "Transatlantic Friendships and the German Influence on American Law in the First Half of the Nineteenth Century," *American Journal of Comparative Law* 35 (1987): 599–611.

14. Robert Wiseman, *The Law of Laws, or, The Excellencie of the Civil Law above All Humane Laws Whatsoever*, 4th ed. (London, 1795); William Fulbecke, *A Parallele or Conference of the Civil Law, the Canon Law, and the Common Law of this Realme of England* (London, 1618); Thomas Wood, *A New Institute of the Imperial or Civil Law* (London, 1704); Sir Arthur Duck, *De usu et authoritate juris civilis Romanorum per dominia principum Christianorum* (London, 1679); Alexander C. Schomberg, *An Historical and Chronological View of Roman Law* (Oxford, 1785); Samuel Hallifax, *An Analysis of the Roman Civil Law*, 4th ed. (Cambridge, 1795).

15. Morison, *John Austin*, 19.

16. In theory, we might suppose that the most philosophically minded students might study Austin, but in so doing, they would gain little of value for actual courtroom or office practice.

17. This essay is printed in John Austin, *The Province of Jurisprudence Determined*, ed. H. L. A. Hart (London, 1954), 365–93; quotation on 365.

18. On Bentham and Austin, see Morison, *John Austin*, 38–48; on the concept of a "science of legislation" as opposed to scientific jurisprudence, see Austin, *Lectures*, 144–70.

19. It is political philosophy in the sense that the *Lectures* deal with the definition of law and the relationship of law to sovereignty, concepts now considered to be part of public law or politics.

20. Blackstone's *Commentaries* was the basic textbook for law students both during his lifetime and in the nineteenth century, being replaced only by the work of Henry John Stephen, which depended heavily on Blackstone. See Julius S. Waterman, "Thomas Jefferson and Blackstone's Commentaries," in *Essays in the History of Early American Law*, ed. David H. Flaherty (Chapel Hill: University of North Carolina Press, 1969), 451–57.

21. Austin, *Lectures*, vol. 1, 34.

22. In so doing, Austin was able to construct an "ideal" system of laws, the purpose of jurisprudence.

23. On the forms of action, see the classic work of F. W. Maitland, *The Forms of Action at Common Law*, ed. A. H. Chaytor and W. J. Whittaker (1909; rpt. Cambridge: Cambridge University Press, 1948).

24. Ibid., 10–15, 7.

25. On Cowell and Wood, see Alan Watson, "*Justinian's Institutes* and Some English Counterparts," in *Studies in* Justinian's Institutes: *In Memory of J. A. C. Thomas*, ed. Peter Stein and A. D. Lewis (London: Sweet & Maxwell, 1983), 181–86; Peter Stein, "Continental Influences on English Legal Thought, 1600–1900," *La formazione storica del diritto moderno in Europa, atti del III Congresso Internazionale della Societa Italiana di Storia del diritto* (Florence: Olschki, 1977), 3:210–18. On Finch and the *Nomotechnia*, see Wilfred Prest, "The Dialectical Origins of Finch's Law," *Cambridge Law Journal* 36 (1977): 326–52.

26. Hale's *Analysis* is also found as an appendix to editions of Hale's *History of the Common Law*, published after 1705. Watson "*Justinian's Institutes*," 185; for an opinion *contra*, see the essay of W. G. Hammond in T. C. Sandars, *The Institutes of Justinian*, ed. W. G. Hammond (Chicago, 1876), vii–xli.

27. This precursor of the *Commentaries* was modeled closely on Hale's earlier work. On the significance of the *Commentaries* as an educational tool, see e.g., Dennis Nolan, "Sir William Blackstone and the New American Republic: A Study of Intellectual Impact," *New York University Law Review* 51 (1976): 731.

28. John Langbein, "Introduction," in William Blackstone, *Commentaries on the Laws of England*, ed. Langbein, vol. 3 (Chicago: University of Chicago Press, 1979); Duncan Kennedy, "The Structure of Blackstone's Commentaries," *Buffalo Law Review* 28 (1979): 205; Alan Watson, *Roman Law and Comparative Law* (Athens: University of Georgia Press, 1991), 166–81; see also the classic study of Daniel J. Boorstin, *The Mysterious Science of the Law* (Cambridge, Mass.: Harvard University Press, 1941); Peter King, "Utilitarian Jurisprudence in America: The Influence of Bentham and Austin on American Legal Thought in the Nineteenth Century" (Ph.D. dissertation, University of Illinois, 1961).

29. Jeremy Bentham, "A General View of a Complete Code of Laws," in *The Works of Jeremy Bentham* (Edinburgh, 1843), 155–210; Jeremy Bentham, *Supplement to Papers Relative to Codification and Public Instruction* (London, 1817); see also Paul A. Palmer, "Benthamism in England and America," *American Political Science Review* 35 (1941): 855.

30. Austin, *Lectures*, 2:669–704; see also Enid Campbell, "German Influences in English Legal Education."

31. Tony Weir, "The Common Law System," in *International Encyclopedia of Comparative Law: Structures and Divisions of Law* (Tübingen: J. C. B. Mohr, 1974), 2:77–114.

32. Robert B. Stevens, *Law School: Legal Education in America from the 1850s to the 1980s* (Chapel Hill: University of North Carolina Press, 1983); Boorstin, *Mysterious Science*, 11–25. Indeed, the "science of law" as a moral rather than a deductive science came into fashion in the United States a half-century before Langdell.

33. Stevens, *Law School*, 35–76.

34. Austin, *Lectures*, 1:127–29.

35. Patrick Atiyah, *The Rise and Fall of Freedom of Contract* (Oxford: Clarendon Press, 1979), 345.

36. On Austin's treatment of natural law, see Morison, *John Austin*, 76–78; see also Peter Stein, *Roman Law and English Jurisprudence Yesterday and Today* (London: Cambridge University Press, 1969), 12, wherein Stein suggests that Austin was indirectly influenced by the natural lawyers through the Pandectists. See also Stein, "Continental Influences on English Legal Thought," 1105–25.

37. Kennedy, "Structure of Blackstone's Commentaries," 205.

38. Langbein, "Introduction"; Kennedy, "Structure of Blackstone's Commentaries," 205; King, "Utilitarian Jurisprudence."

39. On Austin's conservative political views, see Morison, *John Austin*,

122–32; Wilfrid Rumble, "The Legal Positivism of John Austin and the Realist Movement in American Jurisprudence," *Cornell Law Review* 66 (1981): 989, calls Austin "an arch-conservative."

40. W. G. Hammond, "Preface," in Blackstone, *Commentaries on the Laws of England*, ed. Hammond (San Francisco, 1890).

41. See on the early common law of *ferae naturae*, Thomas A. Lund, "Early American Wildlife Law," *New York University Law Review* 51 (1976): 703–30.

42. See, e.g., Stein, *Roman Law*, 11.

43. Stein, "Legal Theory and the Reform of Legal Education in Mid-Nineteenth Century England," 185, 195; see also Schwarz, "John Austin," 196.

44. Austin, *Lectures*, 1:358–65. Austin used the term "legal person."

45. Weir, "Common Law." Interestingly, Austin seems to have approved of Hale's *Analysis*; see Austin, *Lectures*, 1:44: "In his 'Analysis of the Law,' which *abounds with acute and judicious remarks*, it is stated expressly by Sir Matthew Hale" (emphasis added).

46. Peter Stein, "The Attraction of the Civil Law in Post-Revolutionary America," *Virginia Law Review* 52 (1966): 403, 406–7; Watson, "*Justinian's Institutes*"; and Klaus Luig, "Institutionen Lehrbucher des nationalen Rechts im 17. und 18. Jahrhundert," *Ius Commune* 3 (1970): 64.

47. Austin, *Lectures*, 1:525–704.

48. The principal treatment of Austin's use of Roman and civil law is Schwarz, "John Austin," 178, 192–97, reprinted in German as A. B. Schwarz, *Rechtsgeschichte und Gegenwart* (Karlsruhe: C. F. Muller, 1960), 73–92. Schwarz comments at 195: "Here [in the main course of the *Lectures*] we may incontrovertibly recognize the characteristic training in Roman and Pandect law." I take the phrase "map of the legal system" from Morison, *John Austin*, 107.

49. On the right/wrong distinction, see Kennedy, "Structure of Blackstone's Commentaries," 221–72. The first two books of the *Commentaries* are devoted to a discussion of the rights of persons and the rights of things respectively, while the latter two books are devoted to private wrongs and public wrongs.

50. Austin, *Lectures*, 1:416–17, 476–77; cf. Morison, *John Austin*, 107–08 (which draws out the Austinian distinction between "primary rights and sanctioning rights").

51. See Morison, *John Austin*, 113–14: "If we ask why Austin did this [focus on rights], the answer is probably that this was what the writers who presented him with models for his map did. If he had gone against the grain in this respect, he would have had a hopeless task in his limited time because he would

have got so little help." It is noteworthy (but ignored by Morison) that Roman law does not focus on concepts of subjective rights, as modern legal theorists understand the term; see H. F. Jolowicz, *Roman Foundations of Modern Law* (1957; rpt. Oxford: Clarendon Press, 1961), 66–67; on the development of the concept of "right" among the civilians, see Richard Tuck, *Natural Rights Theories* (Cambridge: Cambridge University Press, 1979). It is unfair to suggest, however, that Austin's emphasis on rights was solely derivative. In fact, Austin did have the alternative model of a right/wrong distinction presented by Blackstone. That he deliberately rejected this distinction is not without significance.

52. Jolowicz, *Roman Foundations*, 61–81.

53. It is interesting that Anglo-American jurisprudence has generally employed dichotomy rather than trichotomy.

54. Austin, *Lectures*, 2:751.

55. Ibid., 1:416. Interestingly, here, Austin was in agreement with both Hale and Blackstone and so stated; see Jolowicz, *Roman Foundations*, 48–53.

56. Austin, *Lectures*, 1:416: "The former [public law] regards persons as bearing political characters."

57. Ibid., 1:416: "In a word, Public Law is the law of political *Status*; and, instead of standing opposed to the body of law, is a branch of one of its departments: namely, of the *law* of Persons."

58. Thomas Wood, *An Institute of the Laws of England*, 2d ed. (London, 1722).

59. Schwarz, "John Austin," 192–93. Schwarz recognizes, however, that on a fundamental level Falck and Austin differed. Falck, for instance, ultimately looked to a "higher source" of law, akin to natural law, whereas Austin, in *The Province*, did not, as the analysis of the categories of law clearly illustrates. Stein, "Legal Theory," 193, echoes H. L. A. Hart's unfavorable comparison of Bentham and Austin, quoting Hart to the effect that "had it [Bentham's posthumously published *Of Laws in General*] been published in his lifetime, it rather than John Austin's later and obviously derivative work, would have dominated English jurisprudence."

60. Schwarz, "John Austin," 192–93. The full citation to Falck's work is Niels N. Falck, *Juristische Encyclopaedie*, 2d ed. (Kiel, 1830). A copy is listed as being in Austin's library (Campbell in Austin, *Lectures*, 1:xii).

61. Austin, *Lectures*, 1:44.

62. The first chapter of the *Juristische Encyclopaedie* begins with section 26, entitled "Oeffentliches und Privatrecht; deren Verhaltniss zu einander"; sec-

tion 28 is entitled "b) Sachenrecht"; section 29 is entitled "c) Obligationen-recht."

63. Falck, *Juristische Encyclopaedie*, section 26; for Austin's comments, see *Lectures*, 1:69–70.

64. See, e.g., Austin's critical remarks on Ulpian's use of the phrase *jus naturale* to refer to the "instincts of animals" rather than to law properly so-called. He comments: "But these metaphorical laws which govern the lower animals, and which govern (though less despotically) the human species itself, should not have been blended and confounded, by a grave writer upon jurisprudence, with laws properly so-called."

65. Maitland, *Forms*. It is interesting, in this context, to notice Austin's attack on Blackstone in *Lectures*, 1:71: "It is true that Sir William Blackstone, also rejects that division, and also considers the law which is concerned with political conditions a member of the Law of Persons. But the method observed by Blackstone in his far too celebrated Commentaries, is a slavish and blundering copy of the very imperfect method which Hale delineates roughly in his short and unfinished Analysis. From the outset to the end of his Commentaries, he blindly adopts the mistakes of his rude and compendious model, missing invariably, with a nice and surprising infelicity, the pregnant but obscure suggestions which it proffered to his attention, and which would have guided a discerning and inventive writer to an arrangement comparatively just. Neither in the general conception, nor in the detail of his book, is there a single particle of original and discriminating thought. He had read somewhat (though far less than is commonly believed); but he had swallowed the matter of his reading, without choice and without rumination. He owed the popularity of his book to a paltry but effectual artifice, and to a poor, superficial merit. He truckled to the sinister interests and to the mischievous prejudices of power; and he flattered the overweening conceit of their national or peculiar institutions, which then was devoutly entertained by the body of the English people, though now it is happily vanishing before the advancement of reason. And to this paltry but effectual artifice he added the allurement of a style which is fitted to tickle the ear, though it never or rarely satisfies a severe and masculine taste. For that rhetorical and prattling manner of his is not the manner which suited the matter in hand. It is not the manner of those classical Roman jurists who are always models of expression, though their meaning be never so faulty. It differs from their unaffected, yet apt and nervous style, as the tawdry and the flimsy dress of a milliner's doll, from the graceful and imposing nakedness of a Grecian statue."

66. Austin, *Lectures*, 1:482.

67. Schwarz suggests that because of Austin, "English jurisprudence does not bear the same home-grown character which gives its peculiar greatness to English law" ("John Austin," 197). This allegation is, perhaps, too strong. Austin's positivism is not civilian, and though his systematization efforts reflect the influence of Roman and civilian sources, there was a native English tradition. Indeed, it is important to recognize that while Austin rejected the unsystematic nature of the common law and looked to the civil law for inspiration and language, even in rejecting common law he was inevitably influenced by it.

68. Alan Watson, *The Making of the Civil Law* (Cambridge, Mass.: Harvard University Press, 1981), 83–98; Hoeflich, "Legal Education."

69. Alan Watson, *Sources of Law, Legal Change, and Ambiguity* (Philadelphia: University of Pennsylvania Press, 1984), 1–24; see also Fritz Pringsheim, "The Inner Relationship Between English and Roman Law," *Cambridge Law Journal* 5 (1935): 347–65.

70. Biographical details are drawn primarily from Gerald T. Dunne, *Justice Joseph Story and the Rise of the Supreme Court* (New York: Simon and Schuster, 1970), and James McClellan, *Joseph Story and the American Constitution* (Norman: University of Oklahoma Press, 1971); see also Gerhard Kegel, "Joseph Story," *Rabels Zeitschrift für auslandisches und internationales Privatrecht* 43 (1979): 609.

71. Since much of Story's practice was centered on commercial subjects and admiralty, he probably encountered works by Robert Joseph Pothier and others.

72. W. W. Story, ed., *Life and Letters of Joseph Story*, vol. 1 (Boston, 1851).

73. Reprinted in Joseph Story, *The Miscellaneous Writings of Joseph Story*, ed. W. W. Story (Boston, 1852), 66–92.

74. Ibid., 198–241.

75. Story, ed., *Life*, 496–97.

76. See Daniel R. Coquillette, "Justinian in Braintree: John Adams, Civilian Learning, and Legal Elitism, 1758–1775," in *Law in Colonial Massachusetts, 1630–1800*, ed. Frederick S. Allis, Jr. (Boston: Colonial Society of America, 1984), 359–418.

77. Peter Stephen DuPonceau was born in St. Martin, France, on June 3, 1760. He arrived in Portsmouth, New Hampshire, in 1777 and joined the Continental army soon after. In 1781, he became a citizen of Pennsylvania and served as Robert Livingston's under secretary of foreign affairs until 1783. He was admitted as a lawyer in Philadelphia in 1786. His knowledge of foreign

law and languages led to his continuing involvement in international law. DuPonceau translated many major works and authored books and articles on several topics, which included law, linguistics, and philology. He died on April 1, 1844. For more information and references, see *Dictionary of American Biography*, s.v. "DuPonceau, Pierre Etienne."

James Kent was born in Fredericksburgh, New York, on July 31, 1763. He became an apprentice of Attorney General Egbert Benson in 1781, the same year he graduated from Yale. He was elected for three terms to the New York Assembly. He was associated with the Federalists but left the political arena when he was appointed to a professorship in Columbia University. He remained there until 1798. He then became a judge and then chief judge of the New York Supreme Court and in 1814 was named chancellor of the New York Court of Chancery. He retired in 1823, only to reaccept a position at Columbia University. There he published the first volume of his *Commentaries on American Law* in 1826. Kent died in December 1847. For more information and references, see *Dictionary of American Biography*, s.v. "Kent, James."

78. William Kent, *Memoirs and Letters of James Kent, LL.D.* (Boston, 1898), 27, 36–37.

79. On Kent's use of Roman law viewed by a modern-day expert, see Alan Watson, "Chancellor Kent's Use of Foreign Law," in *The Reception of Continental Ideas in the Common Law World, 1820–1920*, ed. Matthias Reimann (Berlin: Duncker and Humblot, 1993), 45–62. On Kent's broad intellectual interests (including classics and Roman law), see John Langbein, "Chancellor Kent and the History of Legal Literature," *Columbia Law Review* 93 (1993): 547.

80. John Duer, *A Discourse on the Life, Character, and Public Services of James Kent.* (New York, 1898), 17.

81. Ibid., 38–39.

82. *Supplement to the Catalogue of the Law Library of Harvard University* (Cambridge, Mass., 1835).

83. Livermore was the author of books on the conflict of laws and agency; on Livermore, see Rodolfo De Nova, "The First American Book on Conflict of Laws," *American Journal of Legal History* 8 (1964): 136.

84. Robert Joseph Pothier was one of the most important civilian private law theorists of the eighteenth century. His works on contract laws were of immense importance in the development of Anglo-American contract doctrine. On Pothier's influence on American law, see the comments of Roscoe Pound, "The Influence of French Law in America," *Illinois Law Review* 3 (1909): 354.

85. See *The Centennial History of the Harvard Law School, 1817–1917* (Cambridge, Mass.: Harvard Law School Association, 1918), 92–93.

86. Joseph Story, *Commentaries on the Law of Bailments with Illustrations from the Civil and the Foreign Law* (Cambridge, Mass., 1832).

87. Joseph Story, *Commentaries on the Law of Agency* (Boston, 1839).

88. Joseph Story, *Commentaries on the Law of Partnership* (Boston, 1841).

89. Joseph Story, *Commentaries on the Conflict of Laws Foreign and Domestic* (Boston, 1834).

90. Hoeflich, "Transatlantic Friendships," 605–6.

91. *Dictionary of American Biography*, s.v. "Pickering, John."

92. John Pickering, "The Civil Law," *American Jurist* 3 (1829): 39–62.

93. On Follen, see the memoir published in Charles Follen, *The Works of Charles Follen* (Boston, 1841), 1:3–582.

94. In his diary for April 20, 1825, Follen wrote that he had "enrolled by name with Du Ponceau as a law student" (ibid., 153).

95. Ibid., 157–58, 617.

96. Kurt H. Nadelmann, "De l'organisation et de la jurisdiction des cours de justice, aux Etats Unis d'Amerique par M. Joseph Story," in *Joseph Story*, ed. Mortimer D. Schwartz and John C. Hogan (New York: Oceana Publications, 1959), 80–81.

97. See Hoeflich, "Transatlantic Friendships," 604.

98. On Story's inability to read German, see Story, ed., *Life*, 82. On the importance of this lack to Story's scholarly work, see C. J. A. Mittermaier, "Collision der Gesetze verschiedener Staate," *Kritische Zeitschrift für Rechtswissenschaft und Gesetzorbung des Auslandes* 7 (1835): 228–49.

99. Story, ed., *Life*, 38–39.

100. Like Story, American legal scholars were able to follow German scholarship through translations. See M. H. Hoeflich, "Savigny and His Anglo-American Disciples," *American Journal of Comparative Law* 37 (1989): 18–19.

101. There are occasional hints that Story at least checked his sources. See Story, *Agency*, 12n.4: "Mr. Livermore has cited another passage . . . from Cujaccius; but after considerable research I have not been able to verify the citation." On Story's use of secondary sources in his *Commentaries on the Conflict of Laws*, see Kurt H. Nadelmann, "Joseph Story's Contribution to American Conflicts Law: A Comment," *American Journal of Legal History* 5 (1961): 230, reprinted in Nadelmann, *Conflict of Laws: International and Interstate* (The Hague: Nijhoff, 1972), 21; and Nadelmann, "Bicentennial Observations on the Second Edition of Joseph Story's Commentaries on the Conflict of Laws," *American Journal of Comparative Law* 28 (1980): 67; see also Ernest G. Loren-

zen, "Story's Commentaries on the Conflict of Laws—100 Years After," *Harvard Law Review* 48 (1934): 15. A fascinating contemporary evaluation of Story's achievements in his conflicts treatise is to be found in Mittermaier, "Collision," 228.

102. See A. W. B. Simpson, "The Rise and Fall of the Legal Treatise: Legal Principles and the Forms of Legal Literature," in *Legal Theory and Legal History: Essays on the Common Law*, by Bruce Simpson (London: Hambledon, 1987), 273–320.

103. Anthony Fitzherbert, *La Graunde Abridgement*, 3 vols. (London, 1514–16).

104. See Simpson, "Rise and Fall," 635, 633; T. F. T. Plucknett, *Early English Legal Literature* (Cambridge: Cambridge University Press, 1958), 19.

105. On English legal education, see Stein, "Legal Theory and the Reform of Legal Education in Mid-Nineteenth Century England," 185; on the U.S. system, see Stevens, *Law School*.

106. The most important American edition of Blackstone's *Commentaries*, that by St. George Tucker, was published in Virginia in 1803.

107. Nathan Dane, *A General Abridgement and Digest of American Law* (Boston, 1823).

108. The *General Abridgement* consists primarily of categorical arrangements of case extracts and summaries supplemented by textual material, especially from Pothier's works.

109. Stewart Kyd, *A Treatise on the Law of Bills of Exchange and Promissory Notes* (London, 1790).

110. John J. Powell, *A Treatise on the Law of Mortgages* (Dublin, 1785); John J. Powell, *An Essay Upon the Law of Contracts and Agreements* (Dublin, 1790); see generally, C. K. Shipton, *Early American Imprints, 1639–1800* (Worchester, Mass.: American Antiquarian Society, 1955); Eldon Revare James, "A List of Legal Treatises Printed in the British Colonies and the American States Before 1801," in *Harvard Legal Essays Written in Honor of and Presented to J. H. Beale and S. Williston* (Cambridge, Mass.: Harvard University Press, 1934), 159; Simpson, "Rise and Fall," 303–9.

111. Stein, "Attraction of the Civil Law"; Watson, *"Justinian's Institutes"*; Luig, "Institutionen," 64; Kelley, "Gains Noster," 619.

112. Story, *Bailments*, xi; see also Simpson, "Rise and Fall," 309–20. Simpson believes that Story was particularly attracted to the "natural lawyers" as well as to the Romanists.

113. For an interesting parallel among the early civilians, see Watson, *Making of the Civil Law*, 23–38; see Simpson, "Rise and Fall," 312.

114. See, e.g., Story, *Bailments*.

115. 2 Ld. Raymond 909.

116. Raymond, 47–55.

117. George Sharswood, *Lectures Introductory to the Study of the Law* (Philadelphia, 1870), 153; see also William R. Leslie, "Similarities in Lord Mansfield's and Joseph Story's View of Fundamental Law," *American Journal of Legal History* 1 (1957): 278.

118. On Mansfield, see Edmund Heward, *Lord Mansfield* (Chichester: Barry Rose, 1979); C. H. S. Fifoot, *Lord Mansfield* (Oxford: Clarendon Press, 1936).

119. See, e.g., Arthur T. von Mehren and James Gordley, *The Civil Law System*, 2d ed. (Boston: Little, Brown, 1977).

120. Sir William Jones, *An Essay on the Law of Bailments* (1781; rpt. London, 1806); James Kent, *Commentaries on American Law*, 11th ed. (Boston, 1867).

121. Jones, *Essay on the Law of Bailments*, 4–48, quotation on 4.

122. Ibid., Contents.

123. Ibid., 34–110.

124. Y.B 8 Edw.II 275, cited by Lord Holt, at 2 Ld. Raymond 914 (also styled *Bowdon v. Pelleter*); on this case, see Samuel Stoljar, "The Early History of Bailment," *American Journal of Legal History* 1 (1957): 5.

125. Schwarz, "John Austin," 187, 191; Kelley, "Gaius Noster," 619.

126. Jones, *Essay on the Law of Bailments*, 36–40.

127. Kent, *Commentaries*, 749–813, 66.

128. Story, *Bailments*, 53–60.

129. Ibid., vii–ix; 58. "The rule is certainly *strictissimi juris*; and the incorporation into our law ought not readily to be admitted." It is thus difficult for me to agree entirely with Roscoe Pound that Story used Roman law to show the congruence of common law with natural law because all had the same rule. Clearly this is untrue as regards places, such as this, where Story disagrees with the Roman rule. See Roscoe Pound, *The Formative Era of American Law* (1938; rpt. Boston: Little, Brown, 1939), 147.

130. On the notion of Roman law as *ratio scripta*, see Watson, *Making of the Civil Law*, 83–98; Hoeflich, "Legal Education"; see also Peter Stein, "Elegance in Law," *Law Quarterly Review* 77 (1961): 242; Alejandro Guzman, "Ratio Scripta," *Ius Commune Sonderhefte* (Frankfurt am Main: C. V. Klosterman, 1981), 14.

131. See Pound, *Formative Era*, 147.

132. Story, *Bailments*, 219–22; quotations on 222.

133. Story, *Agency*, 11–12; quotation on 11.

134. Story, *Conflict.*

135. Nadelmann, *Conflict of Laws*, and Nadelmann, "Bicentennial Observations." See also Eduard Lambert and J. R. Xirau, *L'ancetre americain du droit compare; la doctrine du Juge Story* (Paris: Recueil Sirey, 1947) (concerning *Swift v. Tyson*).

136. On these works and their influence on Story, see Nadelmann's articles. On Livermore, see De Nova, "First American."

137. Story, *Conflicts*, v.

138. See Roscoe Pound, "The Place of Judge Story in the Making of American Law," *Massachusetts Law Quarterly* 1 (1915–16): 121–40.

139. Story, *Bailments*, 55.

140. Pound, "Place of Judge Story," 121, 137.

141. On Savigny's doctrines, see Reddie, *Historical Notices*; see also Gooch, *History*, 42–54, and Gutzwiller, *Der Einfluss.*

142. On Austin's conservatism, see Enid Campbell, "John Austin and Jurisprudence in Nineteenth Century England" (Ph.D. dissertation, Duke University, 1959), 81–181.

143. Andrew Johnson, "The Influence of Nathan Dane on Legal Literature," *American Journal of Legal History* 7 (1963): 29.

144. See Nadelmann, *Conflict of Laws*, and Nadelmann, "Bicentennial Observations." See also Lambert and Xirau, *L'ancetre americain.*

145. Joseph Story to Chancellor Kent, May 17, 1834, Story Manuscripts, Massachusetts Historical Society, Boston, quoted in Morgan D. Dowd, "Justice Joseph Story: A Study of the Legal Philosophy of a Jeffersonian Judge," *Vanderbilt Law Review* 18 (1965): 643, 649.

146. Kent Newmyer, "A Note on the Whig Politics of Justice Joseph Story," *Mississippi Valley Historical Review* 48 (1961): 480; Dowd, "Justice Joseph Story."

147. Notions of republican virtue played a role of great importance in American life during this period, inspiring not only education and law but politics. For example, the Society of Cincinnati was composed of soldiers from the Revolutionary War army and named in memory of the great Roman republican general Lucius Cincinnatus; see Gary Wills, *Cincinnatus, George Washington and the Enlightenment* (Garden City, N.Y.: Doubleday, 1984). According to his son W. W. Story, Justice Story had a particular liking for Cicero's works; see Story, ed., *Life*, 564. See also R. A. Ferguson, *Law and Letters in American Culture* (Cambridge, Mass.: Harvard University Press, 1984).

148. Stein, "Attraction of the Civil Law," attributes much of the early popularity of civil law to anti-British sentiment resulting from the Revolution and

the War of 1812. Although this is surely true to a degree, it is not the complete answer.

149. Many of the radical codification theorists saw codes as a means of democratizing the law and breaking the hold of the legal elite; see Charles M. Cook, *The American Codification Movement* (Westport, Conn.: Greenwood Press, 1981).

150. See Joseph Story, "Law, Legislation, Codes," in *Readings in American Legal History*, ed. Mark D. Howe (Cambridge, Mass.: Harvard University Press, 1949), 460–72.

151. Foremost among these has been Professor Peter Stein of Cambridge University; see Stein's articles cited above; see also Stein, "Logic and Experience in Roman and Common Law," *Boston University Law Review* 59 (1979): 433; Stein, "Continental Influences on English Legal Thought," 3:1119.

152. Rudolf Schlesinger, "The Common Core of Legal Systems: An Emerging Subject of Comparative Study," in *XXth Century Comparative and Conflicts Law: Legal Essays in Honor of Hessel E. Yntema*, ed. Kurt Nadelmann, Arthur T. von Mehren and John Hazard (Leiden: A. W. Sijthoff, 1961), 65–79.

2. Roman and Civil Law in the Anglo-American World Before 1850: Lieber, Legaré, and Walker, Roman Lawyers in the Old South

1. "Hugh Swinton Legaré," *Southern Review* 8 (1870): 123; Michael O'Brien, *Rethinking the South* (Baltimore: Johns Hopkins University Press, 1988), 24.

2. See Noble E. Cunningham, Jr., *In Pursuit of Reason: The Life of Thomas Jefferson* (Baton Rouge: Louisiana State University Press, 1987); perhaps the best study of southern legal culture to date is Donald J. Senese, "Legal Thought in South Carolina, 1800–1860" (Ph.D. dissertation: University of South Carolina, 1970). On Theophilus Parsons, see Isaac Parker, *A Sketch of the Character of the Late Chief Justice Parsons* (Boston, 1813).

3. Robert Bevier Kirtland, *George Wythe: Lawyer, Revolutionary, Judge* (New York: Garland, 1986), 115.

4. On the University of Virginia, see Edgar Finley Shannon, *The University of Virginia: A Century and Half of Innovation* (New York: New Camen Society in North America, 1969). On the University of Georgia, see Thomas Dyer, *The University of Georgia: A Bicentennial History* (Athens: University of Georgia Press, 1985). Paul Carrington, "The Revolutionary Idea of University Legal

Education," *William and Mary Law Review* 31 (1990): 527; Paul Carrington, "Teaching Law in the Antebellum Northwest," *University of Toledo Law Review* 23 (1991): 3.

On Transylvania University, see Carrington, "Revolutionary Idea" and "Teaching Law." On Tulane, see John Percy Dyer, *Tulane: The Biography of a University* (New York: Harper & Row, 1966).

5. The *Southern Review* was published quarterly beginning in 1828. It contained poetry, book reviews, and articles on law, science, mathematics, history, language, medicine, and other topics. Chief contributors included T. C. Wallace, Robert Hayne, Thomas Cooper, Stephen Elliot, and Hugh Swinton Legaré. The last volume appeared in 1832. The *Southern Literary Messenger* was a magazine published for the Virginia Historical and Philosophical Society, starting in 1834. It published travelogues, reviews, poetry, and articles on varied topics. Contributors included Edgar Allan Poe, Lydia Sigourney, Oliver Oldschool, and W. Gilmore Simms. T. W. White was replaced as an editor by John R. Thompson in 1848. The last volume appeared in 1864. See Richard J. Calhoun, "Literary Magazines in the Old South," in *The History of Southern Literature*, ed. Louis D. Rubin (Baton Rouge: Louisiana State University Press, 1985), 157–63.

6. O'Brien, *Rethinking the South*. See also Michael O'Brien, ed., *All Clever Men, Who Make Their Ways* (Fayetteville: University of Arkansas Press, 1982).

7. See Michael O'Brien, ed., *Intellectual Life in Antebellum Charleston* (Knoxville: University of Tennessee Press, 1986). See also E. Merton Coulter, *College Life in the Old South* (1928; rpt. Athens: University of Georgia Press, 1983), 181–82.

8. Michael O'Brien, *A Character of Hugh Legaré* (Knoxville: University of Tennessee Press, 1985).

9. There has not been done for the southern legal tradition what Perry Miller did for the northern. One may hope that the new journal *Southern Legal History* will help correct this imbalance. See also M. H. Hoeflich, "Roman Law in American Legal Culture," *Tulane Law Review* 66 (1992): 1723–44.

10. See Lawrence M. Friedman, *A History of American Law*, 2d ed. (New York: Simon and Schuster, 1985).

11. M. H. Hoeflich, "Savigny and His Anglo-American Disciples," *American Journal of Comparative Law* 37 (1989): 17 -37; M. H. Hoeflich, "Transatlantic Friendships and the German Influence on American Law in the First Half of the Nineteenth Century," *American Journal of Comparative Law* 35 (1987): 599–611.

12. See Carl Holliday, *A History of Southern Literature* (1906; rpt. Port Washington, N.Y.: Kennikat Press, 1969).

13. On Lieber, see Frank Freidel, *Francis Lieber, Nineteenth-Century Liberal* (Baton Rouge: Louisiana State University Press, 1947); see also Thomas Sergeant Perry, *The Life and Letters of Francis Lieber* (Boston, 1882). On Legaré, see Linda Rhea, *Hugh Swinton Legaré, a Charleston Intellectual* (Chapel Hill: University of North Carolina Press, 1934); see also O'Brien, *A Character of Hugh Legaré*. Legaré's major writings are collected along with a memoir by his sister (of which the original is in the Caroliniana Collection, University of South Carolina, Columbia), in Legaré, *The Writings of Hugh Swinton Legaré*, ed. Mary Legaré, 2 vols. (Charleston, 1846). On Walker, see John Belton O'Neall, "James M. Walker," in *Biographical Sketches of the Bench and Bar of South Carolina* (Charleston, 1859).

14. Freidel, *Lieber*, 366.

15. James Murdock Walker, *An Inquiry into the Use and Authority of Roman Jurisprudence in the Law Concerning Real Estate* (Charleston, S.C., 1850); James Murdock Walker, *The Theory of the Common Law* (Boston, 1852); Walker, *Tract on Government* (Boston, 1853).

16. Francis Lieber, *Legal and Political Hermeneutics* (Boston, 1839); Lieber, *Manual of Political Ethics* (Boston, ca. 1838; 2d ed. rev. Philadelphia, 1875); Lieber, *On Civil Liberty and Self-Government* (Philadelphia, 1859).

17. Arthur Schiller, "Roman Interpretation and Anglo-American Interpretation and Construction," *Virginia Law Review* 27 (1940–41): 733–68.

18. Ballantyne and Hughes began printing the *Edinburgh Review* in October 1802. The *Review* ran until October 1929.

19. Hoeflich, "Transatlantic Friendships," 602–6.

20. Freidel, *Lieber*, 98, 118–19, 161, vii, 35–40, 57–58, 98–102, 115.

21. Hoeflich, "Transatlantic Friendships," 602–6.

22. Ibid. See also Huntington Library, Lieber Papers MS. LI3255 cited in Kurt Nadelmann, "Joseph Story's Sketch of American Law," *American Journal of Comparative Law* 3 (1954): 4.

23. Rhea, *Legaré*, 1–45, 48, 51.

24. Legaré, *Writings*, xlv; Rhea, *Legaré*, 54.

25. Rhea, *Legaré*, 54.

26. By jurists' law, I refer to the legal principles established by the Roman jurists of the period before the Digest whose works were extracted and included in the Digest.

27. On Heineccius see Michael Stolleis, *Juristen. Ein biographisches Lexikon von der Antike bis zum 20. Jahrhundert* (Munich: C. H. Beck, 1995), 279–80.

28. Dugald Stewart, *Elements of the Philosophy of the Human Mind*, vol. 1 (London, 1792).

29. George Davie, *The Democratic Intellect* (1961; rpt. Edinburgh: Edinburgh University Press, 1982), 147.

30. Legaré, *Writings*, xlv.

31. Rhea, *Legaré*, 131–55.

32. Legaré, *Writings*, lxi.

33. O'Neall, "Walker," 574.

34. O'Neall, "Walker," 574–75.

35. Lieber was raised in Prussia during the time of the Napoleonic occupation. Therefore, it is understandable that he spoke German and French. As for his knowledge of the classical languages and his linguistic ability, see Freidel, *Lieber*, 18, 178–82.

36. Legaré was also learned in Italian, Spanish, and Portuguese (Rhea, *Legaré*, 40). But although the number of languages with which Legaré was familiar was large, the quality of his linguistic ability was less than Lieber's.

37. Samuel Livermore was born on August 25, 1786, in Concord, New Hampshire. After graduating from Harvard College in 1804, he was accepted to the Bar in Essex County. Livermore authored a variety of works; his key point was to call attention to the works of medieval authors. For further information and references, see *Dictionary of American Biography*, s.v. "Livermore, Samuel."

38. *Catalogue of Books Belonging to the South Carolina Library* (Columbia, 1807). See also M. H. Hoeflich, "Edward Gibbon, Roman Lawyer," *American Journal of Comparative Law* 39 (1991): 808–18.

39. *Catalogue of the South Carolina Library*. On Cicero, see M. H. Hoeflich, "Ciceronian Ethic and Nineteenth Century American Law," forthcoming.

40. See Duck, *De usu et authoritate juris civilis Romanorum*. See also Daniel Coquillette, *The Civilian Writers of Doctors' Commons, London: Three Centuries of Juristic Innovation in Comparative, Commercial and International Law* (Berlin: Duncker & Humblot, 1988), 161–65; Walker, *Inquiry*, 47.

41. There are two printed catalogs of Hugh Legaré's library: *Catalogue of the Library of the Honorable Hugh Legaré* (Washington, D.C., 1843), which appears to have been prepared by his executors immediately after his death, and *Catalogue of the Rare and Valuable Private Library of the Late Honorable H. S. Legaré* (Washington, D.C., 1848), which was prepared by an auction house. Copies of both are at the Caroliniana Library at the University of South Carolina, Columbia.

42. *The 1812 Catalogue of the Library of Congress, a Facsimile* (1812; rpt.

Washington D.C.: Library of Congress, 1982).

43. *Library of the Law School of Harvard University* (Cambridge, Mass., 1826).

44. Lieber, *Hermeneutics*, 135.

45. Ibid., 162.

46. George Staunton, trans. of *Ta Tsing Leu Lee*, trans. Ta Ch'ing lu (London, 1810); originally published in Peking, in Chinese.

47. See Chapter 1.

48. Hoeflich, "Ciceronian Ethic."

49. Freidel, *Lieber*, 432–35.

50. See the unpublished manuscripts of Francis Lieber's "Lectures on International Law," found in the Lieber Archives, 1863–64, Columbia University Library.

51. See Samuel Pufendorf, *Of the Law of Nature and Nations*, trans. Basil Kennet and George Carew, 8 vols. (London, 1729). See also Hugo Grotius, *The Rights of War and Peace (De Juri Belli et Pacis)*, trans. A. C. Campbell (Westport, Conn.: Hyperion Press, 1979).

52. Grant Gilmore and Charles L. Black, *The Law of Admiralty* (Brooklyn: Foundation Press, 1957).

53. Hugh Swinton Legaré, "The Origin, History and Influence of Roman Legislation," in *Writings*, 1:502–58; Legaré, "Kent's *Commentaries*," ibid., 2: 102–41; Legaré, "D'Aguesseau," ibid., 559–98; Legaré, "Codification," ibid., 482–501.

54. Gustav Hugo, *Lehrbuch eines civilistischen Cursus* (1799; rpt. Berlin, 1835); Joseph Story, *Commentaries on the Conflict of Laws Foreign and Domestic* (Boston, 1834); Christian Gottlieb Haubold, *Institutionum Juris Romani Privati Historico-Dogmaticarum Lineamenta observationibus maxime litteräriis distincta* (Leipzig, 1826); *Gaii Jurisconsulti Institutionum Commentarius*, ed. August W. Heffter (Berolini, 1827); *Corpus Juris Civilis*, ed. Heinrich Schräder (Berolini, 1832).

55. Legaré, "Origin," 502.

56. Henry Hallam, *Constitutional History of England*, 3 vols. (Boston, 1829).

57. Henry Hallam, *History of Europe During the Middle Ages*, rev. ed., 3 vols. (New York, 1899).

58. Legaré, "Origin," 504.

59. Joseph Story, "Tribute to Mr. Legaré," *Boston Daily Advertiser*, June 30, 1843. A copy of the original newspaper article can be found in the University of South Carolina Library.

60. Legaré, "Origin," 524–25.

61. Charles Fearne, *An Essay on the Learning of Contingent Remainders and Executory Devises* (London, 1772).

62. Legaré, "Origin," 517.

63. Legaré, "Origin," 515, 522, 517, 518.

64. See Peter Stein, "The Attraction of the Civil Law in Post-Revolutionary America," in *The Character and Influence of the Roman Civil Law Historical Essays* (London: Hambledon Press, 1988).

65. Legaré, "Origin," 518.

66. B. G. Struve, *Corpus Juris Publici Imperii Nostri Romano-Germanici*, 3d ed. (Jena: I. F. Bielckum, 1738).

67. Legaré, "Origin," 518.

68. Ibid., 511.

69. See Legaré, "Kent's *Commentaries*"; Legaré, "Codification."

70. It predates the seminal work by Roscoe Pound by more than fifty years.

71. John Reeves, *History of English Law*, 5 vols. (London, 1814–29).

72. Walker, *Inquiry*, 8.

73. Walker, *Theory*, 1.

74. John Austin, *Lectures on Jurisprudence*, ed. Robert Campbell (Jersey City, 1869).

75. Walker, *Theory*, 3–4.

76. Legaré, "Origin," 517.

77. Walker, *Theory*, 129–30.

78. See Daniel Mayes, "An Address to the Students of Law in Transylvania University," in *The Gladsome Light of Jurisprudence: Learning and the Law in England and the United States in the 18th and 19th Centuries*, ed. Michael H. Hoeflich (Westport, Conn.: Greenwood Press, 1988), 145–64.

79. On Lieber's participation during the Civil War, see Freidel, *Lieber*, 317–59.

80. There is little evidence of widespread distribution of *Hermeneutics* in either private or public libraries.

81. See Chapter 1, note 77.

82. Edward Everett was born in Dorchester, Massachusetts, on April 11, 1794. He graduated from Harvard in 1811 and received his Ph.D. from Göttingen in 1817. See Edward Everett, *Orations and Speeches on Various Occasions*, 4 vols. (Boston, 1853–68). For more information and references, see *Dictionary of American Biography*, s.v. "Everett, Edward."

Edward Livingston was born in Clermont, New York, on May 28, 1764. He graduated from Princeton in 1781 and then studied law at the office of John Lansing, along with Alexander Hamilton, James Kent, and Aaron Burr. For information on his work, see Edward Livingston, *The Complete Works of Edward Livingston on Criminal Jurisprudence*, 2 vols. (New York, 1873); Charles Havens Hunt, *Life of Edward Livingston* (New York, 1864); William B. Hatcher, *Edward Livingston: Jeffersonian Republican and Jacksonian Democrat* (Baton Rouge: Louisiana State University Press, 1940). See also *Dictionary of American Biography*, s.v. "Livingston, Edward."

Rufus Choate was born on October 1, 1799. He graduated from Dartmouth College in 1819 and was admitted to the Massachusetts court of common pleas in September 1822 and to the supreme judicial court in November 1825. For more information and references to his works, see *Dictionary of American Biography*, s.v. "Choate, Rufus."

Charles Sumner was born on January 6, 1811, in Boston. He graduated from the Harvard Law School in 1833, having been a pupil of Joseph Story. For more information and references, see *Dictionary of American Biography*, s.v. "Sumner, Charles."

83. Lieber to Mittermaier, October 1840, Lieber Papers, Caroliniana Library, University of South Carolina, Columbia; C. J. A. Mittermaier, "Collision der Gesetze vershiedener Staate," *Kristische Zeitschrift für Rechtswissenschaft und Gesetzgebung des Auslandes* 7 (1835): 228.

84. Lieber to his wife, Matilda, on March 20, 1840, Lieber Papers, Caroliniana Library; University of South Carolina.

85. W. G. Hammond, Preface to Francis Lieber, *Legal and Political Hermeneutics*, rev. ed., ed. Hammond (St. Louis, 1880), iii.

86. *California State Library Catalogue* (Sacramento, 1857).

87. Robert M. Cover, *Justice Accused: Antislavery and the Judicial Process* (New Haven: Yale University Press, 1975).

88. See Robert A. Ferguson, *Law and Letters in American Culture* (Cambridge, Mass.: Harvard University Press, 1984).

89. Hoeflich, "Ciceronian Ethic."

90. Ferguson, *Law and Letters*. See also Perry Miller, *The Life of the Mind in America* (San Diego: Harcourt Brace Jovanovich, 1965).

91. Legaré, *Writings*, lv.

92. Walker, *Inquiry*, 46.

93. Story, "Tribute."

94. "Hugh Swinton Legaré," *Southern Review* 8 (1870): 138.

95. P., "An Inquiry into Roman Jurisprudence," *Southern Quarterly Review* 3 (April 1851): 544.

96. J. L. Petigru was born on May 10, 1789, in Abbeville District, South Carolina. He was admitted to the Bar in 1812 and elected solicitor in 1816.

For further information and references, see *Dictionary of American Biography*, s.v. "Petigru, J. L."

97. Mrs. E. J. Eames, "To My Own Little Girl," *Southern Literary Messenger* 8 (1842): 255; N. C. Brooks, "Moses Smiting the Rock," *Southern Literary Messenger* 3 (1837): 25.

98. A Lawyer of North Carolina, "The Civil Law," *Southern Literary Messenger* 8 (1842): 249–55, quotation on 249.

99. Ibid., 253.

100. "Study of the Law," *Southern Literary Messenger* 3 (1837): 25–31, reprinted in *The Gladsome Light of Jurisprudence*, ed. Hoeflich, 201–13.

101. On Harvard, see Charles Warren, *History of the Harvard Law School and of Early Conditions in America*, 2 vols. (1908; rpt. New York: Da Capo Press, 1970). On Transylvania, see Charles Kerr, "Transylvania University's Law Department," *Americana* 31 (1937): 3; Carrington, "Revolutionary Idea."

102. Benjamin Butler was born on December 14, 1795, in Columbia County, New York. Admitted to the Bar in 1817, he then joined the law office of Martin Van Buren. For further information and references, see *Dictionary of American Biography*, s.v. "Butler, Benjamin."

103. Benjamin Butler, *Plan for the Organization of a LAW FACULTY in the University of the City of New York* (New York, 1835), reprinted in *The Gladsome Light of Jurisprudence*, ed. Hoeflich, 165–82.

104. Ibid., 166.

105. "Study of Law," *Southern Literary Messenger* 3 (1837): 30.

106. Hamilton Bryson, "The Use of Roman Law in Virginia Courts," *American Journal of Legal History* 28 (1984): 135–46.

3. Roman Law, Comparative Law, and the Historical School of Jurisprudence in England and America After 1850: Maine, Cushing, Hammond, and Pomeroy

1. See Lawrence M. Friedman, *A History of American Law*, 2d ed. (New York: Simon and Schuster, 1985). See also Peter Stein, "The Attraction of the Civil Law in Post-Revolutionary America," in *The Character and Influence of the Roman Civil Law Historical Essays* (London: Hambledon Press, 1988), 411–42.

2. See Daniel R. Coquillette, *The Civilian Writers of Doctors' Commons, London: Three Centuries of Juristic Innovation in Comparative, Commercial and International Law* (Berlin: Duncker & Humblot, 1988). See also Sir William Holdsworth, *A History of English Law*, vol. 12 (London: Methuen, 1938), 677.

3. Friedman, *History of American Law*.

4. For a brief biographical note on Savigny with bibliography, see Gerd Kleinheyer and Jan Schröder, *Deutsche Juristen aus Funf Jahrhunderten* (Heidelberg: C. F. Muller, 1983), 229–40; Stolleis, *Juristen*, 540–44. The leading biography continues to be Adolf Stoll, *Friedrich Carl von Savigny: Ein Bild seines Lebens mit einer Sammlung seiner Briefe*, 3 vols. (Berlin: Heymann, 1927–39). See also James Whitman, *The Legacy of Roman Law in the German Romantic Era: Historical Version and Legal Change* (Princeton: Princeton University Press, 1990).

5. On Theodor Mommsen, see Antoine Guilland, *Modern Germany and Her Historians* (London: Jarrold and Sons, 1915), 120–70.

6. Friedrich Carl von Savigny, *Vom Beruf unserer Zeit für Rechtswissenschaft und Gesetzgebung* (Heidelberg, 1814). For a history on the translation of Savigny's work, see M. H. Hoeflich, "Savigny and His Anglo-American Disciples," *American Journal of Comparative Law* 37 (1989): 19. Savigny, *Geschichte des römischen Rechts im Mittelalter* (Heidelberg, 1834); Savigny, *System des heutigen römischen Rechts*, 8 vols. (Berlin, 1840–49). On Savigny and his historical approach, see, above all, Matthias Reimann, *Historiche Schule und Common Law. Die deutsche Rechtswissenschaft des 19 Jhrdts im amerikanischen Rechtsdeuken. Comparative Studies in Continental and Anglo-American Legal History* Bd. 14 (Berlin: Duncker & Humblot, 1993).

7. Savigny, *Vom Beruf.*

8. See Hoeflich, "Savigny," 17–37.

9. Hugh Swinton Legaré, *The Writings of Hugh Swinton Legaré*, ed. Mary Legaré (Charleston, 1846), 1, 135.

10. Hoeflich, "Savigny," 17, 25, 21–22, 19–20; George Long, *Two Discourses Delivered in the Middle Temple Hall* (London, 1847); David Irving, *An Introduction to the Study of the Civil Law*, 4th ed. (London, 1837); James Reddie, *Historical Notices of the Roman Law and of the Recent Progress of Its Study in Germany* (Edinburgh, 1826).

11. Hoeflich, "Savigny," 19, 23, 27.

12. On the notion of *ratio scripta*, see Alejandro Guzman, *Ratio Scripta*, in *Ius Commune Sonderhefte* (Frankfurt am Main: C. V. Klosterman, 1981).

13. See Hoeflich, "Savigny."

14. The best biography of Maine is R. C. J. Cocks, *Sir Henry Maine* (Cambridge: Cambridge University Press, 1988). George Feaver, *From Status to Contract* (London: Longmans, Green, 1969), remains important; see also Stephen G. Uts, "Maine, Ancient Law and Legal Theory," *Connecticut Law Review* 16 (1984): 821; and the collection on Maine and his achievement, Alan

Diamond, ed., *The Victorian Achievement of Sir Henry Maine* (Cambridge: Cambridge University Press, 1991).

15. Holdsworth, *History of English Law*, 83–84; Cocks, *Maine*, 9–12; Feaver, *From Status to Contract*, 18; see also Peter G. Stein, "Maine and Legal Education," in Diamond, *Victorian Achievement*, 195–208; R. C. J. Cocks, *Foundations of the Modern Bar* (London: Sweet & Maxwell, 1983), 96–100.

16. Feaver, *From Status to Contract*, 64.

17. Henry Maine, *Ancient Law*, ed. Frederick Pollock, 10th ed. (1861; New York, 1884); see Cocks, *Maine*, 52–78.

18. Henry Maine, *Village Communities and Miscellanies* (New York, 1889); Cocks, *Maine*, 101–11; Maine, *Dissertations on Early Law and Custom* (New York, 1886); Cocks, *Maine*, 125–30; Maine, *Popular Government* (New York, 1885); Cocks, *Maine*, 131–40; Maine, *Lectures on International Law* (London, 1888).

19. There are nineteen endnotes, numbered A–S, which span pages 387–447.

20. Hoeflich, "Savigny," 27.

21. Maine, *Ancient Law*, 115–65. To be exact, Maine states, "The movement of the progressive societies has hitherto been a movement from *Status to Contract.*"

22. See John W. Cairns, "Blackstone, an English Institutist: Legal Literature and the Rise of the Nation State," *Oxford Journal of Legal Studies* 4 (1984): 318–60.

23. William G. Hammond, "System of Legal Classification of Hale and Blackstone in Its Relation to the Civil Law," in T. C. Sandars, *The Institutes of Justinian*, ed. Hammond (Chicago, 1876).

24. Maine, *Ancient Law*, 1–108; and see Alan Diamond, "Fictions, Equity and Legislation: Maine's Three Agencies of Legal Change," in Diamond, *Victorian Achievement*, 242–55.

25. Maine, *Ancient Law*, 70–108.

26. Ibid., 22–23, 116–18, 18, 147–58, 190–92, 221, 271.

27. John Taylor, *Elements of the Civil Law*, 3d ed. (London, 1755); Samuel Hallifax, *An Analysis of the Roman Civil Law*, 4th ed. (Cambridge, 1795); Luther S. Cushing, *An Introduction to the Study of the Roman Law* (Boston, 1854).

28. Edward Gibbon, *The History of the Decline and Fall of the Roman Empire*, 6 vols. (London, 1788–89); Gustav Hugo, *Lehrbuch eines civilistischen Cursus* (1799; rpt. Berlin, 1835). On Gibbon, see M. H. Hoeflich, "Edward Gibbon, Roman Lawyer," *American Journal of Comparative Law* 39 (1991): 803–18.

29. Maine, *Ancient Law*, 163–65, 178; Maine, *Village Communities*, 332, 336.

30. See Rudolf Schlesinger, *Formation of Contracts: A Study of the Common Core of Legal Systems* (New York: Oceana, 1968).

31. See Cocks, *Maine*, esp. 24–27.

32. Henry S. Maine, "Roman Law and Legal Education," *Fortnightly Review* and *International Law: A Series of Lectures Delivered Before the University of Cambridge* (1887; rpt. London, 1888), reprinted in *Village Communities*, 330–83.

33. *Report from the Select Committee on Legal Education* (London, 1846); see also Stein, "Maine and Legal Education."

34. Sir Arthur Duck, *De usu et authoritate juris civilis Romanorum per dominia principum Christianorum* (London, 1679). See also Coquillette, *Civilian Writers*, 161–65.

35. Maine, *Village Communities*, 332.

36. Ibid.

37. Ibid., 4.

38. See Frederick Pollock, "History of Comparative Jurisprudence," in *Essays in the Law* (London: Macmillan, 1922).

39. Maine, *Village Communities*, 345–50.

40. Ibid., 337.

41. Sir Robert Wiseman, *The Excellencie of Civil Law Above All Humane Laws Whatsoever* (London, 1664).

42. Maine, *Village Communities*, 364–66.

43. Ibid., 337.

44. See George E. Davie, *The Democratic Intellect* (1961; rpt. Edinburgh: Edinburgh University Press, 1982). See also Davie, *The Crisis of the Democratic Intellect* (Edinburgh: Plygon Press, 1986).

45. Maine, *Village Communities*, 361.

46. M. H. Hoeflich, "The Americanization of British Legal Education in the Nineteenth Century," *Journal of Legal History* 8 (1987): 244–59.

47. On Cushing, see *Dictionary of American Biography*, s.v. "Cushing, Luther Stearns."

48. Jean Domat, *Civil Laws in Their Natural Order*, trans. William Strahan, ed. Luther S. Cushing, 2 vols. (Boston, 1850); Friedrich Carl von Savigny, *Law of Possession*, trans. Luther S. Cushing (Berlin, 1838); Robert Joseph Pothier, *Treatise on the Contract of Sale*, trans. Luther S. Cushing (Boston, 1839); C. J. A. Mittermaier, *Effects of Drunkenness on Criminal Responsibility*, trans. Luther S. Cushing (Boston, 1840); Luther S. Cushing, *An Introduction to the Study of the*

Roman Law (Boston, 1854); Cushing, *Manual of Parliamentary Practice*, 2d ed. (Boston, 1845).

49. *Dictionary of American Biography*, s.v. "Cushing, Luther Stearns."

50. Cushing, *Introduction*, v.

51. Alexander C. Schomberg, *An Historical and Chronological View of Roman Law* (Oxford, 1785); John Taylor, *Elements of the Civil Law*, 3d ed. (London, 1755).

52. Cushing, *Introduction*, 180.

53. Ibid., 180–82.

54. Ibid., 181.

55. Ibid., 129.

56. See Mark Tushnet, *The American Law and Slavery* (Princeton: Princeton University Press, 1981). See also Alan Watson, "Slave Law: History and Ideology," *Yale Law Journal* 91 (1982): 1034–47.

57. See Kurt Nadelmann, "Joseph Story's Sketch of American Law," *American Journal of Comparative Law* 3 (1954): 3–8.

58. Cushing, *Introduction*, 183–200.

59. Ibid., 184–86.

60. Sir William Jones, *An Essay on the Law of Bailments* (1781; rpt. Albany, 1806).

61. Cushing, *Introduction*, 187–200.

62. Ibid., 199.

63. Ferdinand Mackeldey, *Lehrbuch des heutigen römischen Rechst* (Vienna, 1851–52), trans. as *Handbook of Roman Law*, trans. and ed. Moses A. Dropsie (Philadelphia, 1883).

64. Cushing, *Introduction*, 140.

65. Ibid., 144–45.

66. On Hammond, see Emlin McClain, "William G. Hammond," in *Great American Lawyers*, ed. William Draper Lewis (Philadelphia: John C. Winston Co., 1909), 8:189–238. See also William Gardiner Hammond, *Remembrance of Amherst*, ed. George F. Whicher (New York: Columbia University Press, 1946).

67. McClain, "Hammond," 194, 199, 198, 202–3.

68. The *Western Jurist* was one of the most remarkable legal literary productions of the mid-nineteenth century, largely because of Hammond's influence. It not only published articles on American law but also featured work in comparative law, legal history, and international law.

69. On the University of Iowa, see Emlin McClain, "Law Department of the State University of Iowa," *Green Bag* 1 (n.d.): 374–94.

70. McClain, "Hammond," 214.

71. T. C. Sandars, *The Institutes of Justinian*, ed. William G. Hammond (Chicago, 1876).

72. Hammond, "System of Legal Classification of Hale and Blackstone."

73. Francis Lieber, *Legal and Political Hermeneutics*, ed. William G. Hammond (St. Louis, 1880).

74. William Blackstone, *Commentaries*, ed. W. G. Hammond (San Francisco, 1890).

75. W. G. Hammond, "The Civil Law," *Western Jurist* 4 (1870): 173–75.

76. Hammond, "Civil Law," 173–75.

77. See Michael H. Hoeflich, "Introduction," in *The Gladsome Light of Jurisprudence: Learning and the Law in England and the United States in the 18th and 19th Centuries*, ed. Hoeflich (Westport, Conn.: Greenwood Press, 1988), 6–8.

78. Hammond, "Civil Law," 175, 177.

79. Ibid., 177–78.

80. William G. Hammond, "Ancient Law," *Western Jurist* 2 (1868): 1–11.

81. Ibid., 7: "Mr. Maine therefore has rendered a very great service indeed in setting the example of a new and more liberal treatment of legal topics. By following in the path he leads, the cultivated lawyer will learn how to connect the peculiar walks of his profession with those wider fields of learning and speculation which he shares with all educated and thinking men. *It is for this, rather than for any positive contributions of the works to legal science, that it will be longest remembered.*"

82. Ibid., 6, 7.

83. Stein, "Attraction of Civil Law."

84. See, e.g., *Western Jurist* 9–12 (1875–78), passim.

85. W. A. Hunter, "The Place of Roman Law in Legal Education," *Western Jurist* 9 (1875): 461–72.

86. Ibid., 462, 463, 465–66.

87. See *The Catalogue of the Hammond Historical Law Collection* (Iowa City, 1895), a copy of which can be found in the University of Iowa Law Library.

88. McClain, "Hammond," 222–26, 230–35, 213, 215.

89. On Pomeroy, see John Norton Pomeroy Jr., "John Norton Pomeroy," in *Great American Lawyers*, ed. William Draper Lewis (Philadelphia: John C. Winston Co., 1909), 8:89–136.

90. Ibid., 91, 95.

91. Ibid., 100.

92. Ibid., 108, 121.

93. John Norton Pomeroy, *An Introduction to Municipal Law*, 2d ed. (San Francisco, 1883), 445–49.

94. Ibid., xxxii–xxxvi, 565–66. In the first paragraph of Part 1, Pomeroy states that the "attention will be directed, among the ancients, principally to Rome."

95. Pomeroy, *Introduction*, 298.

96. Ibid., 103, 113.

97. See M. H. Hoeflich, "Law and Geometry: Legal Science from Leibniz to Langdell," *American Journal of Legal History* 30 (1986): 95–121.

4. The Domestication of Roman Law in the Anglo-American World After 1850: The Last Generation of the Nineteenth Century and the First of the Twentieth Century

1. See Robert Gordon, "Legal Thought and Legal Practice in the Age of American Enterprise, 1870–1920," in *Professions and Professional Ideologies in America*, ed. Gerald L. Geison (Chapel Hill: University of North Carolina Press, 1983). See also Anton-Hermann Chroust, *The Rise of the Legal Profession in America*, 2 vols. (Norman: University of Oklahoma Press, 1965).

2. See the next section of this chapter.

3. For works by Samuel Williston, see note 46 of this chapter.

4. See Oliver Wendell Holmes, *The Common Law and Other Writings* (1881; Birmingham, Ala.: Legal Classics Library, 1982). See also F. W. Maitland, *English Law and the Renaissance* (1901; Littleton, Colo.: Fred B. Rothman, 1985).

5. See Maitland, *English Law*. See also John H. Baker, "English Law and the Renaissance," *Cambridge Law Journal* 44 (1985): 46–61.

6. There has always been an antiquarian branch of Roman legal scholarship, but in the late nineteenth century it flourished; see, for instance, the works of the Anglo-Catholic barrister and historian Charles Butler, e.g., *Horae Juridicae Subsecivae* (London, 1806).

7. M. H. Hoeflich, "Introduction," in *The Gladsome Light of Jurisprudence: Learning and the Law in England and the United States in the 18th and 19th Centuries* (Westport, Conn.: Greenwood Press, 1988), 6–8. See Robert Stevens, *Law School: Legal Education in America from the 1850s to the 1980s* (Chapel Hill: University of North Carolina Press, 1983). See also Albert J. Harno, *Legal Education in the U.S.* (San Francisco: Bancroft-Whitney, 1953).

8. M. H. Hoeflich, "The Bloomington Law School," in *Property Law and*

Legal Education: Essays in Honor of John E. Cribbet, ed. Peter Hay and M. H. Hoeflich (Urbana: University of Illinois Press, 1988), 204–5.

9. See Charles Warren, *History of the Harvard Law School and of Early Conditions in America.*

10. Roman law was a subject that had academic appeal for the professionals who were trying to differentiate themselves from the pure practitioners. See Robert Stevens, "Two Cheers for 1870: The American Law School," in *Law in American History,* ed. Donald Fleming and Bernard Bailyn (Boston: Little, Brown, 1971), 405–550. See also Jerold S. Auerback, "Enmity and Amity: Law Teachers and Practitioners," ibid., 551–604.

11. See James Hadley, *Introduction to Roman Law* (New York, 1873).

12. See M. H. Hoeflich, "Savigny and His Anglo-American Disciples," *American Journal of Comparative Law* 37 (1989): 17–37.

13. On Gibbon, see M. H. Hoeflich, "Edward Gibbon, Roman Lawyer," *American Journal of Comparative Law* 39 (1991): 803–18.

14. See Chapter 3.

15. On Hammond and Maine, see Chapter 3.

16. See Francis W. Kelsey, ed., *Latin and Greek in American Education* (New York: Macmillan, 1911), 121–53.

17. For an example, see William Warwick Buckland, "Interpolations in the *Digest,*" *Yale Law Journal* 33 (1924): 343–64.

18. F. H. Lawson, *The Oxford Law School, 1850–1965* (Oxford: Clarendon Press, 1968), appendix.

19. On William Wetmore Story, see Henry James, *William Wetmore Story and His Friends,* 2 vols. (1903; rpt. New York: Da Capo Press, 1969).

20. William Wetmore Story, *Treatise on the Law of Contracts,* 2 vols., 4th ed. (Boston, 1856).

21. James, *Story,* 1:215–16, 93–103.

22. William Wetmore Story, *A Roman Lawyer in Jerusalem: First Century* (N.p.: National Military Home, 1895).

23. Both the *Southern Review* and the *Southern Literary Review* are replete with poetry written by people of various professions, including lawyers. For more information on these publications, see note 5 of Chapter 2.

24. See W. A. Hunter, "The Place of Roman Law in Legal Education," *Western Jurist* 9 (1875): 461–72.

25. Ibid., 462–66.

26. Ibid., 469.

27. See Erwin Grueber, *Der römische Recht als Theil des Rechtsunterrichtes an den englischen Universitäten. zugleich ein Beitrag zur Reform unserer juristischen*

Studien und Prufungen (1888; rpt. Hamburg: Verlagsanstalt und Druckerei A. G., 1889).

28. Erwin Grueber, *The Lex Aquilla: The Roman Law of Damage to Property* (Oxford, 1886).

29. Of course, such an idea was also found in the United States; see above, Chapter 2, at note 65.

30. For a biographical account of Bryce, see H. A. L. Fisher, *James Bryce*, 2 vols. (New York: Macmillan, 1927).

31. James Bryce, "Inaugural Lecture," in *Studies in History and Jurisprudence* (New York: Oxford University Press, 1901), 2:860–88; Bryce, "Valedictory Lecture," ibid., 887–907.

32. Bryce, "Inaugural," 867, 869, 871, 873, 875–76.

33. Bryce, "Valedictory," 892–94.

34. Ibid., 898–99.

35. Hunter, "Place of Roman Law," 471.

36. See M. H. Hoeflich, "Roman and Civil Law in American Legal Education and Research Prior to 1930: A Preliminary Survey," *University of Illinois Law Review* (1984): 719–37.

37. *Catalog of the Law School at the University of Nebraska* (N.p., n.d.); *Catalog of the Law School at Chicago–Kent College of Law* (N.p., n.d.).

38. James S. Ewing, "The Study of Law in Popular Education," paper read before the Illinois State Bar Association on June 13 and 14, 1885, Springfield.

39. Munroe Smith, "Roman Law in American Law Schools," *American Law Register and Review* 36 (1897): 176–78.

40. Ibid., 178–79, 181.

41. Ibid., 181–84.

42. See Rudolph Leonhard, "The Vocation of America for the Science of Roman Law," *Harvard Law Review* 26 (1913): 389.

43. Hoeflich, "Roman and Civil Law," 735–36.

44. See Rudolf von Jhering, *Der Kampf um's Recht* (Vienna, 1884).

45. Of course, Roman law continued to exercise practical influence. See, for instance, James Whitman, "Commercial Law and the American Volk: Notes on Llewellyn's German Sources for the Uniform Commercial Code," *Yale Law Journal* 97 (1987): 156–75.

46. John Couch, "Women in Early Roman Law," *Harvard Law Review* 8 (1894): 39; Lawrence Lowell, "The Judicial Use of Torture I, II," *Harvard Law Review* 11 (1898): 220, 290; John Chipman Gray, "Judicial Precedents: A Short Study in Comparative Jurisprudence," *Harvard Law Review* 9 (1895): 27; C. S. Lobingier, "Napoleon and His Code," *Harvard Law Review* 32 (1928): 114;

Peter Hamilton, "The Civil Law and the Common Law," *Harvard Law Review* 36 (1922): 180; Samuel Williston, "Contracts for the Benefit of a Third Person in the Civil Law," *Harvard Law Review* 16 (1902): 43; Williston, "Dependency of Mutual Promises in the Civil Law," *Harvard Law Review* 13 (1899): 80; Williston, "The Risk of Loss After an Executory Contract of Sale," *Harvard Law Review* 9 (1895): 72; Ernst Freund, "The New German Civil Code," *Harvard Law Review* 13 (1900): 627; Walter Neitzel, "Non-Contentions Jurisprudence in Germany," *Harvard Law Review* 21 (1908): 476; Neitzel, "Specific Performance, Injunctions, and Damages in German Law," *Harvard Law Review* 22 (1908): 161; S. C. Weil, "Waters: American Law and French Authority," *Harvard Law Review* 33 (1919): 133.

47. Fisher, *Bryce*, 1:9, 58.

48. James Bryce, *The Holy Roman Empire* (Oxford, 1864); Fisher, *Bryce*, 1:64.

49. James Bryce, *Studies in History and Jurisprudence*, 2 vols. (Oxford: Clarendon Press, 1901).

50. James Bryce, "The Methods of Legal Science," ibid., 2:607–37.

51. Ibid., 607–23, 628–30.

52. Ibid., 632.

53. James Bryce, "The Roman Empire and the British Empire in India," in *Studies in History and Jurisprudence*, 1:1–71; Bryce, "The Extension of Roman and English Law Throughout the World," ibid., 72–123; Bryce, "Flexible and Rigid Constitutions," ibid., 124–215; Bryce, "Methods of Law Making in Rome and in England," ibid., 2:699–744; Bryce, "The History of Legal Development at Rome and in England," ibid., 745–81; Bryce, "Marriage and Divorce in Roman and English Law," ibid., 782–859.

54. On Maitland's large array of correspondence, see C. H. S. Fifoot, ed., *The Letters of Frederic William Maitland* (Cambridge: Cambridge University Press, 1965). See also DeLloyd G. Guth and M. H. Hoeflich, "F. W. Maitland and Roman Law: An Uncollected Letter with Comments and Notes," *University of Illinois Law Review* (1982): 441–48.

55. Fifoot, ed., *Letters*, 369–70.

56. For a biographical account of W. W. Buckland's life and works, see Percy H. Winfield and Arnold D. McNair, eds., *Cambridge Legal Essays* (Cambridge: W. Heffer and Sons, 1926), 9–13.

57. W. W. Buckland and Arnold McNair, *Roman Law and Common Law* (Cambridge: Cambridge University Press, 1936).

58. For a bibliography of Alan Watson's work, see Watson, *Failures of the Legal Imagination* (Philadelphia: University of Pennsylvania Press, 1988), x–xi.

59. The vast majority of Buckland's work was oriented toward the exposition and recovery of the substantive rules of classical Roman law.

60. W. W. Buckland, *Equity in Roman Law* (1911; rpt. Littleton, Colo.: F. B. Rothman, 1983); Buckland, *A Manual of Roman Private Law*, 2d ed. (Cambridge: Cambridge University Press, 1947); Buckland, *The Roman Law of Slavery: The Condition of the Slave in Private Law from Augustus to Justinian.* (1908; rpt. Cambridge: Cambridge University Press, 1970); Buckland, *A Text-Book of Roman Law from Augustus to Justinian*, 3d ed., ed. Peter Stein (Cambridge: Cambridge University Press, 1966); Samuel Hallifax, *An Analysis of the Roman Civil Law*, 4th ed. (Cambridge, 1795). See also J. G. Phillimore, *An Introduction to the Study and History of the Roman Law* (London, 1848).

61. Buckland, *Roman Law of Slavery*, preface.

62. See W. W. Buckland, "Interpolations in the *Digest*: A Criticism of Criticism," *Harvard Law Review* 54 (1941): 1273–1310.

63. See Herman Kantorowicz and W. W. Buckland, *Studies in the Glossators of the Roman Law* (1938; rpt. Darmstadt: Scientia Verlag Aalen, 1969).

64. Winfield and McNair, eds., *Cambridge Legal Essays*, 10–12.

65. Hoeflich, "Roman and Civil Law," 731.

66. See Charles Sherman, *Academic Adventures* (New Haven: Tuttle, Morehouse, and Taylor, 1947), 104–8.

67. Hoeflich, "Roman and Civil Law," 731.

68. Sherman, *Academic Adventures*.

69. Fernand Bernard, *The First Year of Roman Law*, trans. Charles Sherman (New York: Oxford University Press, 1906).

70. Sherman's introductory lectures on Roman law are drawn from unpaginated notes taken by Walter L. Summers, Esq. (Yale LL.B.), now in the author's possession. A copy of these lecture notes is on deposit at the offices of the *University of Illinois Law Review*.

71. Hoeflich, "Roman and Civil Law," 732.

72. Charles Sherman, *Roman Law in the Modern World*, 3 vols. (Boston: Boston Book Company, 1917).

73. Hoeflich, "Roman and Civil Law," 731.

74. See Henry Adams, et al., *Essays in Anglo-Saxon Law* (Boston, 1876).

75. For a biographical account of Pound's life, see Paul Sayre, *Life of Roscoe Pound* (1948; rpt. Littleton, Colo.: Fred B. Rothman, 1981).

76. Ibid., 1–4.

77. Ibid., 1–4, 137.

78. See Jhering, *Der Kampf um's Recht*.

79. Sayre, *Pound*, 344–48, 384–90, 402–5.

80. See Franklyn C. Setaro, *A Bibliography of the Writings of Roscoe Pound* (Cambridge, Mass.: Harvard University Press, 1942).

81. Roscoe Pound, *Readings in Roman Law and the Civil Law and Modern Codes as Developments Thereof*, 2d ed. (Cambridge, Mass.: Harvard University Press, 1914).

82. I have come to own several hundred of these pamphlets and reports through the generosity of Professor Philip Hamburger.

83. Pound, *Readings*, iv.

84. Ibid., 74–158.

85. Setaro, *Bibliography*, 21.

86. Setaro, *Bibliography*, 187.

87. Setaro, 187.

88. Unfortunately, such a thesis is impossible to prove.

89. Pound, *Readings*, 88–93.

90. Roscoe Pound, *The Formative Era of American Law* (1938; rpt. Boston: Little, Brown, 1939); Pound, "The Influence of French Law in America," *Illinois Law Review* 3 (1909): 354–63; Pound, "The French Civil Code and the Spirit of Nineteenth Century Law," *Boston University Law Review* 35 (1955): 77–97; Pound, "The Influence of the Civil Law in America," *Louisiana Law Review* 1 (1938): 1–16; Pound, "Comparative Law in the Formation of American Common Law," *Actorum Academiae Universalis Iurisprudentiae Comparativae* 1 (1928): 183–97.

91. Thomas Edward Scrutton, *The Influence of the Roman Law on the Law of England* (1885; rpt. Littleton, Colo.: Fred B. Rothman, 1985).

92. Oliver Wendell Holmes, *The Common Law* (Boston, 1881); Matthias Reimann, "Holmes's *Common Law* and German Legal Science," in *The Legacy of Oliver Wendell Holmes*, ed. Robert W. Gordon (Stanford: Stanford University Press, 1992), 72–114.

Conclusion

1. See R. H. Helmholz, "Use of the Civil Law in Post-Revolutionary American Jurisprudence," *Tulane Law Review* 66 (1992): 1649–84.

2. See Richard A. Cosgrove, *Our Lady of the Common Law: An Anglo-American Legal Community, 1870–1930* (New York: New York University Press, 1987).

3. Peter Stein, "The Attraction of the Civil Law in Post-Revolutionary

America," in *The Character and Influence of the Roman Civil Law Historical Essays* (London: Hambledon Press, 1988), 411–42.

4. See A. W. B. Simpson, "The Rise and Fall of the Legal Treatise: Legal Principles and the Forms of Legal Literature," *University of Chicago Law Review* 48 (1981): 623, 670.

5. Alan Watson, *Roman Law and Common Law* (Athens: University of Georgia Press, 1991), 147–81; Klaus Luig, "The Institutes of National Law in the Seventeenth and Eighteenth Centuries," *Juridical Review* 17 (1972): 193; John W. Cairns, "Blackstone, an English Institutist: Legal Literature and the Rise of the Nation State," *Oxford Journal of Legal Studies* 4 (1984): 318.

6. William Blackstone, *Commentaries*, ed. W. G. Hammond (San Francisco, 1890).

7. On Pothier, see Michael Stolleis, *Juristen*, 160, 380.

8. M. H. Hoeflich, "Lieber, Legaré and Walker: Roman Lawyers in the Old South," in *Comparative Studies in Continental and Anglo-American Legal History, Bd. 13, The Reception of Continental Ideas in the Common Law World, 1820–1920*, ed. Matthias Reimann (Berlin: Duncker & Humblot, 1993).

9. M. H. Hoeflich, ed., *The Gladsome Light of Jurisprudence: Learning and the Law in England and the United States in the 18th and 19th Centuries* (Westport, Conn.: Greenwood Press, 1988).

10. Ibid.

11. Hoeflich, "Lieber."

12. Paul M. Hamlin, *Legal Education in Colonial New York* (New York: New York University Law School Quarterly Review, 1939).

13. Morton Horwitz, *The Transformation of American Law* (Cambridge, Mass.: Harvard University Press, 1977).

14. Charles M. Cook, *The American Codification Movement* (Westport, Conn.: Greenwood Press, 1981).

15. David Mellenkoff, *The Language of the Law* (Boston: Little, Brown, 1963).

16. Daniel Boorstin, *The Mysterious Science of the Law* (Cambridge, Mass.: Harvard University Press, 1941).

17. Francis Leiber, *Legal and Political Hermeneutics* (Boston, 1839).

18. W. W. Buckland, "Casus and Frustration in Roman Law and Common Law," *Harvard Law Review* 46 (1933): 1281.

19. Hamlin, *Legal Education*.

20. See Duck, *De usu et authoritate juris civilis Romanorum*. See also Daniel R. Coquillette, *The Civilian Writers of Doctors' Commons, London: Three Centuries*

of *Juristic Innovation in Comparative, Commercial and International Law* (Berlin: Duncker & Humblot, 1988), 161–65.

21. F. H. Lawson, *The Oxford Law School, 1850–1965* (London: Oxford University Press, 1968).

22. See, e.g., William Fulbecke, *A Parallele of the Civil Law, the Canon Law, and the Common Law of This Realme of England* (London, 1602).

23. Frederick Pollock and F. W. Maitland, *A History of English Law Before the Time of Edward I* (Cambridge: Cambridge University Press, 1923).

24. See *Memorials of Old Haileybury College* (Westminster: A. Constable, 1894); *A Preliminary View of the Establishment of the Honorable East India Company in Hertfordshire* (Haileybury, 1806).

25. See W. G. Hammond, "System of Legal Classification of Hale and Blackstone in Its Relation to the Civil Law," in *The Institutes of Justinian*, ed. T. C. Sandars (Chicago, 1876); Erwin Grueber, *The Lex Aquilia: The Roman Law of Damage to Property* (Oxford, 1886).

26. H. S. Legaré, *The Writings of Hugh Swinton Legaré*, 2 vols., ed. Mary Legaré (Charleston, 1846).

27. On the use of Cicero as a model in the early republic, see S. Botein, "Cicero as a Role Model for Early American Lawyers: A Case Study in Classical 'Influence,'" *Classical Journal* 73 (1978): 313–31; see also Richard J. Hoffman, "Classics in the Courts of the United States, 1790–1800," *American Journal of Legal History* 22 (1978): 55–84; M. Reinhold, *Classica Americana: The Greek and Roman Heritage in the United States* (Detroit: Wayne State University Press, 1984).

28. Tony Weir, "Friendships in the Law," *Tulane Civil Law Forum* 6–7 (1991–92): 61–93.

29. Hoeflich, "Roman and Civil Law in American Legal Education and Research Prior to 1930," 719–37.

30. Paul Sayre, *Life of Roscoe Pound* (1948; rpt. Littleton, Colo.: Fred B. Rothman, 1981).

31. Marcus Lutter, Ernst Stiefel, and M. H. Hoeflich, *Der Einfluss deutscher Emigranten auf die Rechtsentwicklung in den USA und in Deutschland* (Tübingen: JCB Mohr, 1993).

32. Ibid.

33. Karl Llewellyn, "A Realistic Jurisprudence—The Next Step," *Columbia Law Review* 30 (1930): 431; Underhill Moore, "The Lawyer's Law," *Yale Law Journal* 41 (1932): 566; Jerome Frank, "Are Judges Human?" *University of Pennsylvania Law Review* 80 (1931): 17, 223; Robert M. Hutchins, "Modern Movements in Legal Education," *American Law School Review* 6 (1929): 402.

SELECT BIBLIOGRAPHY

Adams, Henry, et al. *Essays in Anglo-Saxon Law*. Boston, 1876.

Atiyah, Patrick. *The Rise and Fall of Freedom of Contract*. Oxford: Clarendon Press, 1979.

Auerbachk, Jerold S. "Enmity and Amity: Law Teachers and Practitioners." In *Law in American History*, edited by Donald Fleming and Bernard Berlyn. Boston: Little, Brown, 1971.

Austin, John. *Lectures on Jurisprudence*. 2 vols. Edited by Robert Campbell. Jersey City, 1869.

———. *The Province of Jurisprudence Determined*. Edited by H. L. A. Hart. London, 1954.

Baker, John H. "English Law and the Renaissance." *Cambridge Law Journal* 44 (1985): 46–61.

Bentham, Jeremy. "A General View of a Complete Code of Laws." In *The Works of Jeremy Bentham*. Edinburgh, 1843.

———. *Supplement to Papers Relative to Codification and Public Instruction*. London, 1817.

Bernard, Fernand. *The First Year of Roman Law*. Translated by Charles Sherman. Oxford: Oxford University Press, 1906.

Blackstone, William. *Commentaries on the Laws of England*. Edited by W. G. Hammond. San Francisco, 1890.

Boorstin, Daniel J. *The Mysterious Science of the Law*. Cambridge, Mass.: Harvard University Press, 1941.

Botein, S. "Cicero as a Role Model for Early American Lawyers: A Case Study in Classical 'Influence.'" *Classical Journal* 73 (1978): 313–31.

Brooks, N. C. "Moses Smiting the Rock." *Southern Literary Messenger* 3 (1837): 25.

Bryce, James. *The Holy Roman Empire*. Oxford, 1864.

———. *Studies in History and Jurisprudence.* 2 vols. Oxford: Clarendon Press, 1901.

———. "Valedictory Lecture." *Studies in History and Jurisprudence,* 1901.

Bryson, Hamilton. "The Use of Roman Law in Virginia Courts." *American Journal of Legal History* 28 (1984): 135–46.

Buckland, William Warwick. "Casus and Frustration in Roman Law and Common Law." *Harvard Law Review* 46 (1933): 1281–1300.

———. *Equity in Roman Law.* 1911. Reprint. Littleton, Colo.: F. B. Rothman, 1983.

———. "Interpolations in the *Digest.*" *Yale Law Journal* 33 (1924): 343–64.

———. "Interpolations in the *Digest*: A Criticism of Criticism." *Harvard Law Review* 54 (1941): 1273–1310.

———. *A Manual of Roman Private Law.* 2d ed. Cambridge: Cambridge University Press, 1947.

———. *The Roman Law of Slavery: The Condition of the Slave in Private Law from Augustus to Justinian.* 1908. Reprint. Cambridge: Cambridge University Press, 1970.

———. *A Text-Book of Roman Law from Augustus to Justinian.* Edited by Peter Stein. 3d ed. Cambridge: Cambridge University Press, 1966.

Buckland, W. W., and Arnold McNair. *Roman Law and Common Law.* Cambridge: Cambridge University Press, 1936.

Butler, Benjamin. *Plan for the Organization of a LAW FACULTY in the University of the City of New York.* New York, 1835.

Butler, Charles. *Horae Juridicae Subsecivae.* London, 1806.

Cairns, John W. "Blackstone, an English Institutist: Legal Literature and the Rise of the Nation State." *Oxford Journal of Legal Studies* 4 (1984): 318–60.

Calhoun, Richard J. "Literary Magazines in the Old South." In *The History of Southern Literature,* edited by Louis D. Rubin. Baton Rouge: Louisiana State University Press, 1985.

California State Library Catalogue. Sacramento, 1857.

Campbell, Enid. "German Influences in English Legal Education and Jurisprudence in the 19th Century." *University of Western Australia Law Review* 4 (1959): 357–90.

———. "John Austin and Jurisprudence in Nineteenth Century England." Ph.D. dissertation, Duke University, 1959.

Carrington, Paul. "The Revolutionary Idea of University Legal Education." *William and Mary Law Review* 31 (1990): 527–74.

————. "Teaching Law in the Antebellum Northwest." *University of Toledo Law Review* 23 (1991): 30.

Catalogue of Books Belonging to the South Carolina Library. Columbia, 1807.

The Catalogue of the Hammond Historical Law Collection. Iowa City, 1895.

Catalogue of the Library of the Honorable Hugh Legaré. Washington, D.C., 1843.

Catalogue of the Rare and Valuable Private Library of the Late Honorable H. S. Legaré. Washington, D.C., 1848.

The Centennial History of the Harvard Law School 1817–1917. Cambridge, Mass.: Harvard Law School Association, 1918.

Chroust, Anton-Hermann. *The Rise of the Legal Profession in America.* 2 vols. Norman: University of Oklahoma Press, 1965.

Cocks, R. C. J. *Foundations of the Modern Bar.* London: Sweet & Maxwell, 1983.

————. *Sir Henry Maine.* Cambridge: Cambridge University Press, 1988.

Cook, Charles M. *The American Codification Movement.* Westport, Conn.: Greenwood Press, 1981.

Coquillette, Daniel R. *The Civilian Writers of Doctors' Commons, London: Three Centuries of Juristic Innovation in Comparative, Commercial and International Law.* Berlin: Duncker & Humblot, 1988.

————. "Justinian in Braintree: John Adams, Civilian Learning, and Legal Elitism, 1758–1775." In *Law in Colonial Massachusetts, 1630–1800,* edited by Frederick S. Allis, Jr. Boston: Colonial Society of America, 1984.

Corpus Iuris Civilis. Edited by Heinrich Schräder. Berolini, 1832.

Cosgrove, Richard A. *Our Lady of the Common Law: An Anglo-American Legal Community, 1870–1930.* New York: New York University Press, 1987.

Couch, John. "Women in Early Roman Law." *Harvard Law Review* 8 (1894): 39–50.

Coulter, E. Merton. *College Life in the Old South.* 1928. Reprint. Athens: University of Georgia Press, 1983.

Cover, Robert M. *Justice Accused: Antislavery and the Judicial Process.* New Haven: Yale University Press, 1975.

Cunningham, Noble E., Jr. *In Pursuit of Reason: The Life of Thomas Jefferson.* Baton Rouge: Louisiana State University Press, 1987.

Cushing, Luther S. *An Introduction to the Study of the Roman Law.* Boston, 1854.

————. *Manual of Parliamentary Practice.* 2d ed. Boston, 1845.

Dane, Nathan. *A General Abridgement and Digest of American Law.* Boston, 1823.

Dargo, George. *Politics and the Clash of Legal Traditions.* Cambridge, Mass.: Harvard University Press, 1975.

Davie, George E. *The Crisis of the Democratic Intellect*. Edinburgh: Polygon Press, 1986.

―――. *The Democratic Intellect*. 1961. Reprint. Edinburgh: Edinburgh University Press, 1982.

De Nova, Rodolfo. "The First American Book on Conflict of Laws." *American Journal of Legal History* 8 (1964): 136–56.

Dewey, Frank L. *Thomas Jefferson, Lawyer*. Charlottesville: University Press of Virginia, 1986.

Diamond, Alan, ed. *The Victorian Achievement of Sir Henry Maine*. Cambridge: Cambridge University Press, 1991.

Domat, Jean. *Civil Laws in Their Natural Order*. Translated by William Strahan, edited by Luther S. Cushing. 2 vols. Boston, 1850.

Dowd, Morgan D. "Justice Joseph Story: A Study on the Legal Philosophy of a Jeffersonian Judge." *Vanderbilt Law Review* 18 (1965): 643–62.

Duck, Sir Arthur. *De usu et authoritate juris civilis Romanorum per dominia principum Christianorum*. 1648. Reprint. London, 1679.

Duer, John. *A Discourse on the Life, Character, and Public Service of James Kent*. New York, 1898.

Dunne, Gerald T. *Justice Joseph Story and the Rise of the Supreme Court*. New York: Simon and Schuster, 1970.

Dyer, John Percy. *Tulane: The Biography of a University*. New York: Harper & Row, 1966.

Dyer, Thomas. *The University of Georgia: A Bicentennial History*. Athens: University of Georgia Press, 1985.

Eames, Mrs. E. J. "To My Own Little Girl." *Southern Literary Messenger* 8 (1842): 255.

The 1812 Catalogue of the Library of Congress, a Facsimile. 1812. Reprint. Washington, D.C.: Library of Congress, 1982.

Everett, Edward. *Orations and Speeches on Various Occasions*. 4 vols. Boston, 1853–68.

Ewing, James S. "The Study of Law in Popular Education." Paper read before the Illinois State Bar Association on June 13 and 14, 1885, Springfield.

Falck, Niels N. *Juristische Encyclopaedie*. 2d ed. Kiel, 1830.

Fearne, Charles. *An Essay on the Learning of Contingent Remainders and Executory Devises*. London, 1772.

Feaver, George. *From Status to Contract*. London: Longmans, Green, 1969.

Ferguson, Robert A. *Law and Letters in American Culture*. Cambridge, Mass.: Harvard University Press, 1984.

Fifoot, C. H. S. *Lord Mansfield*. Oxford: Clarendon Press, 1936.

———. *The Letters of Frederic William Maitland*. Cambridge: Cambridge University Press, 1965.

Fisher, H. A. L. *James Bryce*. 2 vols. New York: Macmillan, 1927.

Fitzherbert, Anthony. *La Graunde Abridgement*. 3 vols. London, 1514–16.

Follen, Charles. *The Works of Charles Follen*. 5 vols. Boston, 1841.

Frank, Jerome. "Are Judges Human?" *University of Pennsylvania Law Review* 80 (1931): 17–53, 223–67.

Freidel, Frank. *Francis Lieber, Nineteenth-Century Liberal*. Baton Rouge: Louisiana State University Press, 1947.

Freund, Ernst. "The New German Civil Code." *Harvard Law Review* 13 (1900): 627–37.

Friedman, Lawrence M. *A History of American Law*. 2d ed. New York: Simon and Schuster, 1985.

Friedman, Lawrence M., and Robert V. Percival. *The Roots of Justice: Crime and Punishment in Alameda County, California, 1870–1910*. Chapel Hill: University of North Carolina Press, 1981.

Fulbecke, William. *A Parallele of the Civil Law, the Canon Law, and the Common Law of This Realme of England*. London, 1602.

———. *A Parallele or Conference of the Civil Law, the Canon Law, and the Common Law of This Realme of England*. London, 1618.

Gaii Jurisconsulti Institutionem Commentarius. Edited by August W. Heffter. Berolini, 1827.

Gibbon, Edward. *The History of the Decline and Fall of the Roman Empire*. 6 vols. London, 1778–89.

Gilmore, Grant, and Charles L. J. Black. *The Law of Admiralty*. Brooklyn: Foundation Press, 1957.

Gooch, G. P. *History and Historians in the Nineteenth Century*. London: Longmans, Green, 1913.

Gordon, Robert. "Legal Thought and Legal Practice in the Age of American Enterprise, 1870–1920." In *Professions and Professional Ideologies in America*, edited by Gerald L. Geison. Chapel Hill: University of North Carolina Press, 1983.

———, ed. *The Legacy of Oliver Wendell Holmes*. Stanford: Stanford University Press, 1992.

Gray, John Chipman. "Judicial Precedents: A Short Study in Comparative Jurisprudence." *Harvard Law Review* 9 (1895): 27–41.

Grotius, Hugo. *The Rights of War and Peace (De Juri Belli et Pacis)*. Translated by A. C. Campbell. Westport, Conn.: Hyperion Press, 1979.

Grueber, Erwin. *The Lex Aquilia: The Roman Law of Damage to Property.* Oxford, 1886.

———. *Der römische Recht als Theil des Rechtsunterrichtes an den englischen Universitäten. zugleich ein Beitrag zur Reform unserer juristischen Studien und Prufungen.* 1888. Reprint. Hamburg: Verlagsanstalt und Druckerei A. G., 1889.

Guilland, Antoine. *Modern Germany and Her Historians.* London: Jarrold and Sons, 1915.

Guth, DeLloyd G., and M. H. Hoeflich. "F. W. Maitland and Roman Law: An Uncollected Letter with Comments and Notes." *University of Illinois Law Review* (1982): 441–48.

Gutzwiller, Max. *Der Einfluss Savignys auf die Entwicklung des Internationalprivatrechts.* Freiburg, Schweiz: Kommissionsverlag: Gschwend, Tschopp und Co., 1923.

Guzman, Alejandro. *Ratio Scripta.* In *Ius Commune Sonderhefte.* Frankfurt am Main: C. V. Klosterman, 1981.

Hadley, James. *Introduction to Roman Law.* New York, 1873.

Hallam, Henry. *Constitutional History of England.* 3 vols. Boston, 1829.

———. *History of Europe during the Middle Ages.* Rev. ed. 3 vols. New York, 1899.

Hallifax, Samuel. *An Analysis of the Roman Civil Law.* Cambridge, 1774. 4th ed. Cambridge, 1795.

Hamilton, Peter. "The Civil Law and the Common Law." *Harvard Law Review* 36 (1922): 180–92.

Hamlin, Paul M. *Legal Education in Colonial New York.* New York: New York University Law Quarterly Review, 1939.

Hammond, William G. "Ancient Law." *Western Jurist* 2 (1868): 1–11.

———. "The Civil Law." *Western Jurist* 4 (1870): 173–75.

———. *Remembrance of Amherst.* Edited by George F. Whicher. New York: Columbia University Press, 1946.

———. "System of Legal Classification of Hale and Blackstone in Its Relation to the Civil Law." In *The Institutes of Justinian,* edited by T. C. Sandars. Chicago, 1876.

Harno, Albert J. *Legal Education in the U.S.* San Francisco: Bancroft-Whitney, 1953.

Hatcher, William B. *Edward Livingston: Jeffersonian Republican and Jacksonian Democrat.* Baton Rouge: Louisiana State University Press, 1940.

Haubold, Christian Gottlieb. *Institutionum Juris Romani Privati Historico-Dogmaticarum Lineamenta observationibus maxime litteräriis distincta.* Leipzig, 1826.

Helmholz, R. H. "Use of the Civil Law in Post-Revolutionary American Jurisprudence." *Tulane Law Review* 66 (1992): 1649–84.

Heward, E. *Lord Mansfield.* Chichester: Barry Rose, 1979.

Hoeflich, M. H. "The Americanization of British Legal Education in the Nineteenth Century." *Journal of Legal History* 8 (1987): 244–59.

———. "The Bloomington Law School." In *Property Law and Legal Education: Essays in Honor of John E. Cribbet,* edited by Peter Hay and M. H. Hoeflich. Urbana: University of Illinois Press, 1988.

———. "Edward Gibbon, Roman Lawyer." *American Journal of Comparative Law* 39 (1991): 803–18.

———. "Law and Geometry: Legal Science from Leibniz to Langdell." *American Journal of Legal History* 30 (1986): 95–121.

———. "Lieber, Legaré, and Walker: Roman Lawyers in the Old South." In *Comparative Studies in Continent and Anglo-American Legal History, Bd. 13, The Reception of Continental Ideas in the Common Law World, 1820–1920,* edited by M. Reimann. Berlin: Duncker & Humblot, 1993.

———. "Roman and Civil Law in American Legal Education and Research Prior to 1930: A Preliminary Survey." *University of Illinois Law Review* (1984): 719–37.

———. "Roman Law in American Legal Culture." *Tulane Law Review* 66 (1992): 1723–17.

———. "Savigny and His Anglo-American Disciples." *American Journal of Comparative Law* 37 (1989): 17–37.

———. "Transatlantic Friendships and the German Influence on American Law in the First Half of the Nineteenth Century." *American Journal of Comparative Law* 35 (1987): 599–611.

———, ed. *The Gladsome Light of Jurisprudence: Learning and the Law in England and the United States in the 18th and 19th Centuries.* Westport, Conn.: Greenwood Press, 1988.

Hoffman, Richard J. "Classics in the Courts of the United States, 1790–1800." *American Journal of Legal History* 22 (1978): 55–84.

Holdsworth, Sir William. *A History of English Law.* 16 vols. 1903. Reprint. London: Methuen, 1938–66.

Holliday, Carl. *A History of Southern Literature.* 1906. Reprint. Port Washington, N.Y.: Kennikat Press, 1969.

Holmes, Oliver Wendell. *The Common Law and Other Writings.* 1881. Reprint. Birmingham, Ala.: Legal Classics Library, 1982.

Horwitz, M. *The Transformation of American Law.* Cambridge, Mass.: Harvard University Press, 1977.

"Hugh Swinton Legaré." *Southern Review* 8 (1870): 123–58.

Hugo, Gustav. *Lehrbuch eines civilistischen Cursus.* 1799. Reprint. Berlin, 1835.

Hunt, Charles Havens. *Life of Edward Livingston.* New York, 1864.

Hunter, W. A. "The Place of Roman Law in Legal Education." *Western Jurist* 9 (1875): 461–72.

Hutchins, Robert M. "Modern Movements in Legal Education." *American Law School Review* 6 (1929): 402–14.

———. "An Inquiry into Roman Jurisprudence." *Southern Quarterly Review* 3 (April 1851): 541–45.

Irving, David. *An Introduction to the Study of the Civil Law.* 4th ed. London, 1837.

James, Eldon R. "A List of Legal Treatises Printed in the British Colonies and the American States Before 1801." In *Harvard Legal Essays Written in Honor of and Presented to J. H. Beale and S. Williston.* Cambridge, Mass.: Harvard University Press, 1934.

James, Henry. *William Wetmore Story and His Friends.* 2 vols. 1903. Reprint. New York: Da Capo Press, 1969.

Jhering, Rudolf von. *Der Kampf um's Recht.* Vienna, 1884.

Johnson, Andrew. "The Influence of Nathan Dane on Legal Literature." *American Journal of Legal History* 7 (1963): 28–50.

Jolowicz, H. F. *Roman Foundations of Modern Law.* 1957. Reprint. Oxford: Clarendon Press, 1961.

Jones, Howard Mumford. *O Strange New World.* 1952. Reprint. New York: Viking Press, 1964.

Jones, Sir William. *An Essay on the Law of Bailments.* 1781. Reprint. Albany, N.Y., 1806.

Kantorowicz, Herman, and W. W. Buckland. *Studies in the Glossators of the Roman Law.* 1938. Reprint. Darmstadt: Scientia Verlag Aalen, 1969.

Kegel, Gerhard. "Joseph Story." *Rabels Zeitschrift für auslandisches und internationales Privatrecht* 43 (1979): 609–31.

Kelley, D. R. "Gaius Noster: Substructures of Western Social Thought." *American Historical Review* 84 (1979): 619–48.

Kelsey, Francis W., ed. *Latin and Greek in American Education.* New York: Macmillan, 1911.

Kennedy, Duncan. "The Structure of Blackstone's Commentaries." *Buffalo Law Review* 28 (1979): 205.

Kent, James. *Commentaries on American Law.* 11th ed. Boston, 1867.

Kent, William. *Memoirs and Letters of James Kent, L.L.D.* Boston, 1898.

Kerr, Charles. "Transylvania University's Law Department." *Americana* 31 (1937): 3–43.

King, Peter. "Utilitarian Jurisprudence in America: The Influence of Bentham and Austin on American Legal Thought in the Nineteenth Century." Ph.D. dissertation, University of Illinois, 1961.

Kirtland, Robert Bevier. *George Wythe: Lawyer, Revolutionary, Judge.* New York: Garland, 1986.

Kleinheyer, Gerd and Jan Schröder. *Deutsche Juristen aus Funf Jahrhunderten.* Heidelberg: C. F. Muller, 1983.

Kyd, Stewart. *A Treatise on the Law of Bills of Exchange and Promissory Notes.* London, 1790.

Lambert, Eduard, and J. R. Xirau. *L'ancetre americain du droit compare; la doctrine du Juge Story.* Paris: Recueil Sirey, 1947.

Langbein, John. "Chancellor Kent and the History of Legal Literature." *Columbia Law Review* 93 (1993): 547–94.

———. "Introduction." In William Blackstone, *Commentaries on the Laws of England.* Vol. 3. Chicago: University of Chicago Press, 1979.

Lawson, F. H. *The Oxford Law School, 1850–1965.* Oxford: Clarendon Press, 1968.

A Lawyer of North Carolina. "The Civil Law." *Southern Literary Messenger* 8 (1842): 249–55.

Legaré, Hugh Swinton. *The Writings of Hugh Swinton Legaré.* 2 vols. Edited by Mary Legaré. Charleston, 1846.

Leonhard, Rudolph. "The Vocation of America for the Science of Roman Law." *Harvard Law Review* 26 (1913): 389–415.

Leslie, William R. "Similarities in Lord Mansfield's and Joseph Story's View of Fundamental Law." *American Journal of Legal History* 1 (1957): 278–307.

Library of the Law School of Harvard University. Cambridge, Mass., 1826.

Lieber, Francis. *Legal and Political Hermeneutics.* Boston, 1839.

———. *Legal and Political Hermeneutics.* Edited by W. G. Hammond. St. Louis, 1880.

———. *Manual of Political Ethics.* Boston, ca. 1838. 2d ed. rev. Philadelphia, 1875.

———. *On Civil Liberty and Self-Government.* Philadelphia, 1859.

Livingston, Edward. *The Complete Works of Edward Livingston on Criminal Jurisprudence.* 2 vols. New York, 1873.

Llewellyn, Karl. "A Realistic Jurisprudence—The Next Step." *Columbia Law Review* 30 (1930): 431–65.

Lobingier, C. S. "Napoleon and His Code." *Harvard Law Review* 32 (1928): 114–34.

Long, George. *Two Discourses Delivered in the Middle Temple Hall*. London, 1847.

Lorenzen, Ernest G. "Story's Commentaries on the Conflict of Laws—100 Years After." *Harvard Law Review* 48 (1934): 15–38.

Lowell, Lawrence. "The Judicial use of Torture I, II." *Harvard Law Review* 11 (1898): 220.

Luig, Klaus. "The Institutes of National Law in the Seventeenth and Eighteenth Centuries." *Juridical Review* 17 (1972): 193–226.

———. "Institutionen Lehrbucher des nationalen Rechts im 17. und 18. Jahrhundert." *Ius Commune* 3 (1970): 64–97.

Lund, Thomas A. "British Wildlife Law Before the American Revolution: Lessons from the Past." *Michigan Law Review* 74 (1975): 49–74.

———. "Early American Wildlife Law." *New York University Law Review* 51 (1976): 703–30.

Lutter, Marcus, Ernst Stiefel, and M. H. Hoeflich. *Der Einfluss deutscher Emigranten auf die Rechtsentwicklung in den USA und in Deutschland*. Tübingen: JCB Mohr, 1993.

Mackeldey, Ferdinand. *Lehrbuch des heutigen römischen Rechst*. Vienna, 1851–52. Translated as *Handbook of Roman Law*. Translated and edited by Moses A. Dropsie. Philadelphia, 1883.

Maine, Henry Sumner. *Ancient Law*. Edited by Frederick Pollock. 10th ed. 1861. Reprint. New York, 1884.

———. *Dissertations on Early Law and Custom*. New York, 1886.

———. *Lectures on International Law*. London, 1888.

———. *Popular Government*. New York, 1885.

———. *Village Communities and Miscellanies*. New York, 1889.

Maitland, Frederic William. *English Law and the Renaissance* (The Rede Lecture for 1901. 1901. Reprint. Littleton, Colo.: Fred B. Rothman, 1985.

———. *The Forms of Action at Common Law*. Edited by A. H. Chaytor and W. J. Whittaker. Cambridge: Cambridge University Press, 1948.

Mayes, Daniel. "An Address to the Students of Law in Transylvania University." In *The Gladsome Light of Jurisprudence: Learning and the Law in England and the United States in the 18th and 19th Centuries*, edited by Michael H. Hoeflich. Westport, Conn.: Greenwood Press, 1988.

McClain, Emlin. "Law Department of the State University of Iowa." *Green Bag* 1 (n.d.): 374–94.

———. "William G. Hammond." In *Great American Lawyers*, edited by

William Draper Lewis. Vol. 8. Philadelphia: John C. Winston Co., 1909.

McClellan, James. *Joseph Story and the American Constitution*. Norman: University of Oklahoma Press, 1971.

Mehren, Arthur T. von, and James Gordley. *The Civil Law System*. 2d ed. Boston: Little, Brown, 1977.

Mellenkoff, David. *The Language of the Law*. Boston: Little, Brown, 1963.

Memorials of Old Haileybury College. Westminster: A. Constable, 1894.

Miller, Perry. *The Life of the Mind in America*. San Diego: Harcourt Brace Jovanovich, 1965.

Milson, Stroud Francis Charles. *Studies in the History of the Common Law*. London: Hambledon Press, 1985.

Mittermaier, C. J. A. "Collision der Gesetze vershiedener Staate." *Kritische Zeitschrift für Rechtswissenschaft und Gesetzgebung des Auslandes* 7 (1835): 228–49.

———. *Effects of Drunkenness on Criminal Responsibility*. Translated by Luther S. Cushing. Boston, 1840.

Moore, Underhill. "The Lawyer's Law." *Yale Law Journal* 41 (1932): 566–76.

Morison, Samuel Eliot. *The Intellectual Life of Colonial New England*. 1956. Reprint. Ithaca, N.Y.: Cornell University Press, 1960.

Morison, W. L. *John Austin*. Stanford: Stanford University Press, 1982.

Nadelmann, Kurt H. "Bicentennial Observations on the Second Edition of Joseph Story's Commentaries on the Conflict of Laws." *American Journal of Comparative Law* 28 (1980): 67–77.

———. *Conflict of Laws: International and Interstate*. The Hague: Nijhoff, 1972.

———. "De l'organisation et de la jurisdiction des cours de justice, aux Etats Unis d'Amerique par M. Joseph Story." In *Joseph Story*, edited by Mortimer D. Schwartz and John C. Hogan. New York: Oceana Publications, 1959.

———. "Joseph Story's Contribution to American Conflicts Law: A Comment." *American Journal of Legal History* 5 (1961): 230–53.

———. "Joseph Story's Sketch of American Law." *American Journal of Comparative Law* 3 (1954): 3–8.

Neitzel, Walter. "Non-Contentious Jurisdiction in Germany." *Harvard Law Review* 21 (1908): 476–94.

Newmyer, Kent. "A Note on the Whig Politics of Justice Joseph Story." *Mississippi Valley Historical Review* 48 (1961): 480–91.

Nolan. "Sir William Blackstone and the New American Republic: A Study of Intellectual Impact." *New York University Law Review* 51 (1976): 731–68.

O'Brien, Michael. *A Character of Hugh Legaré*. Knoxville: University of Tennessee Press, 1985.

———. *Rethinking the South*. Baltimore: Johns Hopkins University Press, 1988.

———, ed. *All Clever Men, Who Make Their Ways*. Fayetteville: University of Arkansas Press, 1982.

———, ed. *Intellectual Life in Antebellum Charleston*. Knoxville: University of Tennessee Press, 1986.

O'Neall, John Belton. "James M. Walker." In *Biographical Sketches of the Bench and Bar of South Carolina*. Charleston, 1859.

Palmer, Paul A. "Benthamism in England and America." *American Political Science Review* 35 (1941): 855–71.

Parker, Isaac. *A Sketch of the Character of the Late Chief Justice Parsons*. Boston, 1813.

Perry, Thomas Sergeant. *The Life and Letters of Francis Lieber*. Boston, 1882.

Phillimore, J. G. *An Introduction to the Study and History of the Roman Law*. London, 1848.

Pickering, John. "The Civil Law." *American Jurist* 3 (1829): 39–62.

Plucknett, T. F. T. *Early English Legal Literature*. Cambridge: Cambridge University Press, 1958.

Pollock, Frederick. "History of Comparative Jurisprudence." In *Essays in the Law*. London: Macmillan, 1922.

Pollock, Frederick, and F. W. Maitland. *A History of English Law Before the Time of Edward I*. Cambridge: Cambridge University Press, 1923.

Pomeroy, John Norton. *An Introduction to Municipal Law*. 2d ed. San Francisco, 1883.

Pomeroy, John Norton, Jr. "John Norton Pomeroy." In *Great American Lawyers*, edited by William Draper Lewis. Vol. 8. Philadelphia: John C. Winston Co., 1909.

Pothier, Robert Joseph. *Treatise on the Contract of Sale*. Translated by Luther S. Cushing. Boston, 1839.

Pound, Roscoe. "Comparative Law in the Formation of American Common Law." *Actorum Academiae Universalis Iurisprudentiae Comparativae* 1 (1928): 183–97.

———. *The Formative Era of American Law*. 1938. Reprint. Boston: Little, Brown, 1939.

———. "The French Civil Code and the Spirit of Nineteenth Century Law." *Boston University Law Review* 35 (1955): 77–97.

———. "The Influence of the Civil Law in America." *Louisiana Law Review* 1 (1938): 1–16.

———. "The Influence of French Law in America." *Illinois Law Review* 3 (1909): 354–63.

———. "The Place of Judge Story in the Making of American Law." *Massachusetts Law Quarterly* 1 (1915–16): 121–40.

———. *Readings in Roman Law and the Civil Law and Modern Codes as Development Thereof.* 2d ed. Cambridge, Mass.: Harvard University Press, 1914.

Powell, John J. *An Essay Upon the Law of Contracts and Agreements.* Dublin, 1790.

———. *A Treatise on the Law of Mortgages.* Dublin, 1785.

A Preliminary View of the Establishment of the Honorable East India Company in Herfordshire. Haileybury, 1806.

Prest, Wilfred. "The Dialectical Origins of Finch's Law." *Cambridge Law Journal* 36 (1977): 326–52.

Pringsheim, Fritz. "The Inner Relationship Between English and Roman Law." *Cambridge Law Journal* 5 (1935): 347–65.

Pufendorf, Samuel von. *Of the Law of Nature and Nations.* Translated by Basil Kennett and George Carew. 8 vols. London, 1729.

Reddie, James. *Historical Notices of the Roman Law and of the Recent Progress of Its Study in Germany.* Edinburgh, 1826.

Reeves, John. *History of English Law.* 5 vols. London, 1814–29.

Reimann, Matthias. *Historiche Schule und Common Law.* Die deutsche Rechtswiscenschaft des 19 Jhrdts im amerikanischen Rechtdenken. Comparative Studies in Continental and Anglo-American Legal History Bd. 14. Berlin: Duncker & Humblot, 1993.

———. "Holmes's *Common Law* and German Legal Science." In *The Legacy of Oliver Wendell Holmes,* edited by Robert W. Gordon. Stanford: Stanford University Press, 1992.

———, ed. *The Reception of Continental Ideas in the Common Law World 1820–1920.* Duncker and Humblot, 1993.

Reinhold, Meyer. *Classica Americana: The Greek and Roman Heritage in the United States.* Detroit: Wayne State University Press, 1984.

———, ed. *The Classic Pages: Classical Reading of the Eighteenth-Century Americans.* University Park: Pennsylvania State University Press, 1975.

Report from the Select Committee on Legal Education. London, 1846.

Rhea, Linda. *Hugh Swinton Legaré, a Charleston Intellectual.* Chapel Hill: University of North Carolina Press, 1934.

Richard, Carl J. *The Founders and the Classics: Greece, Rome, and the American Enlightenment.* Cambridge, Mass.: Harvard University Press, 1994.

Rumble, Wilfrid. "Austin in the Classroom." *Journal of Legal History* 17 (April 1996): 17–40.

————. "The Legal Positivism of John Austin and the Realist Movement in American Jurisprudence." *Cornell Law Review* 66 (1981): 986–1031.

————. *The Thought of John Austin: Jurisprudence, the British Constitution, and Colonial Reform*. London: Athlone Press, 1985.

Sandars, T. C. *The Institutes of Justinian*. Edited by W. G. Hammond. 1876. Reprint. Chicago 1973.

Savigny, Friedrich Carl von. *Geschichte des römischen Rechts im Mittelalter*. Heidelberg, 1834.

————. *Law of Possession*. Translated by Luther S. Cushing. Berlin, 1838.

————. *System des heutigen römischen Rechts*. 8 vols. Berlin 1840–49.

————. *Vom Beruf unserer Zeit für Rechtswissenschaft und Gesetzgebung*. Heidelberg, 1814.

Sayre, Paul. *Life of Roscoe Pound*. 1948. Reprint. Littleton, Colo.: Fred B. Rothman, 1981.

Schiller, Arthur. "Roman Interpretation and Anglo-American Interpretation and Construction." *Virginia Law Review* 27 (1940–41): 733–68.

Schlesinger, Rudolf. "The Common Core of Legal Systems: An Emerging Subject of Comparative Study." In *XXth Century Comparative and Conflicts Law: Essays in Honor of Hessel E. Ynteima*, edited by Kurt Nadelmann, A. T. von Mehren, and J. Hazard. Leiden: A. W. Sijthoff, 1961.

————. *Formation of Contracts: A Study of the Common Core of Legal Systems*. New York: Oceana, 1968.

Schmidt, Gustav. "The Batture Question." *Louisiana Law Journal* 1 (1841): 84–151.

Schomberg, Alexander C. *An Historical and Chronological View of Roman Law*. Oxford, 1785.

Schwarz, Andreas. "John Austin and the German Jurisprudence of His Time." *Politica* 1 (1934): 178–99.

————. *Rechtsgeschichte und Gegenwart*. Karlsruhe: C. F. Muller, 1960.

Scrutton, Thomas Edward. *The Influence of the Roman Law on the Law of England*. 1885. Reprint. Littleton, Colo.: Fred B. Rothman, 1985.

Sellers, M. N. S. *American Republicanism: Roman Ideology in the United States Constitution*. New York: New York University Press, 1994.

Senese, Donald J. "Legal Thought in South Carolina, 1800–1860." Ph.D. dissertation, University of South Carolina, 1970.

Setaro, Franklyn C. *A Bibliography of the Writings of Roscoe Pound*. Cambridge, Mass.: Harvard University Press, 1942.

Shannon, Edgar Finley. *The University of Virginia: A Century and a Half of Innovation*. New York: New Camen Society in North America, 1969.

Sharswood, George. *Lectures Introductory to the Study of the Law*. Philadelphia, 1870.

Sherman, Charles. *Roman Law in the Modern World*. 3 vols. Boston: Boston Book Company, 1917.

Shipton, C. K. *Early American Imprints, 1639–1800*. Worcester, Mass.: American Antiquarian Society, 1955.

Simpson, A. W. B. "The Rise and Fall of the Legal Treatise: Legal Principles and the Forms of Legal Literature." In *Legal Theory and Legal History: Essays on the Common Law*, by A. W. B. Simpson. London: Hambledon, 1987.

Smith, Munroe. "Roman Law in American Law Schools." *American Law Register and Review* 36 (1897): 175–86.

Squibb, George D. *The High Court of Chivalry: A Study of the Civil Law in England*. Oxford: Clarendon Press, 1959.

Staunton, George. Translation of *Ta Tsing Lev Lee* by Ta Ch'ing lu. London, 1810.

Stein, Peter. "The Attraction of the Civil Law in Post-Revolutionary America." *Virginia Law Review* 52 (1966): 403–34. Also published in *The Character and Influence of the Roman Civil Law Historical Essays*. London: Hambledon Press, 1988.

———. "Continental Influences on English Legal Thought, 1600–1900." *La formazione storica del diritto moderno in Europa, atti del III Congresso Internazionale della Societa Italiana di Storia del diritto*. Vol. 3. Florence: Olschki, 1977.

———. "Elegance in Law." *Law Quarterly Review* 77 (1961): 242–56.

———. "Legal Theory and the Reform of Legal Education in Mid-Nineteenth Century England." *L'Eduicazione Giundica: Profili Storica*. Vol. 2. Edited by A. Giuliani and N. Picardi. Perugia: L'Università degli Studi di Perugia, 1977.

———. "Logic and Experience in Roman and Common Law." *Boston University Law Review* 59 (1979): 433–51.

———. *Roman Law and English Jurisprudence Yesterday and Today*. London: Cambridge University Press, 1969.

Stevens, Robert B. *Law School: Legal Education in America from the 1850s to the 1980s*. Chapel Hill: University of North Carolina Press, 1983.

———. "Two Cheers for 1870: The American Law School." In *Law in American History*, edited by Donald Fleming and Bernard Bailyn. Boston: Little, Brown, 1971.

Stewart, Dugald. *Elements of the Philosophy of the Human Mind*. 3 vols. London, 1792.

Stoljar, Samuel. "The Early History of Bailment." *American Journal of Legal History* 2 (1957): 5–34.

Stoll, Adolf. *Friedrich Carl von Savigny: Ein Bild seines Lebens mit einer Sammlung seiner Briefe.* 3 vols. Berlin: Heymann, 1927–39.

Stolleis, Michael. *Juristen. Ein biographisches Lexicon von der Antike bis zum 20. Jahrhundert.* Munich: C. H. Beck, 1995.

Story, Joseph. *Commentaries on the Conflict of Laws Foreign and Domestic.* Boston, 1834.

———. *Commentaries on the Law of Agency.* Boston, 1839.

———. *Commentaries on the Law of Bailments.* Cambridge, Mass., 1832.

———. *Commentaries on the Law of Partnership.* Boston, 1841.

———. "Law, Legislation, Codes." In *Readings in American Legal History,* edited by Mark D. Howe. Cambridge, Mass.: Harvard University Press, 1949.

———. *The Miscellaneous Writings of Joseph Story.* Edited by W. W. Story. Boston, 1852.

———. "Tribute to Mr. Legaré." *Boston Daily Advertiser,* June 30, 1843.

Story, William Wetmore. *A Roman Lawyer in Jerusalem: First Century.* N.p.: National Military Home, 1895.

———. *Treatise on the Law of Contracts.* 2 vols., 4th ed. Boston, 1856.

———, ed. *Life and Letters of Joseph Story.* Vol. 1. Boston, 1851.

Struve, B. G. *Corpus Juris Publici Imperii Nostri Romano-Germanici.* 3rd ed. Jena: I. F. Bielckum.

"Study of Law." *Southern Literary Messenger* 3 (1837): 25–31.

Supplement to the Catalogue of the Law Library of Harvard University. Cambridge, Mass., 1835.

Taylor, John. *Elements of the Civil Law.* 3d ed. London, 1755.

Tuck, Richard. *Natural Rights Theories.* Cambridge: Cambridge University Press, 1979.

Tushnet, Mark. *The American Law and Slavery.* Princeton: Princeton University Press, 1981.

Uzs, Stephen G. "Maine, Ancient Law and Legal Theory." *Connecticut Law Review* 16 (1984): 821–52.

Walker, James Murdock. *An Inquiry into the Use and Authority of Roman Jurisprudence in the Law Concerning Real Estate.* Charleston, S.C., 1850.

———. *The Theory of the Common Law.* Boston, 1852.

———. *Tract on Government.* Boston, 1853.

Warren, Charles. *History of the Harvard Law School and of Early Conditions in America.* 2 vols. 1908. Reprint. New York: Da Capo Press, 1970.

Waterman, Julius S. "Thomas Jefferson and Blackstone's Commentaries." In *Essays in the History of Early American Law*, edited by David H. Flaherty. Chapel Hill: University of North Carolina Press, 1969.

Watson, Alan. "Chancellor Kent's Use of Foreign Law." *The Reception of Continental Ideas in the Common Law World, 1820–1920*, edited by Matthias Reimann. Berlin: Duncker and Humblot, 1993.

———. *Failures of the Legal Imagination*. Philadelphia: University of Pennsylvania Press, 1988.

———. *"Justinian's Institutes* and Some English Counterparts." In *Studies in Justinian's Institutes: In Memory of J. A. C. Thomas*. Edited by Peter Stein and A. D. E. Lewis. London: Sweet & Maxwell, 1983.

———. *The Making of the Civil Law*. Cambridge, Mass.: Harvard University Press, 1981.

———. *Roman Law and Common Law*. Athens: University of Georgia Press, 1991.

———. *Roman Law and Comparative Law*. Athens: University of Georgia Press, 1991.

———. "Slave Law: History and Ideology." *Yale Law Journal* 91 (1982): 1034–47.

———. *Sources of Law, Legal Change, and Ambiguity*. Philadelphia: University of Pennsylvania Press, 1984.

———. "The Transformation of American Property Law: A Comparative Approach." *Georgia Law Review* 24 (1990): 163.

Weil, Samuel C. "Waters: American Law and French Authority." *Harvard Law Review* 33 (1919): 133–67.

Weir, Tony. "The Common Law System." *International Encyclopedia of Comparative Law: Structures and Divisions of Law*. Vol. 2. Tübingen: J. C. B. Mohr, 1974.

———. "Friendships in the Law." *Tulane Civil Law Forum* 6–7 (1991–92): 61–93.

Whitman, James. "Commercial Law and the American Volk: Notes on Llewellyn's German Sources for the Uniform Commercial Code." *Yale Law Journal* 97 (1987): 156–75.

———. *The Legacy of Roman Law in the German Romantic Era: Historical Version and Legal Change*. Princeton: Princeton University Press, 1990.

Williston, Samuel. "Contracts for the Benefit of a Third Person in the Civil Law." *Harvard Law Review* 16 (1902): 43–51.

———. "Dependency of Mutual Promises in the Civil Law." *Harvard Law Review* 13 (1899): 80–109.

Winfield, Percy H., and Arnold D. McNair, eds. *Cambridge Legal Essays*. Cambridge: W. Heffer and Sons, 1926.

Wiseman, Sir Robert. *The Law of Laws, or, The Excellencie of the Civil Law above All Humane Laws Whatsoever.* 4th ed. London, 1795.

Wood, Thomas. *An Institute of the Laws of England.* 2d ed. London, 1722.

———. *A New Institute of the Imperial or Civil Law.* London, 1704.

Wright, Thomas Goddard. *Literary Culture in Early New England, 1620–1730.* 1920. Reprint. New York: Russell & Russell, 1966.

INDEX

Dernburg, Heinrich, 128
Detinue, 39
Die juristiche Person, 19
Digest, definition of, 17
Dirksen, Heinrich, 57
Divorce, 5, 119
Doctors' Commons, 1, 4
Doctrine, history of, 3
Domat, Jean, 28, 43; *Les loix civiles dan leur ordre naturel*, 56, 85
Domesday Book, 91
Dominium, 137
Donahue, Charles, 144
Donellus, Hugo, 89
Duck, Arthur, 13, 81; *De usu et authoritate juris civlis*, 56
Duer, John, 28
DuPonceau, Peter, 28, 30, 66
Dwight, Theodore, 52

East India Company, 140
Edinburgh Review, 53
Edinburgh University, 54
Edward II, 64
Eichhorn, K. F., 57
Elegantia juris, 62, 118
Emerigon, 28
Enlightenment Europe, 51
Equity jurisdiction, 79
Erskine, Lord, 30
Essex, 26
Everett, Edward, 28, 66

Falck, Nikolaus, 13, 22; *Juristische Encyclopaedie*, 12, 22
Fearne, Charles, 61; *Essay on the Learning of Contingent Remainders*, 65

Ferae naturae, law of, 19
Ferguson, Adam, 54
Ferguson, Robert, 67
Feudal structure, 139
Finch, Henry, 16, 44; *Nomotechnia*, 16
Fitzherbert, Anthony, 32
Florida, 7
Follen, Charles, 30, 106
Forms of action, 15
Foster, William, 123
Founding Fathers, 5, 28, 51
Frank, Jerome, 143
Frederician Code of Prussia, 6
Freund, Ernst, 116
Friedman, Lawrence, 1
Frier, Bruce, 144
Fulbecke, William, 13

Gaius, 62; *Institutes*, 12, 13
Georgia, University of, 50
German: renaissance, 12; aggression, 142
Germanic law, 80
Gibbon, Edward, *History of the Decline and Fall of the Roman Empire*, 56, 91
Goguet, A. B., *Origin of Laws*, 56
Gothofredus, Jacobus, 88–89
Gray, John Chipman, 115
Gridley, Samuel, 6
Grimm, Jakob, 57
Grotius, Hugo, 29, 56, 59
Grueber, Erwin, *Digest 9.2*, 110, 117

Hadley, James, 105; *Introduction to Roman Law*, 105–6
Hadrian's Wall, 4

Powell, John: *Essay Upon the Law of Contracts and Agreements*, 33; *Treatise on the Law of Mortgages*, 36
Practical treatises, 34
Practical virtue concepts, 50
Praetor peregrinus, 119
Praetor urbanus, 119
Primitive society, 80
Privatdozent, 12
Private law doctrine, 127
Propositions, 17
Province, The, 18
Pufendorf, Samuel von, 6, 56, 59

Ratio scripta, 26, 41, 76, 86, 94
Recht, 20
Reconstruction, 74
Reddie, James, *Historical Notices of the Roman Law*, 76
Reeves, John, *History of English Law*, 64
Reform Act of 1832, 45
Regius chairs, 13
Reid, James, 54
Renaissance, 104
Revolutionary War, 1
Right, 20
Roman institutional categories, 18
Rutherforth, Thomas, 56

Sandars, T. C., *Institutes of Justinian*, 92
Savigny, Friedrich Carl von, 10, 11, 55, 75–77; *Vom Beruf unserer Zeit*, 75, 76; *Geschichte des römischen Rechts im Mittelater*, 75, 76; *System des heutigen römischen Rechts*, 75; *Law of Possession*, 85

"Scalawags," 141
Scandinavian law, 80
Schiller, Arthur, 52
Schlegel, A. W., 12
Schlesinger, Rudolf, 48, 81
Schomberg, Alexander C., *Historical and Chronological View of Roman Law*, 13, 85
Schräder, Heinrich, *Corpus Juris Civilis*, 60, 72, 127
Schwarz, Andreas, 11, 22
Science of law, 17, 64
Scientific legal principles, 65, 114
Scotland, 4, 7
Scottish Enlightenment, 54, 84
Scrutton, Thomas, 130
Secession, 51, 69
Selden, John, 29, 81
Sewall, Samuel, 26, 27
Sharswood, George, quoted, 37
Sherman, Charles Phineas, 116, 123–25, 143; *Roman Law in the Modern World*, 124
Simpson, A. W. B., 32
Slavery, 51, 87
Smith, Munroe, 113–14
Society, development of, 84
South Carolina, 51; Charleston, 52; Columbia, 52; Bar, 55
South Carolina College, 55
Southcote's Case, 36
Southern Literary Messenger, 51, 70, 71
Southern Quarterly Review, 70
Southern Review, 51, 60, 63, 67, 68, 70, 72
Stair, Viscount, 30
Statute law, 111
Statute of Uses, 70